WITHDRAWN

THE PRIESTHOOD OF CHRIST

THE PRIESTHOOD
OF CHRIST

CONSIDERATIONS ON
THE PRIESTHOOD

by Ludwig Weikl, S.J.

DUBLIN: CLONMORE AND REYNOLDS LIMITED
LONDON: BURNS OATES AND WASHBOURNE LIMITED

This Edition 1961

© *Copyright by Clonmore & Reynolds Ltd.*

TRANSLATED FROM THE GERMAN BY

ISABEL AND FLORENCE McHUGH

This work is a translation from the German *Entfache
die Glut* by Ludwig Weikl, S.J., published by Frederick
Pustet, Regensburg, Germany and also published in
the United States of America by the Bruce Publishing
Company, under the title *Stir up the Fire*.

MADE AND PRINTED IN THE REPUBLIC OF IRELAND BY
CAHILL AND CO. LTD., FOR CLONMORE AND REYNOLDS LTD.
NIHIL OBSTAT: IOANNES A. SCHULIEN, CENSOR LIBRORUM.
IMPRIMATUR : ✠ALBERTUS G. MEYER, ARCHIEPISCOPUS
MILWAUCHIENSIS. 23 SEPTEMBER 1958.

PREFACE

In his prison in Rome the Apostle Paul writes the epilogue to the drama of his life: " I have fought the good fight, I have finished the course, I have kept the faith " (2 Tim. 4:7). Already he sees the victor's crown which the Just Judge will award him. But the work to which his apostolic life was dedicated is still unfinished. It must go on, and the workers must not be negligent. With these thoughts in his mind the Apostle sends out the call: " *Resuscites gratiam!*" to his beloved and well tried disciple Timothy, the head of the Church at Ephesus: " I admonish thee to stir up the grace of God which is in thee by the laying on of my hands " (2 Tim. 1:6; *cf.* 1 Tim. 4:14).

" The grace of God!" Here it is the call to the ministry of the New Covenant and its principal equipment: *participation in the priesthood of Christ.*

Grace is life, and like every living thing it needs maintenance and care if it is not to wither and even to die. Now, the essential effect of the grace of the priesthood of Christ, namely, the *character sacerdotalis,* definitely cannot be eliminated in the person to whom it has once been given validly, not even by its bearer, the priest himself. The man who is bound to the High Priest Jesus Christ by the *character indelebilis* remains with Him, *sacerdos in aeternum,* because Christ does not dismiss him. But the fullness of life and the effective power of this grace, the same in its essentials in all, nevertheless differs greatly in strength in different persons; in fact, it can be more or less effective in the same person at different times. The " spirit of fear " can hamper it, sometimes more, sometimes less. At such times what should be " the spirit of power, and of love, and of prudence " (*ibid.*) needs to be re-awakened, needs to be rekindled to new life and movement: " *Resuscites gratiam!*"

Let us hope that the following Considerations may serve this end. May the Holy Spirit bless the effort and fan to a new Pentecostal flame the fire which was lit in our souls by the hand of the bishop on the day of our ordination.

INTRODUCTION

The aim of this book is to inspire the reader to reflect on the blessed gift of the priesthood as established by God in His order of salvation and revealed in His saving Word. But the full import of this mystery is to be gleaned not only from the sources of revelation, but also from the teaching of the Church and of theologians under the guidance of the Church. It is therefore our endeavour to make the doctrine of the Church concerning the grace of the priesthood so clear to the minds of our readers that they will esteem it aright, and cherish it as indeed all God's graces need to be cherished.

The purpose of this book is therefore a *contemplative* purpose. If we place it in the category of a book of meditations it gives material for considerations in the sense of the Exercises of St. Ignatius—considerations on the Catholic priesthood. The *consideratio* is essentially an instruction rather than an exhortation; it is addressed primarily to the understanding and *via* this to the will to the ordering of one's life; it does not address itself so directly to the heart as does the meditative method of the (Ignatian) *contemplatio*. But this is not meant in an exclusive sense. Naturally, even in the *consideratio*, there is place for the affections. In its activity the soul tends not only to study calmly the essential characteristics of the object but also to discover its value. If the subject is pleasing the soul desires it; when the soul resolves to possess and enjoy it, it rejoices over it; if the object gives delight, the soul ascends from the gift to the Giver, adores Him, thanks Him, dedicates itself anew to Him, begs Him for further proofs of favour, and is penitent for all disregard and misuse of the gifts of the priesthood.

Thus, the right *consideratio* turns entirely of itself to *affectio,* reflection leads to devotion, recognition to pious affection of the mind, and the emotion of the heart to joyful and active love.

Holy Scripture has always been the best guide from the intellectual consideration of the divine treasures of salvation to their life-giving apprehension. For Holy Scripture is the word of the Holy Spirit Himself, the giver of life, and therefore has that life-giving power which the Lord ascribed to it when He compared it with the seed of the Kingdom of Heaven. The reflections in this book therefore lean in an especial sense on the word of Holy Scripture, not in the merely incidental way in which an outward structure of Scriptural texts is often hung round the writer's own opinions like an ornamentation, but in an essential way which seeks in Holy Scripture the root of all that has been said, and tries to demonstrate this, right down to bedrock.

The author hears the Spirit of God speaking of the priesthood in many texts of the Scriptures which present-day exegetes consider that they must explain less definitely than he does. We do not wish to claim, by any means, that all the texts quoted can be explained *only* as has been done here; only one meaning, which is (affirmatively if not exclusively) contained in the text is brought to the reader's notice in the particular sense in which it is relevant to the facts of the priesthood. This is shown in our references to the Last Supper discourses, to mention but one instance of great importance. Reflecting on these with the priesthood in mind has led the author to the conviction that here the Lord was speaking far more of the conditions of the apostolic mission than of the life of grace of the individual Christian. Present-day exegesis of St. John's Gospel takes the opposite point of view, for instance, in its reading of the parable of the vinestalk and the vine as relating primarily to the Christian life of grace. The Lord speaks, we know, of bringing forth fruit in the apostolic bearing of witness for him. If we assume the existence of the priestly office as instituted by Christ, the prophecies of our Lord at the Last Supper assume an entirely specific meaning, in which they reveal immensely important mysteries of the apostolic, priestly calling—mysteries which remain hidden from us if we understand these texts merely as referring to the relationship of grace existing between Christ and His disciples in general. The Protestant exegesis naturally stands in a far more fundamental contrast to our standpoint; in consequence of the Reformation's denial of the Sacrament of Holy Orders it is inclined, as a matter of course, to deny this relevance to texts which, according to Catholic ideas, may very well be understood to refer to the priesthood. Anyone who bears this in mind will be able to understand, and probably also approve, the particular way in which the texts of Scripture have been assessed in our Considerations.

The frequent references to texts which do not appear in the book also serve to prove the close unity which exists between the mystery of the priesthood and Holy Scripture. The reader should take his Bible and look up the passages referred to; the book is, of course, written for priests; and priests should be used to looking up the Scriptures.

The Scripture reading which is recommended at the end of each Consideration is designed to help the reader to see the object of the Consideration mirrored in particularly valuable testimonies from Holy Scripture, from the liturgical thought and feeling of the Church and from literature of Christian wisdom in general, such as the *Imitation of Christ*, the *Exercises* of St. Ignatius, and so on. Ordinary books of meditations set such texts at the head of each introduction to the meditations, the principle being that the " points " give a spiritual explanation of these texts. We proceed the other way round: the points give the actual material for the meditation; the readings serve as an " explanation " for it. Anyone who takes the trouble to do the readings after each Consideration will be surprised to find how the matter reflected upon is illuminated afresh by the words of Holy Scripture or of the Church. Naturally there is nothing to prevent anyone from taking the readings first, if he finds this suits him better.

There are many books of meditations on the Catholic priesthood. Usually they consist of exhortations to holders of holy orders to offer to the Lord the " gifts and sacrifices for sins " for which they have been appointed to the priesthood. Naturally, this aim is also implicit in our book; but its real intention is not so much to exhort the priest to the right spirit in his pastoral work as to guide him towards a deeper understanding of the bedrock of his priestly being, on which all priestly action is based: this is Ordination itself. Hence, our book sees the Catholic priesthood primarily in the light of and focused on God and the High Priest Jesus Christ; it aims at leading the reader into the depths of the divine Love, which reveals itself to the world in the Catholic priesthood.

In order to do this the book seeks to probe the depths of those movements of life which emanate from the heart of God to the priesthood of the New Covenant. In order to avoid falling into subjective opinions in the course of this endeavour, it had to be solidly based on dogmatic considerations. It was inevitable that this should give it a doctrinal and dogmatic slant here and there. But may not part of our hour of meditation be profitably devoted to a continuation of our schooling recognizing the works of divine love? We were glad to find someone recently expressing in the following words an idea that was uppermost in our mind: " It should be possible to take points for meditation from theology too. The mental habit of having asceticism and knowledge running on two different rails, so to speak, must be progressively abandoned if the result (in the priesthood) is not to be a theology of high intellectual level coupled with a primitive . . . spiritual life " (Prof. Dr. J. M. Reuss in *Wort und Wahrheit*, 1954, p. 101 f.). A clear and deep knowledge of the divine gifts of salvation is, in fact, according to the words of the Apostle, one of the " weapons of our warfare " which we can use for " the demolishing of strongholds, the destroying of reasoning—yes, of every lofty thing that exalts itself against the knowledge of God, bringing every mind into captivity to the obedience of Christ " (2 Cor. 10:4 f.).

CONTENTS

13

PART TWO

THE MISSION OF THE HOLY PRIESTHOOD

PART THREE

THE EQUIPMENT OF THE CATHOLIC PRIESTHOOD

Contents

PART FOUR

THE BLESSINGS OF THE HOLY PRIESTHOOD

THE BLESSINGS OF THE PRIESTHOOD

PART FIVE

THE CATHOLIC PRIESTHOOD IN RELATION TO THE MOST HOLY TRINITY

PART ONE

THE ESSENTIAL CHARACTER OF THE SACRED PRIESTHOOD

> "And he, Son though he was, learned obedience from the things that he suffered; and when perfected, he became to all who obey him the cause of eternal salvation, called by God a high priest according to the order of Melchisedech" (Hebr. 5: 8-10).

THE ESSENTIAL CHARACTER OF THE SACRED PRIESTHOOD

1. THE PRIESTHOOD IN MAN'S YEARNING AND GOD'S PROMISE

" This first tabernacle [namely, the urge towards the priesthood in man's yearning and God's promise] is a figure of the present time, inasmuch as gifts and sacrifices are offered that cannot perfect the worshipper in conscience, since they refer only to food and drink and various ablutions and bodily regulations imposed until a time of reformation " (Hebr. 9:9-10).

HUMANITY CRIES OUT FOR A PRIESTHOOD

1st Consideration

I. The Cry. Aristotle says : " A well-ordered community must consist of the following classes: many peasants for the production of foodstuffs; workpeople and warriors; owners of property; priests and judges " (*Politics*, 1328 b). In a passage closely resembling Hebrews 5, Plato describes the function of the priest: " Our priests are qualified to present our gifts of propitiation to the gods, and by their prayers to win good things in return " (*Politikos*, Chapter 29, 290 c. d).

II. The Answer. God remains silent. He allows this priesthood to continue, but He does not respond to its supplications. For He responds only to priests whom He Himself has called. The impotence of this pagan priesthood is described in the words of St. Thomas: " *Sacerdotium erat ante legem apud colentes Deum secundum humanam determinationem* " (*Summa Th.*,

I-II, q. 103, a. 1). In its whole character and operation this priesthood was a mere creation of human aspirations and, what is more, of blasphemous, diabolical, deception. Yet it was not wholly displeasing to God. It was not contrary to His wishes that the peoples of the earth should single out the finest men from their midst, and commission them as best they knew how to bridge by their prayers and sacrifices the distance between them, and the deity whom they sought, not without hope. For after the Fall God had still left man with his hunger for the Eternal, and to preserve this hunger was the task of the priesthood which man himself commissioned and deputed. For God's plan of salvation was to make contact, when the time should be fulfilled, with this hunger for the Eternal which had been cherished and often purified by the pagan priesthood. Hence, the priesthood *ex humana determinatione* also was and still is in the service of the divine plan of salvation.

III. Humanity's Cry for the Priesthood Is a Cry for Our Priesthood, since our call to the priesthood according to John 15:16, is a call of grace, i.e., *secundum divinam determinationem.* It is not only a call of grace, however. Nature too calls us, uses us, sends us, in so far as lies in its power. We are not always sufficiently conscious of this important fact. The spiritual reading for priests hardly ever speaks of it. And even in Holy Scripture itself the priesthood which unredeemed man creates and deputes for himself is scarcely mentioned except when its aberrations from the true worship of God are depicted (Wisd. 13 and 14; Ps. 113). And yet it is this yearning of humanity for the priest which con-

stitutes the *earthly* proof and justification of all priesthood. Therefore it must not be despised because of
itself it does not make the priesthood efficacious for
the salvation of man. The Roman Catechism says this
with great emphasis: "Quam igitur naturali instinctu
homines agnoscerent Deum colendum esse: consequens
erat, ut in quavis republica aliqui sacrorum et divini
cultus procurationi praeficerentur, quorum potestas
aliquo modo spiritualis diceretur" (Pars II, c. VII, n.
8). God's mercy makes contact with the good will
which the priesthood *ex humana determinatione* possesses, and blesses it by sending to man the priesthood
ex divina determinatione: "And the children of the
stranger, that adhere to the Lord . . . I will bring
them into my holy mount, and will make them joyful
in my house of prayer: their holocausts and their
victims shall please me upon my altar: for my house
shall be called the house of prayer, for all nations"
(Isa. 56:6 f.).

THE LEVITICAL PRIESTHOOD

2nd Consideration

To humanity's call for a true priesthood (1st Consideration) God gives a temporary response which is
recorded in the history of salvation. He founds the
Levitical priesthood (Exod. 29:1 ff.). The hope of fallen
man, to which the priesthood *ex humana determinatione*
had given voice, is answered by God with a priesthood
ex divina determinatione. True, this priesthood does not
yet fulfill that hope, but it confirms, preserves, and purifies it. When the fullness of time came, it found in the

encounter with the fulfilment, i.e., with Jesus, its fate and judgment on it. In the history of the Levitical priesthood God reveals to us a prelude, as it were ("in figura," St. Thomas Aquinas says) of the priesthood in general in its good and evil days.

I. The Blessed Rôle of the Levitical Priesthood. According to God's commandment the duty of the Levitical priesthood was primarily to preserve the Chosen People in the faith and worship of the one true God by the "service of the tabernacle." This service consisted in preaching the holy Law of the Covenant, offering the sacrifices required by it, and performing the prescribed service of prayer. But the Law of the Covenant was given, as the Prophets continually emphasized, with a view to the future Messianic Priest-King, and was meant to be observed for His sake. The sacrifices held out a promise of atonement, it is true, but they did not have the power to effect it, and they were only to find their fulfilment and their full meaning in Christ. The service of prayer, psalms, and canticles was replete with Messianic faith and yearning. Hence, this priesthood was already completely focused upon Christ as the coming Messias. He was already its purport, its joy and its pride, even if it was itself at the same time "but a shadow of the good things to come" (Hebr. 10:1).

II. The Failure of the Levitical Priesthood. The prophecies were fulfilled; the Messias-Priest came. But His own knew Him not and received Him not (Jn. 1: 11). The Parable of the Wicked Vinedressers, in which the Lord Himself expresses this tragic state of things, concludes in Matthew with the remark: " And when the chief priests and Pharisees had heard his parables, they knew that he was speaking about *them* " (Mt. 21: 45). *In what did their failure consist?* Paul throws some light on this mystery when he says (Rom. 9:32): " Because they sought it [the law of justice] not from faith, but as it were from works. For they stumbled at the stumbling-stone, as it is written, ' Behold I lay in Sion a stumbling-stone and rock of scandal: and whoever believes in him shall not be disappointed.' " The stumbling-stone was Christ, the poor humble servant of God (Isa. 53), who fulfilled the Covenant of promise on the altar of the *cross*. God led the Levitical priesthood up to the fulfilment of its calling in Christ. But before the cross, upon which this fulfilment had to be accomplished, it recoiled. For this reason God withdrew Himself from it, and passed the verdict: " Episcopatum ejus accipiat alter " (Ps. 108:8).

III. Thus, Here Already the Cross Is the Dividing Mark which separates a priesthood which is rejected though called by God, and a priesthood which is accepted.

Reading: Mt. 21:31-46.

THE PRIESTHOOD OF MELCHISEDECH

3rd Consideration

In the liturgy of the Eucharistic Sacrifice the Levitical priesthood is passed over in silence; by its rejection of the cross it has shut itself out from enjoyment of the fruits of the cross. The Church, on the other hand, daily commemorates another priesthood which had likewise been sent by God " by promise " and " tamquam in figura ": the priesthood of Melchisedech. In the anamnesis of the Canon she begs God to accept the Eucharistic oblation as He was graciously pleased to accept the pre-Levitical offerings of Abel and Abraham, " et quod Tibi obtulit summus sacerdos Tuus Melchisedech, sanctum sacrificium, immaculatam hostiam."

I. The Priesthood of Melchisedech in Holy Scripture.

Twice before Christ, the Spirit of the Lord speaks of Melchisedech. In Genesis 14: 18-20, it is told how this mysterious priest-king, who was like a being " without father, without mother, without genealogy, having neither beginning of days nor end of life . . ." (Hebr. 7:3), comes forward, offers sacrifice, blesses Abraham, and receives tithes from him. It all reads like a chance historical incident. Centuries pass and no mention is made of the priesthood of Melchisedech until it turns up again in Psalm 109, which interprets for us the mystery of that incident. Here the royal prophet reveals to the Chosen People that a priest " according to the order of Melchisedech " will be given to mankind, and that this priest will be none other than the promised Messias.[1]

---

[1] We refrain from referring here to the seventh chapter of the Epistle to the Hebrews as it is a consideration on the priesthood of Christ rather than on that of Melchisedech.

II. The Importance of the Priesthood of Melchisedech in the History of Salvation. This importance consists not, as is usually maintained, in the fact that Melchisedech offered bread and wine, and thus pointed to the forms of the future Eucharistic Sacrifice, for the Levitical priesthood too offered bread and wine; it lies, rather, in the fact that *by means of it God takes the opportunity of promising to humanity the priesthood which will win His full approval and, at the same time, fulfil mankind's yearning.* He promises this, not by a simple promise, but by an oath of which He will not repent (*juravit Dominus et non poenitebit eum*). It will be a priesthood exercised by One alone, and this One exercises it " in aeternum ". And this One will be the Messias. Hence, according to Psalm 109, Melchisedech's priesthood is the God-given guarantee that the priesthood of man's yearning and God's promise will emerge into fulfilment in the Messianic priesthood, the priesthood of Christ—*our* priesthood.

III. The Priest of the New Covenant should gladly and reverently meditate upon his relation to the priesthood of Melchisedech. The Church instructs us to do so by the prominent position which she gives to Psalm 109 in the Roman Breviary. For has it not first place in the Vespers of all Sundays and feast days? Every time we recite it we should recall that that high priesthood *secundum ordinem Melchisedech* continues, *through us,* to operate in power and in blessing. What power over the heart of God lies, moreover, in our daily prayer after the Consecration, that God may accept our oblation as He was graciously pleased to accept the gifts of the " summus sacerdos Melchisedech." We take God at His word so to speak—the word which He Himself gave on oath, and by which He owes it to Himself to accept with complete approval the oblation which " has become present on the altar solely through the priest's word " (Encyclical, *Mystici Corporis Christi*).

Reading: Gen. 14:18-20.

2. THE PRIESTHOOD OF JESUS CHRIST

> " Having therefore a great high priest
> who has passed into the heavens, Jesus
> the Son of God, let us hold fast our
> confession " (Hebr. 4: 14).

PREFACE

Our considerations up to now have dealt with the
priesthood as the object of human yearning and divine
promise. In Psalm 109 God swears that He will fulfil
man's yearning and His promise. When the fullness of
time came, He made good His word in the glory of
the Messianic Priesthood, the priesthood of Jesus
Christ. The Catholic priesthood is a participation in
the priesthood of Christ. He to whom this gift has
been given only comprehends its value in the measure
that he realizes the fullness and the glory of the priesthood of Christ. The following considerations aim at
helping him to do this.

A KINGLY PRIESTHOOD

4th Consideration

I. The Priesthood of Christ is correlated to His kingly
majesty. The real theme of Psalm 109, which our Lord
Himself declared David had written " in the Spirit "
(Mt. 22:43), is the kingly glory of the coming Messias.
It is revealed, among other things, in His being a priest

secundum ordinem Melchisedech; hence, His priesthood is a function of His Messianic Kingship. In keeping with the basic thought of this psalm, Paul said that "the mystery of his will" was to re-establish all things in Christ, both those in the heavens and those on the earth (Eph. 1:10), "that in all things he may have the first place" (Col. 1:18). But the road which the Messias has to tread to reach this glory is not the way of earthly conquerors and sovereigns (Jn. 18:36), but the way of "making peace by the blood of his cross" (Col. 1:20); this is the priestly Way of the Cross. Hence, the priesthood of Christ is the way which the Messias must tread to His glory. But the glory is the goal.

II. All Participation in the Priesthood of Christ is Participation in His Divine Destiny, and a Call to His Kingly Glory. That is why the Prince of the Apostles cries to all the baptized: "You are a royal priesthood" (1 Pet. 2:9). For Baptism is the basis of our common vocation and common destiny with Christ, the King of the Universe. But the Sacrament of Holy Orders has amplified the participation of us, ordained priests, in the Messianic, Kingly, glory of Christ, in that ordination has augmented our *ability* to work in the building up of the kingdom of Christ; and our mission (*missio apostolica*) has expanded our scope beyond our own souls to those of the people for whom the Church has commissioned us.

III. Cultivation of the Consciousness of His Royal and Messianic Mission in the Priest. In Christ Himself the consciousness of his Messianic and royal mission dwelt

in unbroken purity and depth. Even on Good Friday
He bore witness to it before Pilate (Gospel of the Feast
of Christ the King). It is a characteristic of all great
apostles; indeed, it gives their mission its peculiar
strength and irresistibility. It glows in Paul; from it
Athanasius and Chrysostom draw their steadfast and
combative constancy; Charles Borromeo and Peter
Canisius, their tireless pastoral zeal. Without this consciousness the priest's spirit is weak, worldly and lacking in impetus. It is the fruit of the Holy Spirit, who in
Baptism and ordination has given us the right to it and
the capacity for it. But it does not develop unless
fostered, any more than do the other gifts of grace. It
lives and grows in the priest who prays for understanding of his calling. The considerations " De regno
Christi " in the *Exercises* of St. Ignatius are a classical
school of this sense of the royal and Messianic mission;
they have fanned it to a clear and unquenchable flame
in countless young souls.

To every priestly soul in which it is living and
strong the Lord says each day: " Thou art my servant
Israel, for in thee will I glory " (Isa. 49:3).

Reading: Isa. 49:1-7.

A MEDIATING PRIESTHOOD

5th Consideration

True, the Messias is called by God to eternal kingship. But this kingship is not merely given to Him: He
must acquire and win it as a priest. " For every high
priest taken from among men is appointed for men in

the things pertaining to God, that he may offer gifts and sacrifices for sins" (Hebr. 5:1). It is his office, therefore, to be a mediator between God and man (*Summa Th.*, III, q. 22, a. 1). For no one is his own priest.

Let us, then, consider *the priesthood of Christ: a mediatory priesthood.*

I. Homo Christus Jesus—Mediator Dei et Hominum

(1 Tim. 2:5). The Messias fulfils His office of mediator in a twofold manner: in spirit and in action. *In spirit* because in emerging from the depths of the Godhead (" Ante luciferum, tamquam rorem, genui te," Ps. 109) His desire begins " to be with the children of men," to lead them to the Father (Prov. 8). In His earthly life He describes Himself as the Good Shepherd (Jn. 10:11), who according to Ezechiel 34:23 leads the people of God to the Father. *In action:* in His earthly time His spirit of mediation becomes an effectual act of mediation from the very moment of the Incarnation; in this spirit He takes from the Virgin Mary our human nature in order to offer it up to God; in this spirit He retains the divine nature, which He possessed from all eternity, in order to bring it down to man. Thus the Incarnation is the ordination of the Messianic King, because in it He assumes the equipment for that *admirabile commercium* (work of mediation) in which the " creator generis humani animatum corpus sumens . . . largitus est nobis suam Deitatem " (Vespers of the Feast of the Circumcision). To the execution of this work of mediation He devotes all the energy and love of His most Sacred Heart and all His burning zeal for souls during the whole of His earthly life.

II. The Catholic Priest as Servant of the Mediatory Office of Christ. Since our priesthood is a participation in the priesthood of Christ, it is, like it, essentially mediatory, that is to say, equipped with power for mediation and obliged to mediatory action. The man who receives Holy Orders receives them not merely for his personal sanctification but also for the sanctification of the people of God, for the continuation of that *commercium* in which the Messias from the human race redeems for the heavenly Father " an acceptable people ". For no one is his own priest. Therefore, while we can dispense to others the mysteries of salvation (the sacraments), which our ordination empowers us to dispense, we cannot dispense them to ourselves, with the exception of the Holy Eucharist. In Christ, Messias, Priest and Shepherd of mankind, we have become, as the Apostle says, " God's helpers "; this is a condescension of God to us and at the same time a raising up of our wretchedness to God. For " omnium divinorum divinissimum est, Deo cooperari in conversione animarum " (Ps. Dion).

III. The Strength of Our Priestly Mediatorship is evinced by the strength and purity of our *zeal for souls*. A priest without zeal for souls is like the servant of the parable, who buries the talent which his master had entrusted to him instead of putting it out at interest; even though his personal behaviour is above reproach he cannot escape condemnation, for he has not fulfilled the order of his master; hence he is already judged (Mt. 25:28-31). In this respect the priesthood is never a mere sinecure. Our zeal must not only be lively, however; it must also be pure. As Christ sought souls for the Father (Jn. 17:9), so must our zeal for souls be for the Father and not for the satisfaction of our own desire for self-assertion. To acquire and keep the strength and purity of our zeal for souls demands a constant struggle against nature, which of itself is prone to seek *quae sua sunt,* even in priestly action. To a Francis Xavier the mediation of salvation to souls became such a constant burden as to leave no room for the satisfaction of his natural desires; while still young he consumed his vital forces in the service of the mediatorship of Jesus Christ.

Reading: Ps. 71.

A SACRIFICING PRIESTHOOD

6th Consideration

As a " wonderful barter " the eternal Son of the heavenly Father brings the Divine into the world. He is to pledge it that the " gens perdita " (Soph. 2:5) of the human race may become once more a " populus acquisitionis " (1 Pet. 2:9). But in order that the Divine can become effectual in our mediator, he must, according to the decree of the Father, not only offer up and sacrifice the *human* in his own person but also in " his brothers " to the heavenly Father. Thus the mediator becomes the priest offering sacrifice.

Let us, then, consider *the priesthood of Christ:* a sacrificing *priesthood.*

I. Jesus Offers Himself as a Sacrifice Throughout His Whole Life. Sacrifice is the surrender to God of something which is ours to dispose of. It has a twofold intention: on the one hand, to recognize thereby the supremacy of God, who has unlimited right to dispose of us and of all that we have; on the other hand, to co-ordinate our sacrificial gift and ourselves into the domain of divine consecration and divine blessing, so that we may be " sanctified ". The value of the object sacrificed and the nobility of the sacrificial spirit together determine the degree to which the sacrifice is pleasing in the eyes of God.

In order to make lost humanity into an oblation pleasing in the eyes of the Father, the Mediator Christ Himself joins the ranks of this people. In fact, He becomes their Head. " Christ delivered himself up for us an offering and a sacrifice to God to ascend in fragrant odour " (Eph. 5:2). Moreover He gives to His " purchased people " the nobility of His sacrificial *spirit* by identifying them with His own will to submit to the Father: " And for them I sanctify myself, that they also may be sanctified in truth " (Jn. 17:19 f.). This is the sacrificial spirit in which, according to Hebr. 10:5, He begins and devotes His life, until the " Consummatum est " of His death on the cross.

II. It is Christ's Wish to Sanctify His People by Sacrifice in Our Priesthood Too.

When He laid upon His Apostles and their successors the order " Hoc facite in meam commemorationem," He gave to us priests the power to render present ever anew *among His people* His own sacrificial spirit and His own sacrificial gift; " And as the Divine Redeemer, when He was dying on the Cross, offered Himself to the Eternal Father as the Head of the whole human race, so also in this ' clean oblation ' [the Eucharist] He offers to the Heavenly Father not only Himself as head of the Church, but in

Himself also His mystical members: for He encloses
them all, even the weak and frail among them, most
lovingly in His Sacred Heart." But it is the priest
" whose voice alone renders the Immaculate Lamb
present on the Altar," and in this act of sacrifice " we
represent not only our Saviour but also the whole
Mystical Body and each of its members," so that these
also, united with us in common prayer and supplication,
offer to " the Eternal Father this most pleasing Sacrifice
of praise and propitiation, for the needs of the whole
Church " (Encyclical, *Mystici Corporis Christi*). We are
a sacrificing priesthood, Head and members!

III. His Participation in the Priesthood of Christ will
evince itself in the personal life of the priest in two
ways.

Firstly, in the *disinterestedness* with which he leads,
not to himself but to Christ, the flock entrusted to him.
To him it is not "his" flock, but God's, which God will
one day require at his hand (Ezech. 34:10). Secondly,
in his *apostolic works, prayer and sufferings*. With his
Master Christ he will say: " And for them I sanctify
myself, that they also may be sanctified in truth " (Jn.
17:19). The knowledge that he is called to be " forma
gregis " to the faithful entrusted to him, by an inner
and outward manner of life which is " sanctiorem prae
laicis " (Canon 124), will make him go his way secretly
renouncing the satisfaction of his own heart and inspired
by a loving spirit of sacrifice for the salvation of souls.
His life of prayer will be far removed from that egotism
which seeks only self, even in piety.
Reading: Hebr. 10:5-10.

A PRIESTHOOD IN SUFFERING AND DEATH

7th Consideration

The Messias came to the human race as king, to win it to Himself as " His people." As Priest it is His mission to sanctify this " purchased people " and to offer it in sacrifice to the Father. But the anger of the Father lay upon mankind on account of its sins, and an immeasurable guilt lay upon it because of its unrighteousness. In order that it might become a " people pleasing to the Lord " the anger of the Father had to be placated: the immeasurable debt of guilt had to be paid. The High Priest Jesus Christ takes both upon Himself in His Passion and death.

Let us consider *the priesthood of Christ : a priesthood in suffering and death.*

I. Hence, It Is Christ's Will " to give His life as a ransom for many " (Mt. 20:28). Anyone who would wish to turn Him aside from this is far in mind from " the things of God ": " And he began to teach them that the Son of Man must suffer many things, and be rejected by the elders and chief priests and Scribes, and be put to death. . . . And what he said he spoke openly. And Peter taking him aside, began to chide him. But he, turning and seeing his disciples, rebuked Peter, saying: 'Get behind me, satan, for thou dost not mind the things of God but those of men ' " (Mk. 8:31 ff.; Jn. 10:18). The bitter suffering and death of our Lord is the outward and bloody fulfilment of this Messianic will to expiation; by His obedience unto the death of the cross, He lifts from His people the debt of guilt in which their disobedience had involved them; He changes the anger of the Father into reconciliation with those whom He has signed with His blood. "How much more will the blood of Christ, who through the Holy Spirit offered himself unblemished unto God, cleanse your conscience from dead works to serve the living God?" (Hebr. 9:14.)

II. Let His Will Be Our Will !

Passio Christi enim non salvat nisi configuratos (Summa Th., I-II, q. 85). "Do you not know that all we who have been baptized into Christ Jesus have been baptized into his death?" (Rom. 6:3.) Now, according to the Apostle, we become united to Him in the likeness of His death by crucifying our old self "with him, in order that the body of sin may be destroyed, that we may no longer be slaves to sin" (Rom. 6:5 f.). If even the baptized layman must participate thus in the redemptive death of his High Priest, how much more so must the ordained priest, who daily approaches the altar in order to render present once more in an unbloody manner the sacrifice of Christ for His people?

III. What Is This Dying With Christ ?

J. J. Olier (d. 1657), the holy founder and rector of St. Sulpice, in Paris, gives a horrifying answer: "It means dying to the world to such a degree that it no longer stirs our heart; it may show us its beauties, its honours and its riches; it may threaten and torture us with its trials; all these things will find us dead, as it were, impassive, and unimpressed by all that the world has to offer." "All these things will find us dead." As long as we are in the flesh, we are never really dead to the world; we cannot deaden our susceptibility to its allurements and dangers to such a degree as to make these ineffectual. What, then, does it mean to behave towards the world as if we were dead to it ? The great priests of the Church—the Apostles, after the descent of the Holy Spirit, Paul in his struggle to die to the world and its lusts, Francis Xavier in the loneliness and dereliction of his missionary life and death—tell us this better than any words. To save others from the divine anger they became " as if they were dead " to the world and its claims. Already in life they were dead—dead with Christ. How do I stand ?

Reading : Rom. 6:3-14.

AN EXPIATING PRIESTHOOD

8th Consideration

" From the brook by the wayside he will drink; therefore will he lift up his head " (Ps. 109:7). Thirsting for the salvation of His people, the Servant of God bows His head in death; but His soul, joyful and victorious, passes into the land of freedom and reconciliation: " Agnus redemit oves; Christus innocens Patri reconciliavit peccatores."

" Felix culpa, quae talem ac tantum meruit habere redemptorem!" But the fruit of the Redemption was still hanging on the tree of the cross; in order to effect our salvation, it had to be broken and conveyed to us. In this distribution to us of the fruit of the cross the High Priest Christ accomplishes unceasingly the reconciliation of His people with His heavenly Father.

Let us consider *the Priesthood of Christ, Mediator between God and man.*

I. For This Purpose Christ Founds the New Covenant.
In it He erects an ordered and everlasting realm of
reconciliation which He calls His "Church." He loves
as His bride this product formed of mankind and the
Holy Spirit; He unites Himself to it as the head is
bound to the members. He gives to this Church all
that His people need, that they may live from the
fruit of the Redemption and never have to die again;
above all, the mysteries of salvation, the seven sacraments. Ever since the soldier pierced with his sharp
lance the side of the Good Shepherd, a spring has
been gushing forth from the Shepherd's heart, cleansing
and refreshing His flock and making it pleasing in
the eyes of God; a veritable stream of peace and benediction, from the banks of which resounds the ceaseless
canticle: "Dignus es, Domine, . . . quoniam occisus
es, et redemisti nos Deo in sanguine tuo . . . : et
fecisti nos Deo nostro regnum et sacerdotes!" (Apoc.
5:8-10.)

**II. He Makes Us Priests Ministers of This New
Covenant of Reconciliation** (2 Cor. 3:6). He entrusts us,
as the Apostle says explicitly, with the "ministerium reconciliationis" (2 Cor. 5:18). All the yearning of mankind, which had been trying to build a
bridge to God in the priesthood *ex humana determinatione,* but could not do so (First Consideration),
now receives its fulfilment in abundance of blessing, a
blessing which is to remain inexhaustible as long as
human beings inhabit the redeemed world. We are
able to exercise this service of mediation because
"He also it is who has made us fit ministers of the
new covenant . . ." (2 Cor. 3:6).

III.   The Proof of Our " Ministry of Reconciliation."
When the Church, in her Consecration of a Bishop,
confers upon one of her sons the fullness of the
priesthood, she prays in the Consecration Preface: *Da
ei Domine, ministerium reconciliationis in verbo et
facto, in virtute signorum et prodigiorum.* The priest,
himself a man reconciled with God, serves the work of
reconciliation of his Master, in *verbo*, by the peaceful
words of his preaching, *signis et prodigiis*, by placing
the sacramental signs which accomplish the wonder of
absolution from sin and the rebirth of the sinner: *et
facto*, in whose works of self-sanctification in which we
fill up in our flesh for His body, which is the Church,
what is lacking of the sufferings of Christ (Col. 1:24).
Hence, in the eyes of the faithful, the true priest becomes a reflection of the risen Lord, who announced
the accomplishment of the Redemption to all who
believed in Him with the new salutation: *Pax vobis!*
With the Prophet, the people of the Lord cry to their
priests: " How beautiful upon the mountains are the
feet of him that bringeth good tidings . . . that saith
to Sion: ' Thy God shall reign! ' " (Isa. 52:7.)

Reading : Isa. 55:1-5.

A PRIESTHOOD IN GLORY

9th Consideration

In Psalm 109 the psalmist says to the Messianic
Priest-King: " the sceptre of your power the Lord
will stretch forth from Sion: . . . Yours is princely
power in the day of your birth, in holy splendour . . . "

The royal psalmist sees in spirit the priesthood of his Lord passing from the humility to servitude to the glory of royal triumph.

Let us consider *the priesthood of Christ: a priesthood in glory.*

This glory of the Messianic priesthood is

I. The Glory of Jesus Christ in Heaven as manifested.

(a) *in His glorified person.* For " Jesus, who for the joy set before him, endured a cross, despising shame," now " sits at the right hand of the throne of God " (Hebr. 12:2; *cf.* Ps. 109:1). The Epistle to the Hebrews says so explicitly. The heart of the high priest of humanity did not disdain, then, to allow Himself to be influenced by promises of future glory, to fulfil His mission of redemption.

(b) *in His glorified people.* For the Head draws the members, the King draws His people with Him into the glory of the heavenly Father: " Ascendisti in altum, cepisti captivitatem, accepisti dona in hominibus " (Ps. 67:19). With the Ascension there begins for our Lord that *dies virtutis suae*, the hour of His victorious strength, in which the redeemed people of God shall stream in an uninterrupted procession through the pearl gates of the heavenly Jerusalem, in order to form there " the glorious retinue of His saints." For the Father promised Him this when He said: " Behold I will bring upon her [Jerusalem] as it were a river of peace, and as an overflowing torrent the glory of the Gentiles..." (Isa. 66:12). For He reigns over the peoples as " King of kings and Lord of lords " (Apoc. 19:16).

II.   The Glory of the Mystical Christ on Earth, as it is manifested,

(a) *in the power of our preaching of the cross.* For the glory of the Kingdom of Christ invests with such radiance the doctrine of the folly of the cross, without which we can bring salvation to none, that the cross appears desirable to the faithful;

(b) *in the performance of the holy liturgy,* which, in its essential character and its whole content, is a pre-figuration of the glory of our King, in so far as this can be represented and realized on our earthly battle-field.

III.   This Glory of the Priesthood of Jesus Christ Is in a Particular Way the Portion of Our Priesthood Too, per Participationem. Our Lord confirmed this explicitly when the Apostles put the question to Him through Peter: " Behold, we have left all and followed thee; what then shall we have?" For He solemnly assured them that they would share in His glory (Mt. 19:27 ff.). That is why the Church, on taking us into her priesthood, made us say with the Bishop: " O Lord, my allotted portion and my cup, you it is who hold fast my lot " (Ps. 15:5). Faith in and love of the cross certainly belong to the priestly life; but faith and joy in the victory and glory of Christ belong to it equally certainly. A sacerdotal asceticism which fails to apply this joyful impetus or only applies it sparingly, has something unredeemed about it and cannot deny its kinship to Jansenism, the Christianity of gloom. Like Jansenism, it is full of poison and gall in its essence.

If not sunk in the darkness of sin, the true priest lives in the pure Easter faith and joy of his Church.

Reading.   Psalm 44

AN EVERLASTING PRIESTHOOD

10th Consideration

If the priesthood of Christ is a function of the Messianic kingship, if it is the humble and painful road which the Messias had to tread to His glory (4th Consideration), then it must *come to an end* when the Messianic kingdom is fully realized and when the prince of darkness has been finally rejected. Yet the Holy Scripture says that the Messias is *a priest for ever.* That is what Psalm 109 says. And in the Epistle to the Hebrews (7:24) the Apostle says that Jesus, " because he continues forever, has an everlasting priesthood."

As a final prerogative of our priesthood, let us consider *the priesthood of Christ, an everlasting priesthood.*

I.   The Bearer of This Priesthood Is Everlasting. " But he, because he continues forever, has an everlasting priesthood " (Hebr. 7:24). As the mystery of the Incarnation will not be revoked or dissolved in eternity, Jesus Christ, the bearer of the same, will still retain in eternity the power of priestly reconciliation and combination of the divine and the human. In relation to the Father He is the One who " lives always to make intercession for us " (Hebr. 7:25); in relation to us He remains unique as the one bearer of divine salvation " for in Him dwells all the fullness of the Godhead bodily . . ." (Col. 2:9).

II. The Operation of This Priesthood is Everlasting.
True, the real high-priestly act, the sacrifice on Calvary,
has happened once for all. That same Epistle to the
Hebrews, which speaks of the everlasting priesthood of
Christ, says: " but Jesus, having offered one sacrifice
for sins, has taken his seat forever at the right hand of
God. . . . For by one offering he has perfected forever
those who are sanctified " (Hebr. 10:12 f.). Therefore,
if, Christ, by the one offering of Himself (*una oblatione*),
has already perfected in advance (*consummavit*) all
those who are redeemed (*sanctificatos*), and this, moreover, for the whole future (*in aeternum*), then there is
no scope left for priestly action except in so far as the
fruit of that one redemptive sacrifice can and must be
perpetually applied to the redeemed. And this the
Eternal High Priest carries into effect through the
ministerium Novi Testamenti which He has entrusted
to us.

**III. Our Call to the Service of the Priesthood of
Christ Is Therefore a Perpetual One.**

(*a*) The Catholic priesthood is a perpetual priesthood.
Just as Christ neither grows old nor passes away, so
also the Church, preserved by Him, will continue in
fertile youth and strength to the end of time; just as
the Rock of Peter cannot be overpowered, so also the
priesthood of the Church of Christ possesses the power
to remain indestructible to the end of time. Mighty
orders have blossomed up in the Church, and passed
away because their existence was not essential to the
Church; the priesthood remains because it is essential
to the Kingdom of Christ.

(*b*) The grace of ordination (*potestas sacerdotalis*), which the individual bearer of the priesthood receives, is perpetual. This is the clear teaching of the Church, derived from the constant conviction that the *mysteria Christi* can also be validly administered by a priest who is in the state of mortal sin, or even by one who has fallen away from the unity of the faith. For anyone who has been made an instrument of sanctification by the *sacramentum ordinis* of Christ remains so even if his personal life is unholy. But he remains so solely because Christ does not dismiss again the person whom He has formed into an instrument of His high priesthood by that mysterious conformity which the *character indelebilis* gives to us (Denz. 960, 964). The everlasting priesthood of Christ is the guiding eternal force in the sea of time. We shall indeed be blessed if we so serve it " that, united to You by perpetual charity, we may bring forth an everlasting fruit " (Postcommunion of the Votive Mass of Christ the High Priest).

Reading: Psalm 88, particularly verses 20-38.

THE FULLNESS OF THE PRIESTHOOD

11th Consideration

" *Christus est divini Sacerdotii plenitudo.*" Just as the rays of light which tremble in the clear morning air dissolve into one single light when the sun itself rises over the horizon, so do these words of St. Thomas (*Summa Th.*, III, q. 63, a. 6) embrace in one luminous unity all the power and strength of the priesthood of Christ which we have considered up till now. The priesthood of Christ is simply the fulfilment of everything which God desired from all eternity to effect through the priesthood; and it is the faultless and flawless fulfilment of this. With the consideration of this truth, which admittedly we can never fully grasp in this life, we close the series of considerations on the priesthood of Christ as basis and content of our priesthood.

Let us consider *the priesthood of Christ: Divini Sacerdoti Plenitudo.*

1. Our High Priest Jesus Christ Possesses the Perfection of God-Given Priesthood in a Fivefold Sense :

(*a*) *By vocation :* He was called, not by man but by God Himself, and not for a time but " in aeternum " (Ps. 109) and while God called the world into being with only a simple word of His omnipotence, He sealed with an oath His appointment of Christ as priest.

(*b*) *By the power of ordination :* the priestly power which dwells in Jesus is " all the fullness of the Godhead bodily " (Col. 2:9). With the Incarnate Godhead, which is the unique quality of this High Priest, is combined the Holy Spirit, not as in us, to a limited degree, but with all the fullness of His sanctifying power: " The Spirit of the Lord is upon me " (Lk. 4:18).

(*c*) *By action :* " For it is sanctified by the word of God and prayer " (1 Tim. 4:5). The priestly action of Jesus embraces the whole of humanity; therefore the Church has condemned all doctrines which have sought to limit the redemptive will of Jesus. In Rom. 5:12 ff. we find justification for this attitude. But the priestly action of Jesus extends beyond all humanity and embraces all creation (Rom. 8:19 ff.) in as much as this can be used to the glory of God and the salvation of mankind. Hence, the priesthood of Christ is the priesthood of creation.[1]

(d) *By the fullness of blessing :* The blessed fruit of the priesthood of Jesus Christ is the grace of salvation of the New Covenant. And this is as inexhaustible as the merits of Christ. No use and no misuse can exhaust or even diminish the reserves of salvation which this priesthood has created and left behind in the Church.

(e) *By the divine complaisance :* For our High Priest can say of Himself that He " does always the things that are pleasing to Him [the Father]" (Jn. 8:29). Therefore the Psalmist too hails Him: " Thy throne, O God, is forever and ever, and a sceptre of equity is the sceptre of thy kingdom. Thou hast loved justice and hated iniquity; therefore God, thy God, has anointed thee with the oil of gladness above thy fellows " (Hebr. 1:8 f.; Ps. 44: 7 f.).

---

[1] At the end of the Canon the celebrant refers the heavenly Father to the real Christ present in the consecrated elements, and prays: " Per quem haec omnia semper bona creas—sanctificas—vivificas—benedicis—et praestas nobis." What are these " haec omnia "? To be sure, in the first place the elements of bread and wine, in that these contain, through the true sacrificing priest and the true sacrificial gift, that which the heavenly Father " creat—sanctificat—vivificat—benedicit et praestat,"; in the God-Man too. And this gift represents the whole created universe, from which it was taken by the Incarnate God. Hence, at this " haec omnia " the glance of priest and faithful may wander over the whole domain of visible and invisible creation. In the Primitive Church all the gifts which the faithful had brought were blessed at this point.

II. He Has Called Us to Participate in This Plenitudo Sacerdotii Divini. All that is ours of divine mission and spiritual power, means of salvation and honour before God and the Church, derives from the fullness of the priesthood of Christ, for "of His fullness we have all received" (Jn. 1:16). "For which cause he is not ashamed to call them [i.e., us] brethren, saying, [to the Father] 'I will declare thy name to my brethren; in the midst of the church I will praise thee. . . .' And again, 'Behold I and my children whom God has given me'" (Hebr. 2:11 f.). Therefore with the Apostle the true priest rejoices in the grace of his calling: "For we preach not ourselves, but Jesus Christ as Lord, and ourselves merely as your servants in Jesus. For God, who commanded light to shine out of darkness, has shone in our hearts, to give enlightenment concerning the knowledge of the glory of God, shining on the face of Christ Jesus" (2 Cor. 4:5 f.).

Reading: Hebr. Chap. 2.

3. OUR PARTICIPATION IN THE PRIESTHOOD OF CHRIST

> "And he himself gave some men as apostles, and some as prophets, others again as evangelists, and others as pastors and teachers, in order to perfect the saints for a work of ministry, for building up the body of Christ, until we all attain to the unity of the faith and of the deep knowledge of the Son of God, to perfect manhood, to the mature measure of the fullness of Christ" (Eph. 4: 11 f.).

PREFACE

To realize the splendours of the priesthood of Christ is, of all the obligations for our calling, the first and most necessary one (Considerations 4 to 11). The priest from whom the glories remain hidden and uncomprehended is like a man carrying a heavy load of which he feels the *weight* but does not know the value. He is a coolie of the Kingdom of God.

But the priest who comprehends them, will he not feel an urge to discover also *the bonds which bind him to them*? " Juncturam subministrationis "—" every joint of the system " (under Christ) Paul calls them in his Epistle to the Ephesians (4:16). Through these bonds Christ joins His own to Himself and moves them to that action whereby the community of the faithful which we call His Church and which Paul calls " the body of Christ " (Eph. 4:12) is built up from Christ Himself and his disciples.

The first of these "juncturae" is fastened by Christ in Baptism. By it He takes the baptized into an indissoluble union with Himself, His person and His works, so that the latter are "as living stones, built thereon into a spiritual house, a holy priesthood, to offer spiritual sacrifices acceptable to God through Jesus Christ" (1 Pet. 2:5). Baptism co-ordinates the baptized into the community of the redeemed inasmuch as it is a "kingly priesthood" in the sphere of action of the individual's own person. This bond is called the *character baptismalis* in theology.

In the same part of the Epistle to the Ephesians Paul speaks of another "junctura subministrationis," a bond with Christ which differs from the baptismal bond just described in the first place by the fact that it is not given to all the baptized but only to such as are *specially called*. Paul speaks of the unity of the faithful with each other: all must be careful to preserve "the unity of the Spirit in the bond of peace" (4:3). And this unity must not be endangered by the fact that Christ does not give the same measure of grace to all (4:7). For among the disciples of Christ there are some who are entrusted with special tasks and endowed with special gifts of grace. "And he himself [Christ] gave some men [to the Church] as apostles, and some as prophets, others again as evangelists, and others as pastors and teachers" (4:11). Hence, Christ binds to Himself those baptized persons whom He picks out for particular functions corresponding to the names of these services. He has established certain offices in His Church as fundamental bases of the Kingdom of God, in order that the holders of these offices should work for the building up of His body. Every single believer should do this, it is true, but some have special functions. It emerges from I Corinthians 12 that the purpose of these functions consists in giving to the Body of Christ the structure proper to it so that it may not be an uncomely formation made up of cells one like the other; " for the body is not one member, but many " (1 Cor. 12:14).

According to the teaching of the Church, Christ accomplishes the enrolment of these specially called persons by the *Sacrament of Holy Orders*. Through it He binds the ordinand to Himself by a new *junctura subministrationis*; or, to be more exact, He binds Himself to the ordinand. Theology calls this bond the *character sacerdotalis*, the priestly seal of consecration.

What is the *character sacerdotalis*? The following considerations are intended as an answer to this question; an answer which is somewhat out of the ordinary because it starts out from another viewpoint than that to which we are accustomed, namely, from the theology of holy orders. St. Thomas Aquinas has broadly outlined the essential nature of the *character sacerdotalis* in describing it as a mark imprinted on the soul which exercises a fourfold function on the ordained person: (1) it is a *signum distinctivum*, for it takes him out from the mass of the baptized; (2) it is a *signum configurativum* in that it gives him a conformity with Christ, the High Priest, which nonordained baptized do not have; (3) it is a *signum obligativum* in that it binds him to use his special powers (*potestates sacramentales*) for the good of the Church; (4) it is a *signum disposi-*

tivum in that it makes him fit to receive these special powers and able to exercise them aright.

Hence, one can see the most essential effect of holy orders if one considers what distinguishes the ordained disciple of Christ from the nonordained. But cannot one also consider the same matter by looking to Christ instead and asking *what Christ does when He places a baptized person in this position as defined by St. Thomas and sustains him in it?* Then we see the grace of our participation in the priesthood of Christ (*participationem sacerdotii Christi*) as the effect of an enduring action of the High Priest Jesus upon us, His servants. By it He makes us continually fit ministers (2 Cor. 3:6) to fulfil those functions in the edification of His Body, for which He wills to use us. Then the mystery of the *character sacerdotalis* will no longer be seen as a static ordinance, but rather as a proof of the ever watchful and active love of Christ for His Church.

This action of Jesus, by which He makes us participants in His priesthood, is the object of the following considerations (12th to 15th). It covers four different modes of procedure on the part of the Lord towards us, (1) He *wills* our participation in His priesthood; (2) He *carries it into effect;* (3) He *desires it;* (4) He *measures* its extent.

If the Apostle expresses the wish that all Christians should have knowledge of Christ's love in all its dimensions (Eph. 3: 18 f.), it is surely only reasonable that we priests should make an effort to realize the love with which the Lord makes us " fit ministers " of His priesthood.

OUR PARTICIPATION IN THE PRIESTHOOD OF CHRIST:

I. CHRIST WILLS IT

12th Consideration

Jesus Christ possesses the fullness of the divinely willed priesthood (11th Consideration). Therefore it would be possible for Him alone to effect the sanctification of all humanity, indeed of the whole created universe, without using human helpers. Luther's efforts to deny the specific priesthood were based upon the thought of this possibility. But Christ has willed otherwise in accordance with the decree of His heavenly Father. As the Head, from which all sanctification of the Mystical Body emanates, He determined to permit the members themselves to co-operate in the building up of His Body, though not all with the same powers and the same scope for action. This will of Christ to allow persons whom He calls to participate in the building up of His Kingdom is the root of our participation in His priesthood.

Let us, then, consider *our participation, willed by Christ, in the priesthood of Christ.*

I. The Great Revelation of This Will. This revelation took place when our Lord, before His Ascension, commissioned His Apostles to go forth, saying: " Go, therefore, and make disciples of all nations, baptizing them . . . teaching them . . ." (Mt. 28: 18 ff.). Until the end of the world the Kingdom of God is to be built up with the co-operation of men, and He Himself will work together with them: " And behold, *I* am with you all days." The order is not addressed to all, however, but to those " of his own choosing" (Mk. 3:13). These, the Apostles, He had prepared long and patiently for this mission. The Apostles died, but the order remained, and Christ's promise to be with His own remained too and still remains for all those who will be called to take the place of the Apostles " even unto the consummation of the world." Our part in the world-saving priesthood of Christ is rooted in this will.

II. The Particular Revelation of This Will to the Individual. Christ made this revelation in His earthly life when He said: " Follow me " to one of the crowd who believed in Him. He regarded the individuals He had so chosen as a special gift which the Father had given Him, and He gave thanks for them: " They were thine, and thou hast given them to me " (Jn. 17:6); prayed for them (Jn. 17:9 ff.); rejoiced over them (Mt. 11:25); and was sorrowful when they rejected the call of the heavenly Father (the rich young man, Lk. 18:18 ff.; Judas, Jn. 17:12). Hence, Christ sees the grace of a vocation to the priesthood as a mystery which is bound up with the decrees of God.

This call to official service in the building up of the Body of Christ is something much greater than an ordinary offer of the grace of God; it entails certain effects which go far beyond the general call to salvation and apportionment of grace. From Christ the Church learns to regard as " set apart " from the rest of man-kind the person in whom she perceives the signs of this vocation; she feels for him that responsibility with which the Lord filled the Damascene disciple Ananias when He sent him to Paul, saying: " Go, for this man is a chosen vessel to me. . . . I will show him how much he must suffer for my name " (Acts 9:15 f.).

III. " For Consider Your Own Call, Brethren!" (1 Cor. 1:26.) No one was filled with more elation and gratitude at these words than the Apostle of the Gentiles, who himself spoke them. Ever since the " Follow me " of the Lord was addressed to him before the gates of Damascus he no longer regarded himself as a freeman, who could do what he liked with himself, but as a " prisoner of Jesus Christ." With what wonder he regarded the grace of the apostolic vocation, and how hard he tried to grasp more and more deeply not only the task which it had brought Him, but also the blessing which accompanied it. The value we set on the grace of vocation is a sure indication of our spirit as priests. The worldly priest does not value it; the priest who loves sin regards it as a hard fate, but the priest imbued with the spirit of faith rejoices, with Christ: " I praise thee, Father, Lord of heaven and earth, that thou didst hide these things from the wise and prudent, and didst reveal them to little ones. Yes, Father, for such was thy good pleasure " (Lk. 10:21).

Reading: Eph. 3:1-13.

OUR PARTICIPATION IN THE PRIESTHOOD OF CHRIST:
II. CHRIST EFFECTS IT

13th Consideration

The Messianic Kingdom of God cannot be built by purely human strength; the coming of the Messias was necessary to it, because it was to be erected by His power, the power of the Mediator, Jesus, for " neither is there salvation in any other . . ." (Acts 4:12). Now, if the Lord calls men to work with Him in building up the Messianic Kingdom, He calls them at the same time to participate in the power which none possesses but Himself. From the will of Christ to call me there develops, as from its root, an enduring action of Christ in which He equips with powers which only He possesses those whom He so calls.

Let us consider, then, *our participation in the priesthood of Christ : Christ effects it.*

I. He Effected It in the Apostles. In a series of *transmissions of power.* He rendered the Apostles capable of acting upon believers in a manner which He alone was in a position to do. In His Ascension Day order to go forth He conveyed to the Eleven *His* power to make those who believed in His name children of God (Jn. 1:12); in the power of loosing and binding transmitted on the evening of Easter Sunday He equipped them with *His* power " to save his people from their sins " (Mt. 1:21); in the " Do this in remembrance of me " (Lk. 22:19) He guaranteed to them *His* power to render present His Body and Blood together with His sacrificial spirit and His sacrificial act. He must also have passed on to them the powers to confirm, to anoint the sick and to ordain priests, i.e., the power, in placing the sign of these sacraments, to call down *His* action on the person signed with them. In order that they could exercise these powers rightly He promised and sent the Holy Spirit as the executor of His ordinance. For, so He says: ". . . he will receive of what is mine and declare it to you " (Jn. 16:14).

Thus, by progressive communication of His divine and Messianic powers, He makes the Apostles " fit ministers of the new covenant " (2 Cor. 3:6).

II.   He Effects This Participation in Us, the Successors of His Apostles.   Hence, ever since the days of the Apostles, it has been the conviction of the Church that to all on whom the Apostles, praying, laid their hands, those gifts of God's grace have been passed on (2 Tim. 1:6) which they had received from the Lord and had willed to pass on. By this laying on of hands the ordained persons received a mark in which the Holy Trinity recognizes Christ Himself, so that the person so signed is enabled to act in the name, indeed in the very person of Christ, " quasi ipsemet esset Christus." It is the special attribute of the *character sacerdotalis.* What love on the part of Christ, actually to deliver Himself into the hands and up to the will of sinful men! Paul marvels at it and refers to it when contending with those who flout his authority in Corinth. " Such is the assurance I have *through Christ towards God,*" he says. " Not that we are sufficient of ourselves to think anything, as from ourselves, but our sufficiency is from God. *He* also it is who has made us fit ministers of the new covenant, not of the letter but of the spirit " (2 Cor. 3:4 ff.). " Now the Lord is the spirit " (2 Cor. 3:17).

III.   The True Power and Greatness of Our Participation in the Priesthood of Christ Lies in This Self-Delivery of the Lord to Us.   By the *sacramentum ordinis* the person ordained becomes in truth a ruler in the Kingdom of God; henceforth there is something

Lordly in him, namely, the Lord and Master Jesus Christ, who in His priests proceeds by the way of priesthood to the goal of His glory (4th Consideration). The priest may and should be conscious of this; not in a self-sufficient dictatorial way, however, but in the spirit of a servant. For his power over Christ has been lent him and he has to render an account for it. Nevertheless, the least priest of the New Covenant, because of this power which he wields over Jesus Christ, is more splendid in the eyes of the Holy Trinity than Moses in all the glory with which God enveloped him as he came down the mountain out of the cloud. " For though the former ministration was glorified, yet in this regard it is without glory, because of the surpassing glory of the latter " (2 Cor. 3:10). " Now, to him who is able to accomplish all things in a measure far beyond what we ask or conceive in keeping with the power that is at work in us—to him be glory in the Church and in Christ Jesus down through all the ages of time without end. Amen " (Eph. 3:20 f.).

Reading : 2 Cor. 3:4-11.

OUR PARTICIPATION IN THE PRIESTHOOD OF CHRIST:

III. CHRIST YEARNS FOR IT

14th Consideration

Since the Messianic King wills to impart His kingdom to mankind through the mediation of men, He has to equip these with power over His Kingdom, in fact over Himself (13th Consideration). To do this He places Himself in a state of dependence upon His servants;

but as He can withdraw His order from them, this dependence is not an unconditional one. But as long as He does not withdraw His order—and He will not do so " unto the consummation of the world " (Mt. 28:20)— His dependence is a real dependence, and will remain so " unto the consummation of the world."

From this fact there arises a new relationship of Jesus to our participation in His priesthood. The Lord needs us; our priesthood is the " colt of an ass " which " the Lord has need of " to enter into the New Jerusalem, " Because the Lord has need of it " (Lk. 19:31). Our participation in the priesthood of Christ is born of an ardent urge of the Heart of Jesus!

Let us consider, then, *our participation in the priesthood of Christ : Christ yearns for it.*

I. He Proves This in His Earthly Life. " Now after this the Lord appointed seventy-two others, and sent them forth two by two before him into every town and place where he himself was about to come. And he said to them ' The harvest indeed is great, but the labourers are few. Pray therefore the Lord of the harvest to send forth labourers into his harvest' " (Lk. 10:1 f.). The harvest was great because the will of the masses to enter into the Kingdom of God had become great. But no one gets into the Kingdom of God if the saving grace of the Son does not seize him and draw him into the safe shelter of the Father. But for this the Son needs helpers, and these the Father must acquire and send, so that the human harvest may be brought in from the vineyard and field (cf. Mt. 20:1-16). So actually it is the Son who needs the labourers for whom He asks, and tells us to ask, the Father. The thanksgiving in the High-Priestly prayer for those whom the Father had given Him (Jn. 17:9 ff.) is also an indirect confirmation of our Saviour's desire and yearning for priestly co-operators.

II. The Mystical Christ in the Church Bears Testimony to It. Since the days of the Apostles the Church has of course been aware that she needs ordained ministers and dispensers of the sacraments of Christ, just as she needs those sacraments themselves; that as she lives from the "Memorial of the death of Christ," namely, the Eucharist, she needs those "whose voice alone renders Christ present on the altar" (Encyclical, *Mystici Corporis Christi*). Without an adequate priesthood she would sicken and weaken.

Hence, the yearning of the Heart of Jesus lives on in the yearning and solicitude of the Church for the vocation and education of a priesthood competent to cope with the needs of the time. With the eyes of the woman of the Apocalypse, who is threatened by the raging seven-headed dragon, the Church looks out for the angel who will save her and the child from destruction by the beast (Apoc. 12). And the angel is the priesthood of Christ, realized in the ordained priests who call down the presence of Jesus by placing the saving sign of the Eucharist and the other sacraments.

III. Our Participation in the Priesthood of Christ Is an Obligation We Owe to the Pastoral Solicitude of the Heart of Jesus. By their understanding of that solicitude and their effort to relieve it the good shepherds are distinguished from the hirelings in the priesthood. For the hireling shows his selfishness not merely in his bad treatment of the sheep but also in his indifference to the owner of the herd, who is concerned to have good shepherds. The good priest, on the contrary, is eager to win and train good shepherds. The bishop in particular, who is zealous in forming a good clergy, is the great solace of the Heart of Jesus. " If he who offers even a cup of water to one of the least of Christ's disciples ' shall not lose his reward,' what reward will he receive who puts, so to speak, into the pure hands of a young priest the sacred chalice which contains the Blood of Redemption, and who helps him to lift this chalice up to heaven as a pledge of peace and benediction for mankind?" (Encyclical of Pius XI, "*Ad catholici Sacerdotii culmen.*")

Reading : The High-Priestly Prayer, Jn. 17:6-19.

OUR PARTICIPATION IN THE PRIESTHOOD OF CHRIST:

IV. CHRIST DETERMINES ITS EXTENT

15th Consideration

From Christ's will, Christ's power, and Christ's yearning there arises the bond by which we are bound to Him in participation of His priesthood, the *character sacerdotalis,* which fits us forever to be ministers of the New Covenant. But just as the members of the human body are not bound to the whole frame in the same way and for the same function, and as the one is co-ordinated with and serves the others, so is it also with the ministers of the New Covenant: their participation in the priesthood of the Lord is not uniform but manifold and classified as the Lord thinks fit to communicate

His powers, in the words of the Apostle: "But to each one of us grace was given according to the measure of Christ's bestowal" (Eph. 4:7).

Let us consider, then, *our participation in the priesthood of Christ : Christ determines its extent.*

I. This Has Been a Christian Conviction Since the Days of the Apostles.

Paul speaks of it in detail in the fourth chapter of the Epistle to the Ephesians. Christ, who has established the unity of the Church, gave her manifold variety not only in the gifts of grace but also in offices and functions. "And he himself gave some men as apostles, and some as prophets, others again as evangelists, and others as pastors and teachers, in order to perfect the saints for a work of ministry, for building up the body of Christ" (Eph. 4:11 f.). Did not the Lord Himself already co-ordinate the seventy-two with the Twelve in the leading and service of His flock? Acting on this conviction, the Apostles appointed the seven deacons, and after them the presbyters, who had more power than the deacons and yet not the power of the Apostles and bishops. Under the guidance of the Holy Spirit the variety of the early offices in the Church gradually develops into the three-fold official hierarchy of the ministry of the New Covenant, namely, diaconate, presbyterate, and episcopate. Hence we see that participation in the priesthood of Christ is conveyed "according to the measure of Christ's bestowal" —Christ determines its extent.

II. In This Way Christ Develops Our Participation in His Priesthood Into a Ministry in Holy Orders.

That is why the Church calls the sacramental ministry, with

its three degrees, simply the *"Ordo"* and the communication of the necessary powers, the "Sacrament of Holy Orders." In meting out the various offices of the priesthood the Church sees not only an arrangement dictated by experience but also the realization of divinely ordained harmony and beauty. For as we know, God creates everything in such a way that it is not only beautiful and wise in itself but also co-ordinated with its environment. Similarly, He disposes the priesthood in degrees of participation, so to speak, through His Son. These parts do not exist and work on their own, however, but are co-ordinated with each other, the lower grade of the deacons being co-ordinated in service to the higher grade of the presbyters, and these in turn to the bearer of the fullness of the priesthood, namely, the bishop. The ministry of the New Covenant is thus built up in an order created by Christ Himself, an order similar to that formed by the blessed spirits in their service round the throne of God, a *hiera archia.* Therefore, the Church, with motherly pride, announces to the believing and unbelieving: " Non sunt [clerici] omnes in eodem gradu, sed inter eos sacra hierarchia est in qua alii aliis subordinantur " (Canon 108, a. 2). And: " Qui in ecclesiasticam hierarchiam cooptantur, non ex populi vel potestatis saecularis consensu aut vocatione adleguntur; sed in gradibus potestatis ordinis constituuntur sacra ordinatione . . ." (Canon 109).

III. "To the Building Up of Itself [The Body of Christ] in Love" (Eph. 4:16). "God has set the members, each of them, in the body as he willed " (1 Cor. 12:18). "For in one Spirit we were all baptized into one body. . .   . And the eye cannot say to the hand: ' I do not need thy help '; nor again the head to the feet, ' I have no need of you ' " (1 Cor. 12:13 ff.). According to the measure in which each one is called to co-operate in building up the Kingdom of Redemption, he will strive to prove himself the good and faithful servant, who feeds the master's flock in the service that falls to him and in the grade which his degree in Holy Orders demands of him. He avoids all jealousy towards a colleague to whom a higher office has been entrusted, he shuns any cleavage from the community of the faithful due to insubordination or apostasy, schism or heresy, and he finds his joy in devoting all the powers of his being to working for the good of the whole, and will " practise the truth in love, and so grow up in all things in him who is the head, Christ " (Eph. 4:15).

Reading : Eph. 4:1-16.

THE HOLY SPIRIT, DISPENSER OF THE GRACE OF ORDINATION

16th Consideration

In the Rite of Ordination, the Church bids the bishop pray in the second Oration after the Laying on of Hands: " Exaudi nos, quaesumus, Domine Deus noster, et super hos famulos tuos benedictionem Sancti Spiritus et gratiae Sacerdotalis infunde virtutem. . . ." The Church ascribes to the Holy Spirit the communication of the sacramental priestly powers. That this is not to be interpreted as excluding the action of the Incarnate High Priest Jesus Christ (Considerations 12 to 15) is clear from the fact that the Lord transferred essentially

priestly powers (the Eucharist, the power of binding
and loosing, Mt. 16:18, 18:18; Jn. 21:18) to His
Apostles by His own absolute power. Nevertheless the
Holy Spirit has a special part in fitting us for the
ministry in the priesthood of Christ, and is therefore
the object of this Consideration.

**I. Because of the Special Part He Has in the High
Priesthood of Christ.** The Eternal Word of God became
a priest through the Incarnation (5th Consideration);
but the Incarnation is ascribed to the Holy Spirit as the
efficient cause: " The Holy Spirit shall come upon thee
and the power of the Most High shall overshadow thee;
and therefore the Holy One to be born shall be called
the Son of God " (Lk. 1:35); and " that which is
begotten in her is of the Holy Spirit " (Mt. 1:20). Just
as the Holy Spirit appears as the *originator* of the
priestly character of our Lord, so also Scripture shows
Him as the *constant motive force* of Christ's priestly
action: " The Spirit of the Lord is upon me; because
he has anointed me; to bring good news to the poor he
has sent me," and so on (Lk. 4:18 f.). The apparition
of the Holy Spirit at Christ's baptism in the Jordan
had no other purpose than to show that in fulfilling
His kingly and priestly task during His public life, the
Son of Man was acting on the impetus and in the
power of the Holy Spirit, who is the uncreated Unction
of the priesthood in the new Kingdom of God. Hence,
our participation in the true priesthood originates from
the Holy Spirit in the same sense as the priesthood of
Christ originates from it.

**II. Because of the Special Part Which He Has in
Our Own Priestly Power.** Although the Lord gave His

Apostles the order to celebrate the Eucharist and the power to forgive sins, before Pentecost, He instructed them to refrain from carrying out these works of salvation until after they had been " baptised with the Holy Spirit " (Acts 1:5). Only then were they to be " witnesses for me in Jerusalem and in all Judea and Samaria, and even to the very ends of the earth " (Acts 1:8). Ever since the days of the Apostles the Church, in fulfilment of this instruction of the Lord, has always looked upon the communication of the priestly powers as a continuation of the mystery of Pentecost as accomplished in the Apostles—the giving of the " Advocate " who was to help and stand by the Apostles whom Christ had chosen and equipped with priestly powers, that they might be able to exercise these powers rightly and in a manner pleasing to the Father, for the salvation of the people of God. Hence, the Holy Spirit is the pledge and source of those graces which the priest needs to enable him to use beneficially the holy powers entrusted to him.

III. Therefore, the Good Priest Reveals His possession of the Holy Spirit

1. *Unconsciously :* in every performance of his ministry of the mysteries of salvation, in the celebration of the Holy Eucharist; the administration of the holy sacraments, the preaching of the Word of God, the recital of the daily Office—in all these activities his ministry is " of the spirit " (2 Cor. 3:6, 18). The Holy Spirit moves him to this activity inasmuch as it is priestly, stands by hm, blesses him with success, and loves him.

2. *Consciously :* The good priest is aware of his

state of union with the Holy Spirit, he rejoices in it and gives thanks at all times for the grace of being permitted to be an instrument of His love. He too says, with the High Priest Jesus Christ: *Spiritus Domini super me, unxit me, misit me.* In this knowledge he overcomes the timidity which the realization of his personal inadequacy may cause, and from this knowledge he can say with St. Paul: We conduct ourselves . . . as God's ministers . . . in the Holy Spirit (2 Cor. 6:4, 6).

Reading : Acts 1:4-8.

THE CATHOLIC PRIESTHOOD

RES GRANDIS ET ININTERPRETABILIS

17th Consideration

The author of the Epistle to the Hebrews concludes the first part of his expositions concerning the high priesthood of Jesus Christ with an admission of his inability to explain it adequately, because it is a " res grandis . . . et ininterpretabilis " (Hebr. 5:11). In the Votive Mass of Our Lord Jesus Christ the Eternal High Priest, the Church makes her own the sense of failure of the holy writer when she concludes the Epistle on the splendours of the priesthood of Christ with the words: " De quo nobis grandis sermo et ininterpretabilis ad dicendum." We too propose to conclude our considerations on the essential nature of the Catholic priesthood and our part in it with a consideration of the *character of mystery* of this gift of God to sinful man, as a result of which it can only be comprehended by faith.

I. The Catholic Priesthood "Res Grandis." It is essentially a participation in the high priesthood of Christ; but this is the whole mystery of salvation itself and includes all the other mysteries of the divine dispensation, in particular the Incarnation and the Redemption. For to the priest is given the power to make these mysteries present sacramentally, beyond their historical accomplishment, and to convey them to successive generations of Christians for their salvation. Hence we are in very truth " dispensatores mysterium Dei," so much so that J. J. Olier, the saintly founder-rector of St. Sulpice, even speaks of the priest as participating in the action of the eternal Father which brought forth the Son, and in the procession of the Holy Spirit from the Father and the Son. *Grandis sermo!*[1]

II. The Catholic Priesthood a Mysterium Fidei. Since the Catholic priesthood is part of the phenomena of the mystery of salvation as a whole, it shares with this the common quality of being something which can only be

---

[1] Olier, *SS. Ordres*, IIIe partie, ch. II: " Le Prêtre est appelé à entrer en partre avec le Père Eternel, de la puissance d'engendrer son Fils." Naturally, Father Olier does not mean to convey that the action of the priesthood is a constituent element in the life of the Trinity. His daring words refer, one gathers, to the realization of the Eucharistic mystery: " En effet, il (le prêtre) le (Christ) produit tous les jours sur les autels, tel que le Père Eternel l'engendra autrement au jour de la résurrection." It seems to us that Olier understands the relation of the priestly action to the relations within the Trinity in the sense of a revelation and a benign accomplishment of the same in creation in as much as these are bound to the order of the priesthood. His words: " Le prêtre donne le Saint Esprit " are to be understood in the same sense.

apprehended by faith. It bears Jesus Christ into the world " ut omnes crederent per illum " and in doing so itself finds acceptance in the measure that men are willing to believe in Jesus Christ. Therefore the Lord actually makes applicable to His priests the duty of belief which men owe to Him: " He who hears you, hears me; and he who rejects you, rejects me; and he who rejects me, rejects him who sent me." The glory which invests the " ministers of the new covenant " (2 Cor. 3 : 6 ff.) is the *auctoritas Christi*. But faith is of its nature " argumentum non apparentium," a conviction of the truth of what one does not see. Therefore the glory of the priesthood can only be apprehended through the eyes of faith. *Res ininterpretabilis !*

III. The Catholic Priesthood Is a Mysterium Fidei Sacerdotalis. If the mystery of our priesthood cannot penetrate the souls of others except through faith, neither can it penetrate into the depths of the priest's own soul except through the priest's spirit of faith. Priests weak in faith are faulty instruments in the hands of the High Priest, however brilliant their other gifts and their education may be. That is why the Epistle to the Hebrews, as quoted below, while emphasising the great mystery of the priesthood, points to the misfortune which threatens its bearer who falls away from the spirit of faith : " For it is impossible for those who were once enlightened, who have both tasted the heavenly gift and become partakers of the Holy Spirit, who have moreover tasted the good word of God and the powers of the world to come, and then have fallen away, to be renewed again to repentance; since they crucify again for themselves the Son of God and make Him a mockery "

(Hebr. 6:4 ff.). A prophetic description of the priest who loses his spirit of faith!

RESUSCITES GRATIAM, QUAE EST IN TE!

Great, indeed unspeakably great, is the grace of the Catholic priesthood, and only humble and loving faith can comprehend it. When the heart of the priest is enlightened and warmed by this faith, it becomes a piece of God's land: " For the earth that drinks in the rain that often falls upon it, and produces vegetation that is of use to those by whom it is tilled, receives a blessing from God " (Hebr. 6:7). It is the desire of our holy Mother the Church that we should faithfully foster and preserve this spirit of faith. In the Votive Mass of Our Lord Jesus Christ the Eternal High Priest she makes us pray for this fidelity.

Let us, then, close our considerations on the grace of the Catholic priesthood by praying with the Church: " Oh God, by whom Thine only-begotten Son has been established high and eternal Priest, to the glory of Thy majesty and for the salvation of mankind: grant that those He has chosen as ministers and dispensers of His mysteries, may be found faithful in fulfilling the ministry they have accepted " (Collect of Votive Mass of the Eternal High Priest).

Reading : Hebr. 5:9-6:12.

PART TWO

THE MISSION OF THE HOLY PRIESTHOOD

"Even as thou hast sent me into the world, so I also have sent them into the world" (Jn. 17: 18).

PART TWO

THE MISSION OF THE HOLY PRIESTHOOD

PREFACE

The question as to what the mission of the Catholic priesthood is was answered by Christ Himself when He said to His Apostles: "As the Father has sent me, I also send you" (Jn. 20:21). The Father sent Him to found in the world the Kingdom of God, which would last forever and of which He Himself would be the Head: "For in him were created all things in the heavens and on the earth, things visible and things invisible . . . All things have been created through and unto him, and he is before all creatures, and in him all things hold together . . . he, who is the beginning, the first born from the dead, that in all things he may have the first place. For it has pleased God the Father that in him all His fullness should dwell, and that through him he should reconcile to himself all things, whether on the earth or in the heavens, making peace through the blood of his cross" (Col. 1:16 ff.).

A mission of inexhaustible depth and immeasureable breadth, to lead all creation back to unity and order—that is the mission of Christ. When he says that we, the consecrated priesthood, are entrusted with *His* mission, that can mean nothing else than that we are in the *service* of His unique and irreplaceable mission. What are the services for which He wishes to use us? In the following Considerations (Nos. 18 to 22) we will try to answer this question.

FOR THE CONTINUANCE OF THE INCARNATION
OF THE ETERNAL WORD

18th Consideration

In the Rite of Ordination the bishop says: " For it is the priest's duty to offer sacrifice, to bless, to lead, to preach and to baptise." The history of the Church teaches us that the Christian life weakens and falls away when the bearers of priestly powers execute these tasks in a merely perfunctory manner because they are insufficiently convinced of the meaning and purpose of what they do. For the ultimate purpose of all these activities is the building up of the Kingdom of God in two stages. The first stage is the building up of the Kingdom of God *in the soul of the individual:* in the second stage it is the formation of a holy human community, namely, the Church of God. Now in both stages this aim is realised by Christ being mediated to man; by the individual and the community being bound up with Christ. Hence it can truly be said that the mission of the Catholic priesthood to the individual is a mission for the continuance of the mystery of the Incarnation of Christ in the individual; and that the mission of the priest to the community of Christians is a mission for the building up of the Church, the Mystical Body of Christ.

Let us consider, then, the mission of the Catholic priesthood: *A mission for the continuance of the Incarnation of the Eternal Word.*

I. This Is the Meaning of the Basic Commission Which We Have Received, the Commission to Baptise :

Sacerdotem etenim oportet . . . baptizare. With baptism the Kingdom of God takes its beginning in the individual human soul; for the effect of baptism is that " For as in

Adam all die, so in Christ all will be made to live " (1 Cor. 15:22).

Now, this life is Christ Himself, the life and strength of the vinestalk, who is communicated to the branches. In each person whom we baptise Christ proceeds in a mysterious but real way to continue His life and His action until the stage which the Apostle describes in the words: " It is now no longer I that live, but Christ lives in me " (Gal. 2:20; cf. Jn. 17:23). Hence this is a commission to continue the Incarnation of the Eternal Word in the individual soul.

II. This Is the Meaning of All the Other Offices Which We Have to Fulfill in Relation to the Individual Soul. For inasmuch as our offering sacrifice, blessing, leading, preaching, and baptising concerns the individual soul, it has no other purpose than to bring about or preserve the grace of baptism, that is to say, the union of the soul with Christ, or to restore it, if it has been lost. All individual care of souls is therefore fundamentally a ministry of the grace of Baptism, or the preservation of the Union with Christ which is effected in the soul at Baptism. Was not the solicitude of the Apostles for the individual soul fundamentally a solicitude concerning Baptism and preservation of the grace of Baptism? When the people of Jerusalem, on seeing the miracle of Pentecost, asked: " ' Brethren, what shall we do?' Peter answered: ' Repent and be baptised every one of you in the name of Jesus Christ for the forgiveness of your sins; and you will receive the gift of the Holy Spirit ' " (Acts 2:38 f.).

III. In His Relation to the Christian Child of God the Priest Participates in the Fatherhood of God

through this mission for the continuance of the Incarnation of the Eternal Word. To be sure, Ephesians 3 : 14 f. says: " I bend my knees to the Father of Our Lord Jesus Christ, from whom all fatherhood in heaven and on earth receives its name "; but that same Apostle who so emphasises this exclusive prerogative of God, claims that, if not by always actually administering it himself, at least by leading the faithful to Baptism, he has acquired a father's rights in relation to them, which gives him a share in the authority of the heavenly Father: " For in Christ Jesus, through the Gospel, did I beget you " (1 Cor. 4 : 15). In his anxiety that they should preserve their baptismal grace, threatened by grievous errors of faith, He writes to the Galatians: " My dear children, with whom I am in labour again, until Christ is formed in you " (Gal. 4 : 19). This participation in the fatherhood of God lays upon us priests a duty of fatherly care for the baptised children of God. The true priest will give to the many whom the Church has entrusted to him as his spiritual family the same love and care which the Christian father of a family bestows on his children. That Christ shall live and thrive in them will be his constant concern and desire; and it will be a source of holy pride to him to be privileged to work for the continuance of the mystery of the Incarnation of our Lord, that it may never end but be perfected with the end of all temporal things.

FOR THE BUILDING UP OF THE BODY OF CHRIST

19th Consideration

The priest's office in relation to the individual is essentially for the mediation of the grace of Baptism and preservation in the same (18th Consideration). But the Kingdom of God is something more than a crowd of people who have become children of God through Baptism. It is a community willed by God, a *communio sanctorum*, a well-constructed *civitas Dei*. Christ is the *Head* and the baptised are co-ordinated with Him as the *members* are co-ordinated with the head in the human body. The Apostle therefore calls the realm of the baptised the Body of Christ. Now, the building up of the Body of Christ with baptised persons is the second degree of the mission which the Catholic priesthood has received from the Lord.

Let us consider, then, the mission of the Catholic priesthood: *a mission for the building up of the Body of Christ.*

I. The Will and Prayer of the Heart of Jesus Is the Basis of This Commission.

In the high-priestly prayer our Lord prayed to the Father: " Yet not for these only do I pray, but for those also who through their [i.e., the Apostles'] word are to believe in me, that all may be *one,* even as thou, Father, in me and I in thee; . . . And the glory that thou hast given me [i.e., the glory of the children of God], I have given to them, that they may be one, even as we are one: I in them and thou in me; that they may be perfected in unity, and that the world may know that thou hast sent me, and that thou hast loved them even as thou hast loved me " (Jn. 17:20 ff.). The heavenly Father fulfils this prayer of His beloved Son to the end of time in the mystery of the Mystical Body of Christ, which is revealed to the world in the Church.

II. Christ Has Entrusted to His Priesthood the Building Up of His Mystical Body. True, it is by Christ Himself, as the Apostle says (Eph. 4:16), that the whole body is " closely joined and knit together through every joint of the system "; but by imprinting upon us the *character sacerdotalis* He has created an auxiliary body for the task of incorporating the multitude of the baptised into the well-formed order of His Body, so that this Body may " increase to the building up of itself in love." And so He appointed " some men as apostles, and some as prophets, others again as evangelists, and others as pastors and teachers, in order to perfect the saints [the baptised] for a work of ministry, *for building up the Body of Christ,* until we all attain to the unity of the faith . . . to the mature measure of the fullness of Christ " (Eph. 4:11 f.). Hence, Christ Himself has ordained that it is from the holders of the priestly-apostolic powers in the Body of Christ that the " saints " receive the impulse to " so grow up in all things in him who is the head, Christ " (Eph. 4:15). Thus, our priesthood has been commissioned to build up the Body of Christ.

III. How Does the Catholic Priesthood Fulfill Its Mission of Building Up the Body of Christ ? By permitting itself to be used by the Head, who is Christ, as an inspiring and willing instrument to bind those who believe in Him to that well-formed community which He Himself calls His Church (Mt. 16:18) and Paul calls His Body (Eph. 4:12, 16; 5:23). This is done whenever a bishop, priest or deacon makes his contribution to the " offerre, benedicere, praeesse, praedicare, et baptizare " of the ordained priesthood, not merely for the sanctification of individual souls but also to bind to each other the Christians thus sanctified, to form a body united in Christ. We help them to " grow up in all things in him who is the head, Christ "; in every activity by which we assist them to " attain to the unity of the faith and of the deep knowledge of the Son of God . . . " (4:13); by establishing a basis of reverence and obedience of the faithful towards the pope, the visible representative of Christ on earth, but especially by administration of the sacramental forces of unity, through which Christ Himself joins and holds together the whole Body. Our *ministerium eucharisticum* is the core of this unifying process, for as the Primitive Church put it, the individual souls, like the grains of wheat, are kneaded together to form a sacrificial bread of Christ (cf. Encyclical, *Mystici Corporis Christi*, Part II).

Reading : Eph. 4:1-16.

IN THE SERVICE OF THE PRIESTLY OFFICE OF CHRIST

20th Consideration

The Catholic priesthood has received from its founder Jesus Christ the commission to transmit the divine life to individual souls and thereby incorporate them into His Mystical Body (18th and 19th Considerations). Through its functions, the baptised are caught up into that process of growth in which " the whole body is closely joined and knit together " (Eph. 4:16) by Christ its Head, in fulfilment of His threefold Messianic office of priest, teacher, and shepherd. To this end Christ uses the Catholic priesthood as His visible instrument.

Consequently this priesthood fulfills its commission by *offering sacrifice, teaching, and shepherding souls.*

Of the three offices of Christ the basic one is the priestly office; for from it the functions of teacher and pastor derive their meaning and order. The most essential task of the teaching office is to proclaim the priesthood of Christ, while the pastoral office conveys to the people of God the blessing which the priesthood of Christ has called forth. Now, as the priestly office is the highest one in Christ, so also, in our consecrated priesthood, the priestly function takes precedence of all other functions which mark out the priesthood.

Let us therefore consider our priestly mission *as a mission in the service of the priesthood of Christ.*

I. This Service Is Entrusted to Us. When our Lord, at the Last Supper, spoke the words: " Do this in remembrance of me " (Lk. 22:10), he thereby entrusted the Apostles and their successors not only with the accomplishment of the visible work which He had carried out before their eyes, but He also gave them the commission and the power to evoke the *invisible* happenings by which He wills to give Himself in the sacrificial spirit and action of His death for the world, so that " from the rising of the sun even to the going down . . . in every place there is sacrifice, and there is offered . . . a clean oblation " (Mal. 1:11) in which the Father is well pleased. *Sic sacrificium istud instituit—Cujus officium committi voluit—solis presbyteris.* Because this office is entrusted to priests alone, the Church prays with a burning heart in the Rite of Ordination: " Pour out Thy gracious blessing upon these Thy servants . . . may they change by a holy benediction bread and wine

into the Body and Blood of Thy Son for the worship
of Thy people."

**II. This Office Has First Place Among the Duties of
a Priest.** For, as all the visible achievements of the
earthly life of Christ reached their culmination and
completion in His sacrifice on the cross, so too our function in the Eucharistic Sacrifice is the source from
which the divine energy, which alone can build up the
Kingdom of God, flows into all our other priestly
works, including our sacramental functions. By the
words of Consecration, which we priests alone may
pronounce, we operate, so to speak, the heartbeat of the
Heart of Jesus which carries His Blood and His love
into all the members of the Mystical Body, and draws
them into His oblation which reconciles with the
heavenly Father everything in heaven and on earth (cf.
Encyclical, *Mystici Corporis Christi*).

III. "Agnoscite Quod Agitis!" Of our service in the
priestly office of Christ, the Church says: "If there is
among human activities something completely divine
for which the citizens of heaven, if indeed they be
capable of envy, might envy us, it is certainly the Holy
Sacrifice of the Mass. This gift of God makes it possible for human beings to have a foretaste of heaven
already on earth, since they actually have before their
eyes and hold in their hands the Maker of heaven and
earth Himself " (Urban VIII, Encyclical on *The Roman
Missal*, 2 September, 1634). Are we priests fully conscious of the greatness, holiness, and literal reality of
this function when we approach the altar each day?
" Now we have received not the spirit of the world,

but the spirit that is from God, that we may know the things that have been given us by God " (1 Cor. 2:12).

Reading : *The Imitation of Christ,* Book IV, Chapter 5.

IN THE SERVICE OF THE TEACHING OFFICE OF CHRIST

21st Consideration

In order to come to man, the Eternal Wisdom has chosen the way of *the human word;* in order to speak it, God Himself became man; in the language of the Chosen People of the Old Covenant the Divine Wisdom proclaimed Itself and described Its words as the seeds of the Kingdom of God, as germinative forces which can change human souls into the Kingdom of God. The Divine Wisdom calls the acceptance of Its words by the human soul *faith.* Without faith it is impossible to please God (Hebr. 11:6). Faith is the root of the Kingdom of God.

" But how are they to call upon him in whom they have not believed?" (Rom. 10:14). Since the divine Sower wills to sow the seeds of salvation in every age, He has made the Catholic priesthood His instrument for this office too, when He sent them out and fitted them " to bear witness to the gospel of the grace of God " (Acts 20:24). He has appointed us to be the organs of His Messianic teaching office.

Let us, then, consider our mission *as being in the service of the teaching office of Christ.*

I. He Entrusts Us With This Service.

(*a*) His last command on earth was: " Go, therefore, and *make disciples* of all nations " (Mt. 28:18 f.).

(b) He makes His envoys capable of doing so: " You shall *receive power when the Holy Spirit comes upon you,* and you shall be witnesses for me in Jerusalem and in all Judea and Samaria and even to the very ends of the earth " (Acts 1:8). " But when he, the Spirit of truth, has come, he will teach you all the truth " (Jn. 16:13).

(c) He equips them with His *authority* to do it: " He who hears you, hears me; and he who rejects you, rejects me; and he who rejects me, rejects him who sent me " (Lk. 10:16).

II. He Wills to Effect This Service Through Us " In the Demonstration of the Spirit and of Power "— *in virtute et ostensione Spiritus* (1 Cor. 2:4). For the faith which leads to salvation must not be based upon human wisdom: it comes only from the power of God. " For who among men knows the things of a man save the spirit of the man which is in him? Even so, the things of God no one knows but the Spirit of God." Hence, in addition to the strength of the Holy Spirit already given to the Christian in Confirmation, we ministers of the word receive a special *gratia gratis data,* a vocational grace " that we may know the things that have been given us by God. These things we also speak, not in words taught by human wisdom, but in the learning of the Spirit, combining spiritual with spiritual" (1 Cor. 2: 11 ff.). Hence, we are sent and fitted to teach *in virtute et ostensione Spiritus.*

III. Which Priests Experience and Show Forth This Spiritual Enlightenment? According to the intention of Christ every validly ordained priest should realize in himself the words: " To you it is given to know the mysteries of the kingdom of heaven " (Mt. 13:11). For this gift has been given to each one of us as an additional portion together with the *character sacerdotalis*. But this gift of the Spirit is given us *like an eye* which only sees if it is opened, a capacity to see which only becomes effective if it is not hindered. If the Holy Spirit is to begin to teach in our teaching, we must give Him scope to do so by our recollection, our distrust in the strength of our own light, and our trust in the light which comes from the Pneuma. We must listen for His voice where He is to be heard: in the teaching Church and particularly in the words of Holy Scripture, which are, as we know, " theopneustos," that is to say, inspired by the Holy Spirit. There He speaks to him who seeks Him and shows him what he needs in order that " doctrina vestra sit spiritualis medicina pro populo Dei:" (Rite of Ordination).

Reading : 1 Cor. 2.

IN THE SERVICE OF THE PASTORAL OFFICE OF CHRIST

22nd Consideration

The Lord spoke thus through the prophet Ezechiel: " And my servant David shall be king over them and they shall have *one shepherd :* they shall walk in my judgments, and shall keep my commandments . . . and David my servant shall be their prince for ever " (Ezech. 37:24 f.). In the parable of the Good Shepherd (Jn. 10:1 f.) Jesus applies this prophecy to Himself: " I am the good shepherd." He is this in the uniqueness of His competence and His all-embracing love, but not in an exclusiveness which allows of no helpers or fellow workers in caring for the flock. He speaks of those who come to His flock lawfully and feed it with and for Him, because they have entered the sheepfold " by the door " which is Himself (Jn. 10:9). He leaves no doubt that by these helpers He means his Apostles and their fellow workers and successors.

The Catholic priesthood, then, fulfils its commission as *service in the pastoral office of Christ.*

I. " **Sacerdotem Oportet Praeesse** " (Rite of Ordination), for naturally we receive the priestly powers in order to sanctify others with them, and not for our own benefit; apart from the Eucharist, we cannot even apply them to ourselves. " Go rather to the lost sheep of the house of Israel . . . Freely you have received, freely give " (Mt. 10:6, 8). " Tend the flock of God, which is among you, governing not by constraint, but willingly, according to God " (1 Pet. 5:2). Our *praeesse* is pastoral service.

II. In This Pastoral Service We Are " Stewards of the Mysteries of God." " Let a man so account us, as servants of Christ and stewards of the mysteries of God " (1 Cor. 4:1). Our actual pastoral duty is this: to dispense the gifts of salvation to the flock of Christ in the vehicles of the word of God and the sacraments, which the Good Shepherd has commissioned us to administer. When material concerns threatened to thrust themselves upon the Apostles they did not think this right, and said: " It is not desirable that we should forsake the word of God and serve at tables " (Acts 6:1 ff.). It is not earthly welfare, nor science, nor culture which we have to mediate; our task is to administer the cleansing ordinance for the forgiveness of their sins to the flock of Christ; to guide them to the pasture of the Eucharistic food; and to protect them against the dangers which threaten them by the administration of the Sacraments of Confirmation and Extreme Unction. Scientific, artistic, political, and charitable works only properly become part of the pastoral service of the priest in so far as they serve for the sanctification of the people of God. In these activities also the priest shows himself to be " the steward of the mysteries of God."

III. " Pascite . . . Gregem Dei . . . ex Animo " (1 Pet. 5:2).

The first Chief Shepherd of the flock of Christ, who calls himself " fellow presbyter " or " priestly colleague," sees the right " animus " of the priestly shepherd in two qualities; his *praeesse* is

1. An imitation of the willing care of God for the flock of Christ: " non coacte sed spontanee *secundum Deum* "; the fatherly kindness of God shall be reflected, so to speak, in the fulfilment of our pastoral duties; therefore, in the pastoral service of the right kind of priest there is nothing grudging, nothing of the spirit of the hireling who thinks more about his own good than that of the flock, and whose compelling motive is " *turpe lucrum.*"

2. The good priest shows himself in his *praeesse* as *forma gregis*—a model for the souls entrusted to him. He first makes his own the laws of life laid down for them by Christ. And as Christ's fundamental principle is ministering love, he walks in the sight of God, not " lording it " over his charges, nor governing God's

people " under constraint," but rather, in the spirit of the Master, who said: " Let him who is greatest among you become as the youngest, and him who is the chief as the servant " (Lk. 22:26).

Reading : 1 Pet. 5: 1-4 (Epistle of the Mass *Summorum Pontificum*).

EPILOGUE

Pastoral theology instructs the priest in the details of carrying out his ministry in the threefold office of the High Priest Jesus Christ. As the priest's ministry must never consist of a mere outward fulfilment of duty but must be carried out " in spirit and in truth," (as the Master demands in John 4:23), a good ministry does not mean merely the outward and visible order of a priest's actions, but also the interior order of the instrument which the High Priest Christ deigns to use— the spiritual outlook of the sacred minister. These Considerations for priests have been conceived with the purpose of awakening and fostering in us priests the dispositions suitable to the various priestly functions— the preaching of the Word of God, the administration of the sacraments, the celebration of the Most Holy Eucharist, and the fulfilment of all our other pastoral duties. The liturgical movement of our day has been extremely fruitful in this respect. It suffices merely to refer to it here within the framework of our theme.

PART THREE

THE EQUIPMENT OF THE CATHOLIC PRIESTHOOD

"That the man of God may be perfect, equipped for every good work" (2 Tim. 3: 17).

The Catholic priest is placed in the world to carry on the mission which the High Priest Jesus Christ received from His heavenly Father: " As the Father has sent me, I also send you " (Jn. 20:21). But the fulfilment of this mission calls for powers which man does not have of himself. Christ alone possesses them in virtue of being God Incarnate. If His apostolic servants are to fulfil rigntly the mission they have received from Him, He must equip them with His own powers.

Now, since the power of Christ rests in His divine and human nature, it follows that He has to give to those who are to continue His mission in the world power over Himself; He must place Himself at their disposal, so to speak. He does this through the *Sacrament of Holy Orders*. By this sacrament He gives to the ordained that conformity with Himself which the Church calls the *character sacerdotalis*. This character is, at the same time, the basis of the power to administer the sacraments. Ordination, which gives the priestly character and the sacramental powers, is *essential* to the equipment of the Catholic priest. As an *act of consecration*, ordination is the most essential *act* of that equipment. As the *effect* of this consecration, the sacerdotal character is the most essential *content* of the equipment of the Catholic priesthood.

The Catholic priesthood is therefore able to fulfil its mission when it rightly receives the grace of ordination by the Sacrament of Holy Orders (*gratiam ordinis*) and uses it as it should be used. The right reception and worthy use of the grace of ordination on the part of those called is therefore a constant intention of the Church and the object of her " Prayer for Good Priests."

In order to enable the disciple of Christ who shows signs of a vocation to prepare for the worthy reception of priestly ordination, the Church leads him in a lengthy preparation through the seven degrees of consecration. Step by step she equips the cleric with the sacred powers which render him by degrees more capable of taking over ancillary tasks in the service of the priesthood. By means of these auxiliary services the candidate for the priesthood grows in knowledge of the functions of the real priesthood—the teaching, sacrificial and pastoral functions, and thus becomes fit for the reception of the order of the presbyterate in which the priestly power is conferred. This was how the early Church formed her priests, and in Canon 977 the Church of our time has ratified this educational path, at least in principle, for the clerics of today. In practice, to be sure, she has departed considerably from it. The modern school and seminary education has taken the place of probation in the minor orders.

In Considerations 23 to 31 we shall reflect upon how the Church equips the cleric, step by step, by means of the seven consecrations, for his service as minister of the High Priest Jesus Christ.

But the power of Christ received in ordination must also be rightly used and held by the ordained person. For this, an outwardly adequate formation is not sufficient; the priest requires, over and above, *an inner disposition* which impels him to use the powers he has received wisely and zealously for the salvation of souls, in accordance with the will of God. This inner disposition is called *the priestly spirit*. The priestly spirit does not determine the essential character of the Catholic priesthood; for this is determined by the Sacrament of Holy Orders. But whether the use of our priestly powers is worthy and pleasing to God, or not, depends upon this spirit. Therefore, the priestly spirit is also one of the essentials in the equipment of the *sacerdos recte constitutus.*

Considerations 23 to 53 will deal with it.

1. THE SEVEN ORDERS

Tonsure

23rd Consideration

Orders are gifts of God's grace for the use of the Church. The Church has to govern the application of these gifts of grace. She must not give them to just any member of the faithful. From the multitude of the baptized she has to pick out the most suitable and prepare them for the reception of the various Orders. In fulfilment of this task she starts with a process of selection, before conferring any actual Order, and concludes it with a liturgical action of a provisional nature. This action is accomplished in the ceremony of conferring the tonsure. Tonsure is not a consecration but a public recognition of qualification which opens to the candidate the way to Holy Orders. When we received it, it was a provisional answer of the Church to the question of our hearts: " Who may stand in his holy place?" (Ps. 23:3.)

1. **What Persons Does the Church Disqualify as Unfitted to Receive Holy Orders?** In Canon 1371 she enumerates the unsuitable classes of persons. Among candidates for ordination who must be dismissed are those who resist all education (*dyscoli*), are unamenable to all correction (*incorrigibiles*), tend to rebellion in the community (*seditiosi*), and in general all who appear, to judge by their morals and disposition, unsuited for the priestly state. All those are to be rejected, likewise, who are so unsuccessful in their studies that there is no reasonable hope of their being able to acquire the knowledge sufficient for the clerical profession. But above all, those who have offended gravely against faith or morals (*deliquerint*) must be rejected forthwith. The Church carries out this process of selection in a well-considered scrutiny and so she separates the unsuitable from the suitable even before she opens the way to Minor Orders.

II. **What Does the Church Regard as Signs of Suitability for the Reception of Holy Orders?** She makes this known in the words and actions of the liturgy when conferring the tonsure—the cutting of the hair of the candidate's head and the presentation to him of the surplice. By cutting the hair she expresses confidence that the approved candidate for holy orders is ready to renounce the vanities of the world for the love of Christ, and to deny himself its pleasures; for, " If anyone loves the world, the love of the Father is not in him " (Jn. 2:15). In presenting him with the surplice which he is destined to wear in his office as an ordained priest, the Church exhorts the aspirant to the priesthood to strengthen in himself that attitude of mind and heart which the Apostle of the Gentiles calls the " new man," who has been created by Christ's grace " according to God in justice and holiness of truth " (Eph. 4:20 ff.). She demands the consent of the candidate to these symbolical actions by making him pray: " The Lord is the portion of my inheritance and of my cup: it is thou that wilt restore my inheritance to me." The farther the tonsured candidate progresses in renunciation of the world and takes on the spirit of the new man, the more clearly does the Church recognize in him the signs of a true vocation; in her eyes he belongs to the " *generatio quaerentium Deum.*"

III. In Order to Assure His Vocation, the Church Takes the Tonsured Candidate Into the Company of the Clergy. Like every real calling, the clerical state has its own unwritten law which is the result of common duties and experience and the common will to help those of one's own calling to carry out correctly their share in its duties. The Church herself has striven unceasingly to strengthen and ennoble the rules of life of the clergy; in Canons 124 to 144 of her Code she has laid down these rules. With the tonsure the candidate for the priesthood comes under the law and within the framework of the clerical profession and priests are henceforth his guardians, educators, and colleagues in his progress towards the priesthood. He has to earn for himself the grace of his state by fidelity to the rule of that state. But the ordained priest too must look at himself in the mirror of this rule again and again in order to ascertain whether his will to continue on the way opened to him when he received the tonsure is still active.

Reading: Psalm 23 and Canons 124-144 (De *obligationibus clericorum*).

THE ORDER OF DOORKEEPER (OSTIARIATE)

24th Consideration

On the way to the priesthood the Church places the cleric in whom she perceives the signs of vocation on the first step to ordination, with the Order of Ostiarius. Even as priests we are still holders of this office and as such responsible for the work of building which is to be accomplished by the ostiarius for the Church.

Let us consider, then, *the priest's office as ostiarius or doorkeeper to the people of God.*

I. Its Meaning. By the liturgical Rite of Ostiarius the Church gives us the keys to the house of God and authorizes us to ring the bell at the beginning and in the course of the Holy Sacrifice. Hence, according to the instructions of the Church, the ostiarius has to open and close the earthly edifices of the divine mysteries, to call the faithful to prayer, to keep out intruders, and to maintain the actual places of worship, together with their furnishings, in good condition. " *Sic agite quasi reddituri Deo rationem pro his rebus, quae his clavibus recluduntur.*" And we should do all this " *adjuvante Domino Nostro Jesu Christo,*" that is to say, not by virtue of earthly laws and orders, but through the impetus which the holy union with Christ, effected by the ordination, gives us.

II. The People of God Need Our Service as Ostiarius. *Sancta sancte.* What is reserved for God must be preserved from all profanation and defended against the hatred and contempt of God's enemies. Therefore the people of God look for a *guardian* who can say from his heart: "O Lord, I love the house in which you dwell, the tenting-place of your glory" (Ps. 25:8). They call for the *zealot* who, like Christ, will drive profaners from the Temple, and not allow the house of the Father to become a den of thieves. They call for the priestly *friend of God*, who, gifted with a spiritualized sense of beauty, will know how to choose works of art of sound piety for the house of God and distinguish them from the mere product of a secularized taste or misleading and false piety.

III. My Service as Ostiarius. Since the *ostiarius* as holder of a permanent office has disappeared from the Church, the *rector ecclesiae* is himself the *ostiarius* of the house of God and bears all the responsibility that belongs to the office of *ostiariate*. Do I examine my conscience from time to time regarding my care of the churches and chapels of my parish? Do I superintend my helpers adequately and see that they carry out the obligations of the *ostiarius* reliably and worthily in my stead? Do I instruct my Mass servers in such a way as to make them really understand and love with devout hearts what they do with their hands, and their outward senses? And finally, do I realize that the real door which I have to open to the flock of Christ is none other than Christ Himself, who says: "I am the door. If anyone enter by me he shall be safe, and shall go in and out, and shall find pastures"; and "He who enters not by the door into the sheepfold, but climbs up another way, is a thief and a robber" (Jn. 10:9, 1).

Reading: The Bishop's charge when handing the candidate the key of the church in the liturgical rite of the Order of **Ostiariate.**

THE ORDER OF LECTOR

25th Consideration

The Church sets us on the second step in the ascent to the priesthood when she confers on us the Order of Lector. We have received the grace of this order, too, in order to convey its blessing to the people of God.

Let us consider, then, *the priest's office of Lector to the people of God.*

I. In the Rite of the Order of Lector the bishop passed the book, which is the Missal, Breviary or Bible, to us with the order: " Receive and be readers of the word of God. If you fulfil your office faithfully and profitably, yours will be the reward of those who have duly administered the Word of God from the beginning." Hence, not only an order but also a right to the help of a special grace from Christ has been conferred on us with the first auxiliary office in the apostolic commission to preach the Gospel. In the early Church the task of the *lector,* a man of exemplary Christian life, was to read aloud to the congregation those portions of the Holy Scriptures chosen by the bishop. The bishop or priest then explained the feast or mystery of the day from these readings. St. Felix of Nola fulfilled this humble office of lector in his parish for many years before he was consecrated bishop, and while he still held high worldly offices.

II. The Church's Need of the Services of the Consecrated Lector. The words of our Lord in Jn. 8:47: " The reason why you do not hear is that you are not of God," and in Mt. 4:4: " Not by bread alone does man live, but by every word that comes from the mouth of God " show how necessary the Word of God is to the Christian life. Now, the Word of God is contained in its purest and most direct form in Holy Scripture. If the *Imitation of Christ* (Book IV, chap. 4) compares the faithful soul's need of Holy Scripture with its need for the Eucharistic Body of the Lord, it is clear how greatly the Church has need of the services of the lector, who conveys the words of Scripture to Christendom.

III. My Service as Lector (Reader). The liturgy of the present time confines our service as *lector* to the readings of the portions of Holy Scripture which occur in the Mass of the day. But this is done in a language closed to the people and, particularly at Low Mass, without any communication with those present. Who can deny that this reveals a most regrettable inadequacy in the liturgy of today as compared with the Early Church, in which the liturgical language was the language of the people? The priestly *lector* was forced to seek scope for his zeal outside the liturgy and found it in furthering those efforts which we describe today as " The Bible Movement." In our efforts in this direction we aim not merely at giving the faithful the body of the Scriptural words in the shape of cheap popular editions of the Scriptures, but still more its soul and spirit, its wisdom and its solace. Nor should we overlook the Encyclical of our Holy Father Pope Pius XII of 30 September, 1943, which unfortunately has been so little heeded, in which he gives us a distinct hint to increase for our people the very scanty weekly ration of Scripture offered in the liturgy, when he says that priests should " by their words energetically commend the approved popular translations of Holy Scripture, and also, where the liturgical rules permit, by their use of them. . . ." " *Quod autem ore legitis, corda credatis atque opere compleatis!*"

Reading : The bishop's charge in the Rite of Lector.

THE ORDER OF EXORCIST

26th Consideration

The Kingdom of God grows in its struggle with the enemy of the people of God, the devil and his followers. The priest is the chosen champion in this incessant warfare. For this leadership in the spiritual strife he receives his first commission and equipment in the third step on the way to the priesthood, namely the Order of Exorcist.

Let us consider, then, *the priest's office of exorcist among the people of God.*

I. In the Liturgy of the Order of Exorcist the Church prays God that the candidate, by the imposition of hands, together with the words of the exorcism may have power and authority to subjugate the unclean spirits, and also may be an approved physician of Thy Church, confirmed by the gift of healing and by heavenly virtue. In the early Church this office was regarded as the continuation of, or as substitute for, that power over evil spirits which our Lord gave to His Apostles (Mt. 10:1) and to the seventy-two disciples (Lk. 10:17), when He sent them forth.

II. The Church's Need for the Priestly Service of Exorcist. Looking ahead, it is true, on His approaching Passion, our Lord said: "Now is the judgment of the world; *now* will the prince of the world be cast out" (Jn. 12:31). The Church stands in the midst of this "*now*." But Satan defends himself with all his might against being banished from the world (Apoc. 12:17) and he persecutes the Bride of Christ in his continual blows against her children, which weaken and humiliate them until they fall into mortal sin. Hence the Church desires that her children, like the man in the Gospel who brought his possessed boy to our Lord's disciples, should find help and healing from her priests through the power which the Lord has given them over the demons. She looks for the "*probabiles medici in Ecclesia Dei.*"

III. My Office of Exorcist. The history of actual exorcism *in obsessos* shows that the Apostles' power over demons still lives on in the Church. But the scene at the foot of Mount Thabor, when the disciples were unable to overcome the devil though they had power over devils, because their faith was still too weak and their minds were still held captive by the power of the flesh, is still being constantly repeated. Therefore the Church limits most severely the use of the *potestas exorcismi in daemones.* She still uses it, however, in the liturgy of Baptism—in the exorcisms which precede the rebirth of the person baptized. Otherwise she lays down in Canon 1151, art. 1, that the written permission of the bishop is necessary for any extraliturgical use of exorcism *in obsessos,* that this permission may only be given if the case of possession can be absolutely proved by an experienced person (*sic,* in the judgment of the bishop!), and only to a priest distinguished for piety, prudence, and purity of life. The use of the *potestas exorcizandi* without these safeguards has always proved a snare of the devil and the source of the most pernicious false mysticism.

We exercise our office of exorcist in a wider sense in all the blessings of persons, objects, and places which the Church authorizes us to impart, for by our blessing we banish the evil power of the devil and place under the blessing of God the things which the Christian uses. In order that we may be equal to our office of exorcist, within the limits set for us, we must always bear in mind the warning contained in the liturgy of the Rite of Exorcist: "Learn from your office to overcome your passions so that the enemy of souls can claim nothing in your life as belonging to him. For you will have power over the devils in others only if you first overcome in yourselves their manifold wickedness. May the Lord, by His Holy Spirit, grant that you may do this."

Reading : The charge of the bishop in the Rite of Exorcist.

THE ORDER OF ACOLYTE

27th Consideration

The fourth of the Minor Orders made us acolytes. When the duties of the deacons and subdeacons increased in the primitive Church a new degree of service called the acolythate, or office of attendant, was introduced into the Western Church to assist the higher grades of consecrated persons. Quite early, the Church took the holders of this office by a special consecration into the lower hierarchical order. The Eucharistic service is the sphere of activity of this grade in that the acolyte discharges all the ancillary services in the Eucharistic offices which are not reserved to deacons and subdeacons. The Church of today requires that every priest persevere in the service and spirit of the acolythate.

Let us, then, consider *the service of the priest as acolyte among the people of God.*

I. **The Conferring of the Order of Acolyte.**

In the rite of ordination the conferring of the order of acolyte is symbolized by two actions, namely, the delivery of the candlestick and candle and the delivery of the cruets for the wine and water, accompanied by the words of the Bishop: " Receive the candlestick with the candle, and know that it is your duty to light the lights of the church in the name of the Lord." " Receive the cruet, to minister wine and water for the Eucharist of the blood of Christ, in the name of the Lord." As the office of acolyte embraces other duties, too, the specification of these two services is to be understood as *pars pro toto;* for the consecration gives power and orders for all services pertaining to the celebration of the Eucharist, in so far as these are not the exclusive right and duty of those in Major Orders.

II. **The Church's Need of the True Acolyte's Service.**
This demand is based upon man's need to see in holy

signs and actions the proof of God's gifts of grace. The acolyte is mankind's bearer of these signs. Therefore the bishop prays, in the second prayer after the ordination of the acolyte, that he may *"illuminatus vultu splendoris tui fideliter tibi in Ecclesia deserviat."* The light which the faithful are to see in the acolyte is the spiritual in its outward manifestations—that *devotio pia,* spiritual childlikeness of the Christian before God, that attitude of reverence and love which the Lord simply called "your light" in the Sermon on the Mount, when He said : "Let your light shine before men, in order that they may see your good works and give glory to your Father in heaven." In the acolyte and his service at the altar the Church desires to see "the new man, which has been created according to God in justice and holiness of truth."

III. My Service as Acolyte. This consists essentially in the faithful and reverent care with which I see that others acquit themselves of the duties of acolyte under my authority, as the Church requires; in other words, in my care for the training of good servants of the altar, in particular of young altar boys. Is there any better Catholic educational ideal than that of the perfect acolyte ? For in the eyes of the Church it does not suffice for an acolyte to be adequate in his external service of the altar; his whole deportment both inside and outside the Church must be that of a person illuminated by Christ; whose light shines before the faithful; one "pleasing to God and man," like our Lord Himself is rightly regarded. The service of the altar is the best starting point of a whole programme for the education and training of future leaders of the people of God. The priest whom he serves at the altar should be himself such a perfect reflection of Christ as to fire the zeal of his youthful acolyte.

Reading : The exhortation of the bishop in the rite of the ordination of an acolyte.

THE CONDITIONS FOR PROCEEDING TO MAJOR ORDERS

28th Consideration

" *Qui . . . sanctus est, sanctificetur adhuc* " (Apoc. 22:11). Before the Church permitted us to proceed from the order of acolyte to that of subdeacon, she stood before us with the warning words: " *Filii dilectissimi ad sacrum Subdiaconatus Ordinem promovendi, iterum atque iterum considerare debetis attente, quod onus hodie ultro appetitis.*" For we were in the act of ascending to Major Orders. But what makes the subdiaconate a Major Order is not the sacred powers which it confers—these are apparently identical with those conferred by the Order of Acolyte. What raises it so high above the Minor Orders is the condition upon which the candidate is admitted to it, the " *onus, quod hodie ultro appetitis* "; the threefold obligation imposed by the Church—the *professio fidei*, the *officium divinum*, and the *ligamen coelibatus*. It is only on acceptance of these three obligations, which cut deeply into our right of self-rule, that the Church has opened the way to the priesthood for us. As the threefold burden we have taken on ourselves oppresses us daily the good priest will constantly call to mind the reason why he took it on himself.

We shall therefore consider *the meaning of the three conditions placed upon our admission to Major Orders.*

The way to Major Orders has been opened to us by the Church in return for our binding ourselves:

I. To the Professio Fidei. To be sure, one is already bound by Baptism to the belief of the *fides orthodoxa.* But the Church has made admission to Major Orders dependent upon our binding ourselves to the public profession of this faith in the operation of all powers and functions which the Major Orders confer upon us. For she can only confer higher power in the Kingdom of God upon those who accept the law of this Kingdom without reserve and in its entirety. And the law of the Kingdom of Christ is the *fides salutis orthodoxa.* A State cannot exist if its officers do not know and consent to its law; similarly the outward and inward profession of the true doctrine of salvation by the holders of priestly powers is a necessary condition of existence for the Church. Hence the rite of ordination of a subdeacon demands that the candidates be " *in vera et Catholica fide fundati; quoniam, ut ait Apostolus : Omne, quod non est ex fide, peccatum est, schismaticum est, et extra unitatem Ecclesiae est.*" Anyone unable to assent to this requirement of the Church is unfit to proceed to Major Orders.

II. To the Officium Divinum. The Kingdom of God is a kingdom of the worship of God. True, the basic service of this worship is the Eucharistic Sacrifice, which is offered by Jesus Christ, its Head. But as the elders stand beside the altar in heaven, and accompany the worship of the Lamb with their canticles, so also shall the priestly servants of Christ accompany the daily worship in the earthly Kingdom of God with the daily canticles of the canonical hours. The aspirant to the priesthood of Christ who is alive to the inner meaning and mission of his future calling will joyfully bind himself to the recital of the Divine Office and keep his love for this privileged service throughout his life, to the sanctification of his soul and the benefit of the Church.

III. To the Ligamen Coelibatus. The Church has received from Christ the assurance that "there are eunuchs who have made themselves so for the kingdom of heaven's sake" (Mt. 19:12). These so hunger and thirst after the kingdom of God that not even their sexual instincts can turn them aside from it. They feel the urge of nature, it is true, but the impetus which comes from the Kingdom of God is still stronger. Now, as our Lord says: "Not all can accept this teaching but those to whom it has been given" (Mt. 19:11), the Church seeks out those who have received the grace of this spirit of undivided devotion to the Kingdom of God, fosters it in them, and reserves to them alone the precious gift of the priesthood of Christ. She believes the words of her Bridegroom; and experience too, shows her that she has done well to make the vow of celibacy a condition for conferring the Major Orders. The blessing which the law of clerical celibacy has brought to the Church far outways all the scandals and disappointments which the failure of some priests to keep this vow have caused her.

"No one, having put his hand to the plough and looking back, is fit for the Kingdom of God" (Lk.

9:62). When our Lord appointed as Apostles the twelve men who had already known Him for a long time, they had to leave the domestic circle to which they had hitherto belonged—" house and father and mother, and brother and sister ", and enter completely into a community of life with Him, His life of preaching, prayer, and renunciation of human love. Hence the three obligations which the Church places on us on the threshold of the Major Orders, are solely intended to make and keep us fit for the *perpetuo famulari Deo, cui sevire regnare est.*

Reading : The exhortation of the bishop prior to conferring the subdiaconate.

THE SUBDIACONATE

29th Consideration

When we had said our " Yes " to the threefold *" onus "* which the Church lays down as condition for our continued progress towards the priesthood, she opened our way to the subdiaconate. This Order, too, is given to us for a particular task in the sanctification of the people of God.

Let us therefore consider the function *of the priest's office of subdiaconate among the people of God.*

I. The Power and Mission of the Subdiaconate According to the Rite of Ordination. The bishop hands the candidate the empty chalice and the paten, and as the latter touches them the Bishop says: " *Videte cujus ministerium vobis traditur; ideo vos admoneo, ut ita vos exhibeatis, ut Deo placere possitis.*"

The office which the subdeacon has to accomplish with regard to the chalice and paten consists in preparing the sacrificial offerings, that is to say, the bread and wine, and taking care of the linen and sacred vessels which come into contact with the Eucharist. But he is not yet permitted to touch the consecrated elements, for he has no share as yet in the sacramental priesthood. The delivery of the Book of Epistles or Missal to the subdeacon when conferring on him the authority to read the Epistle at Mass, has only been customary in the Church since the Middle Ages. Hence we see that the power and office of the subdiaconate consists essentially in preparing and looking after the "oblationes," the offerings which have yet to be consecrated. And he is fitted to do this, not by a mere order, but by a consecration and the grace thereby imparted to him.

II. The Need of the People of God for the Services of the Subdeacon. In the days when the faithful themselves brought to the altar their gifts, from which the bread and wine for the Holy Sacrifice were chosen, the office of subdeacon had a directly practical application which is still expressed in the ordination liturgy of today with the words: "*De ipis oblationibus tantum debet in altare poni, quantum populo possit sufficere, ne aliquid putridum in sacrario remaneat.*" Hence it is the exalted duty of the subdeacon to take care that the Church of the New Covenant does not meet with the bitter reproach levelled by God at the priesthood of the Old Covenant through the prophet Malachias: "You offer polluted bread upon my altar, and you say: Wherein have we polluted thee? In that you say:

The table of the Lord is contemptible. . . . If you will not hear and if you will not lay it to heart, to give glory to my name, saith the Lord of hosts: I will . . . curse your blessings, yea, I will curse them" (Mal. 1:7, 2:2). But because oblations always represent the persons who present them, the Church extends the office of the subdiaconate to cover a certain superintendence over the faithful whose gifts the subdeacon places on the altar: she appoints him to be *strenuus sollicitusque excubitor caelestis militae,* to be the zealous guardian of the Church Militant, the watchful supervisor of the divine service. In the present-day office of subdeacon the duty of guardian is hardly in evidence any longer.

III. My Priestly Service as Subdeacon. Every time we go to carry out the most priestly of all tasks, the celebration of the Eucharistic Sacrifice, we are obliged by the law of the Church to wear the maniple. It shall remind us each time afresh that the oblations which are now to be consecrated must be select and worthy oblations. It shall censure any carelessness on the part of the priest concerning the *materia consecranda,* any of that lack of cleanliness which the Lord denounces so severely in the words of Malachias. But the maniple also asks us whether that other oblation—which Christ desires to offer to His heavenly Father through us—namely, the baptised, the people of God entrusted to our care—has been so prepared by us that its faith, devotion and reverence, its purity of heart and its sincere spirit of penance make it an oblation pleasing to the Father. The prayer for the seven gifts of the Holy Spirit with which the Church concluded our ordination as subdeacon must prove its power by enabling us to be competent and devoted guardians of the Temple of the Lord, that is to say, of the people of God. "*Quod ipse vobis praestare dignetur, qui vivit et regnat Deus in saecula saeculorum. Amen.*"

Reading : The bishop's exhortation before he hands to the candidate the empty chalice and the paten. Also Malachias 1 : 2, 9.

THE DIACONATE

30th Consideration

When we came forward to be ordained deacons, the Church asked the bishop : "*Reverendissime Pater, postulat sancta Mater Ecclesia Catholica, ut hos praesentes Subdiaconos ad onus Diaconi ordinetis.*" The Church made this request because she could not accomplish the ordination of deacons by her own holy power; as she could the Minor Orders; only those who have the power with which the Apostles had once ordained the seven deacons can confer the degree of ordination which has now to be conferred. That is to say, only the bishops, because only they are the heirs and ministers of the apostolic power of sacramental ordination. The Church therefore appealed to the bishop because she could not effect herself what she desired to give us. But she also made this request because she has urgent need of the deacon. And she also prayed for the grace conferred by ordination so that we might serve her with it.

Let us, then, consider *the service of the diaconate rendered by the priest to the Church of God.*

I. In the Rite of the Ordination of Deacons the bishop laid his right hand on our heads saying: "*Accipe Spiritum Sanctum, ad robur, et ad resistendum diabolo, et tentationibus ejus. In nomine Domini.*" Not out of mere natural social spirit, but equipped with the power of the Holy Spirit, the deacon shall carry out the duties of assistance to which the Apostles appointed the seven deacons by the imposition of hands; that welfare service to the faithful which the Seven had to carry out under the orders of the Apostles among the needy members of the Church in Jerusalem; a service of assistance to the dispensers of the mysteries of God, the bishops and priests, in the celebration of the Eucharistic Sacrifice and the administration of the sacraments, for which reason the Church, in her rite of ordination, calls the deacon the *comminister et co-operator corporis et sanguinis Domini.*

By our consecration as deacons we were equipped to serve both the actual and the Mystical Body of Christ.

II. The Church's Need of the Diaconate. In the Church today the diaconate has become an intermediate stage of brief duration on the way to the real priesthood. In it the meaning and mission of the diaconate has but scanty scope to fulfill itself. And yet, in actual fact, the scope for the exercise of this office would probably be no whit less comprehensive and urgent today than in the days of the Apostles. The members of the Body of Christ who are in material need call for education and training of future leaders of the people over-burdened with their manifold tasks—the celebration of the Eucharist, the administration of the sacraments and other pastoral duties, call for deacons even today with the words: " It is not desirable that we should forsake the word of God and serve at tables " (Acts 6:2). To be sure, lay people and religious who are not priests have taken over to a fairly large extent the tasks and services proper to the clerical deaconship; but since deaconship is the love of Christ which is to be shown to priests and people, it is fitting that the bearers of this love should come from the altar as persons dedicated to the Lord.

III. My Priestly Service as Deacon. As long as the Church of today fails to restore the early Christian diaconate, the priest, particularly the parochial priest, will continue to be overburdened with tasks proper to the diaconate. For the deacon's service in the celebration of the Eucharist and the administration of the sacraments has been taken over almost completely by him. True, he has helpers, if he is lucky, for the charitable services of the diaconate, but the management of welfare work within the parish falls to the lot of the parish clergy almost everywhere as an onerous heritage from the diaconate. Like St. Paul, who did not neglect to care charitably for the poor in Jerusalem even in the midst of his missionary work among the pagan, the priest of today will wish to make the charity of Christ manifest to the needy members of his parish (2 Cor. 8 ff.). But as Paul said: " And if I contribute all my goods to feed the poor . . . yet do not have charity, it profits me nothing " (1 Cor. 13:3). The priest of today too will bear in mind that the relief of the material needs of his flock is definitely not the work for which he has been ordained. The priest is essentially *dispensator mysteriorum Dei* (cf. Jn. 6:27). As modern man has a greater desire for the earthly bread than for the heavenly, he prefers to see the deacon in us than the priest. Hence, the priest runs the risk of letting his zeal for the charitable diaconate make him undervalue the need of divine grace for the true salvation of the world. We shall cope with this danger successfully if we cherish within us that esteem for the real gifts of salvation which moved the Apostles to appoint deacons to serve the tables of the poor (Acts 6:1-6).

Reading: The admonition in the ordination of deacons.

ORDINATION TO THE PRIESTHOOD

31st Consideration

When the deacon has proved his worth [to priests and people] in his auxiliary office, then in the eyes of the Church he is a suitable candidate for the grace of the priesthood of Christ. Accordingly, she now requests the bishop to place him at the sacrificial altar of the Lord and complete the long way of preparation by conferring upon him the fulness and perfection of the equipment of a priest. For this was, in truth, given to us by the Sacrament of Holy Orders. No lack of personal gifts or abilities on our part could curtail, in its essentials, this divine gift of grace.

Let us, then, consider that: *the Sacrament of Holy Orders gives the completion of our equipment as priests.*

I. Our Ordination to the Priesthood Was the Fulfilment of All the Other Consecrations. It is not only the last in order of time and the strongest in order of power of the seven ordinations, but it also constitutes *the raison d'être of all the others* because it confers that power which all the others exist to serve. Even the episcopal power, in as much as it is a sacramental entity, is co-ordinated to the priesthood for the additional power which it possesses over and above this: namely, the competence of the imposition of hands by which baptised persons are made priests. Hence, the ordination to the priesthood is as the sun to the pleiades of the seven Holy Orders.

II. Our Ordination to the Priesthood Gave Us the Perfection of Priestly Power. The rite of ordination expresses this with the words that the newly ordained are given *purum et immaculatum ministerii Christi donum*. Ordination gives to the youngest of us, even if he be full of personal weaknesses, the true and irrevocable power to call, in fact, to compel Christ to offer Himself mysteriously but really, "unblemished unto God. . . . For by one offering he has perfected forever those who are sanctified" (Hebr. 9:14, 10:14). "He also it is who has made us fit ministers of the new covenant" (2 Cor. 3:6). Even if the world cannot comprehend it, it is nevertheless true that a young, newly ordained priest brings more blessings upon the world with his first Mass than a great world-renowned sage can bring by his thought or a mighty statesman by his works.

III. Our Ordination Gave Us the Right and the Power to Achieve the Perfection of Personal Sacerdotal Sanctity. It gave us the *right* when the bishop, addressing us, said: "Realise what you are doing, model yourselves on what you handle, and as you celebrate the mystery of the Lord's death, see that your bodies are wholly dead to every vice and carnal impulse. Let your teaching bring spiritual healing to God's people; the fragrance of your lives delight the Church of God. By preaching and example build up the house—that is, God's family." The young priest may be dismayed when he is exhorted: "May the beauty of every virtue shine forth in you." Yet he can be full of confidence, for with the obligation he is also given *the strength* to fulfill it. When the bishop, immediately after the laying on of hands, prayed: "Hear us and heed us, we pray thee, Lord our God, and pour down on these thy servants, the blessing of the Holy Spirit and the power of priestly grace," he besought for us, in addition to the power of the priesthood just received, a rich fund of helping graces, to enable us to fulfil the high requirements of priestly sanctity. These helping graces are "the graces of the priestly vocation." They are sufficient to bring the priest to the perfection required of him, and we can fail to reach this perfection only if we neglect to avail ourselves of the graces of our state. Hence we see the manifold reasons for the Church's exhortation, *Custodiatis purum et immaculatum ministerii Christi donum.*

Reading : The preface to the rite of ordination.

THE BISHOP AS DISPENSER OF THE SACERDOTAL POWERS

32nd Consideration

The rite of ordination gives to the person called the remainder of those powers which he requires for the exercise of his priestly mission. Its prime author and minister is Christ in that, by His Holy Spirit, Christ invisibly draws us into a mysterious conformity to His own high priesthood, but also in that He has created a visible organ, namely, *the bishop* to imprint upon us the sign of our transformation into priests. Christ permits none to participate in His high priesthood except through a bishop.

We shall therefore conclude our consideration on the equipment of the priest by means of holy orders with a consideration of *the bishop as dispenser of our sacerdotal powers.*

I. The Episcopal Power Is the Source Whence the Catholic Priesthood Springs. In the liturgy of the consecration of a bishop the episcopal power is described as " *cornu gratiae sacerdotalis* "—the source whence springs the priestly power of grace. It was not the community of the faithful who made Timothy and Titus priests, but the Apostle; and the Apostle made them priests, not by merely appointing them. On the contrary, by prayer and the laying on of hands he transmitted to them what he himself had received. Now, what he had received, he had received direct from the Lord, and the community of the faithful awaited it from the Apostle as a gift of the Lord. The bishop, as the vehicle, not merely of priestly but also of apostolic power, is alone in a position to transform men into priests by the laying on of hands (*"creare,"* *"generare,"* as the primitive Church says). Hence the Church declares: "Whoever says that the bishops are not placed over priests, or that they have not got the authority . . . to ordain, or that the power which they have is common to priests also, or that the Holy Orders which they confer without the faithful consenting to or calling upon them to confer, are invalid . . . let him be anathema." Hence, if no one can become a priest without the action of a bishop, the episcopal power is, in a true sense, the source of life of the Catholic priesthood.

II. The Priest's Relation to the Bishop Is Therefore One of Spiritual Sonship. The relation between priest and bishop is certainly also the relation between one who holds office and one who confers it, between employer and employed. But it is more than this; it is the relation of the begotten to the begetter, of the son to the father, that is to say in the domain of the priesthood, in its essential character and functions. In Christ's plan the bishop is an image of His heavenly Father, from whom He Himself has received His priesthood (Ps. 109). Hence, Paul looks upon Titus and Timothy as his sons (1 Tim. 1:18; 2 Tim. 1:2, 2:1; Tit. 1:4) not merely in the sense of sharing the same spirit, but also in the sense of a likeness in being received from him, by which they have the same power of generating life from Christ, which he, the Apostle, has himself received from Christ.

"Filii dilectissimi" has therefore become the con-

ventional expression in the official language of the Church with which the bishop greets his priests.

III. The Right Attitude of the Priest Towards His Bishop Springs From This Spiritual Sonship. In the rite of ordination the Church has instructed the bishop to take the hands of the newly ordained priest between his own and to ask him: " Do you promise to me and my successors reverence and obedience?" When we answered our " *Promitto* " to this, and the bishop kissed us on the right cheek, this was the kiss of the father to the spiritual son who had been given to him by God. When our reverence and obedience are animated by devout knowledge and grateful admission of this sacramental relationship founded on grace, bishop and priest are bound one to another in a " *familia sacra.*" Then reverence is unfeigned and obedience is loving, for both are shown to the bishop, not as a human master, but, as Ignatius of Antioch wrote, " *tamquam Patri Jesu Christi omnium Episcopo* " (*Ad Magnes. Ch. III*).

Reading: The picture of the fatherly shepherd as drawn in that part of the preface to the rite of consecration of a bishop which follows the anointing of the head.

2. THE PRIESTLY SPIRIT

PREFACE

The essential equipment which the Catholic priest receives for the fulfilment of his mission is given by the sacrament of Holy Orders. Every priest who has received this gift of grace validly and has the will to do in his use of it what Christ has ordained becomes a mediator of the graces of salvation even if he is, personally, a man of little holiness or actually a great sinner. " For if one person is baptised by a just and holy man, and another by one who has little merit and is lower in the eyes of God—is less temperate and lives a less worthy life, both receive absolutely one and the same baptism." And what is the reason of this? None other than " because He (Christ) is the (real) dispenser of baptism " (St. Augustine: *John, Homily for the Octave of the Epiphany*). For the priest is the instrument of Christ, not because he is *holy* but because *Christ* has fitted him to be His instrument.

Nevertheless, our moral and religious feelings condemn the priest who combines possession of the holy powers with an unworthy spirit and way of life. God confirms our feelings by demanding holiness of the priesthood of the Old as of the New Covenant, and punishing the lack of holiness severely. Consequently the Sacrament of Holy Orders gives to the priest, together with the sacerdotal powers, the *essential* but not the whole equipment which he needs for the accomplishment of his mission. He must bring to the exercise of his holy powers an attitude of soul in keeping with the sacred character of his duties. This attitude of soul we call priestly sanctity or the priestly spirit. One might also call it the divinely willed " *ethos* " of the Catholic priesthood.

This priestly spirit is not given to us as a *gratia gratis data*, as the priestly powers are; it has to be *acquired with effort*. To be sure, it is also a gift of grace in that our efforts to acquire it are inspired, accompanied and perfected by the Holy Spirit. In the rite of ordination our claim to this assistance of the Holy Spirit was given to us as a divine and fundamental gift by which the newly ordained priest is placed in the position of being able to acquire with normal effort that degree of priestly sanctity corresponding to the fulfilment of his mission. The impious priest does not avail of this claim, and therefore does not receive the graces necessary for his state; and if he becomes a degenerate priest it is always because he has definitely rejected the divine spirit which would have sanctified him.

The following Considerations, Nos. 33 to 45, are designed to help us to strive to preserve the priestly spirit, and where necessary, to awaken it anew.

THE NECESSITY OF SELF-SANCTIFICATION FOR THE PRIEST

33rd Consideration

Since the priestly spirit must be acquired with effort, our *prudentia carnalis* seeks to save us from this trouble. It tries to persuade us that one can be a good priest without being a holy one, and it draws the conclusion that while striving for holiness is praiseworthy, it is not absolutely necessary. Now, it is quite true that not every good priest is a saint who would qualify for canonization, but it is equally true that no one can be a good priest who does not strive constantly and methodically to be holy. The beginning of the priestly spirit is an earnest will to priestly self-sanctification.

Let us therefore consider that *the priestly spirit consents to self-sanctification as a necessity.*

The priest is persuaded of this because of

I. The Nearness to God Into Which His Calling Brings Him.

Because we are mediators between God and man (Hebr. 5:1), we are obliged to approach near to God. We do this in our vicarious sacrifices and prayers and whenever we approach people, not in our own name but in our official capacity, by virtue of which we were told: "He who hears you, hears me; and he who rejects you rejects me" (Lk. 10:16). If we were to see, as a visible happening, the nearness to God into which our functions at the altar and in the confessional, at the baptismal font and in the pulpit bring us, we would feel as the Prophet Isaias did when the nearness of the Lord was revealed to him in the vision of his mission (Isa. 6), and we would feel impelled to say, as he did: "Woe is me, because . . . I am a man of unclean lips, and I dwell in the midst of a people that hath unclean lips, and I have seen with my eyes the King the Lord of hosts." Now, is not the nearness of the Lord all the more terrible the less we strive for holiness, the more complacent and tepid we are in our spiritual life? Therefore, the Holy Spirit reveals Himself in the soul of the good priest in the first place by preserving the priest's *awe in the face of that nearness to God* into which all priestly action leads him. But this impels the priest to strive after holiness. "They shall be holy to their God, and shall not profane his name: for they offer the burnt offering of the Lord, and the bread of their God, and therefore they shall be holy" (Lev. 21:6).

II. The Union With Christ Which the Character Sacerdotalis Gives Him. This is in itself a *gratia gratis data,* given to him not primarily for his personal sanctification but for the sanctification of those to whom he is sent. But since it binds the priest indissolubly to Christ, and Christ to the priest, it establishes a relationship which can only be salutary for the priest if he treads the way of Christ, and which must of necessity be damning and terrible in its consequences if he tries to go the way of the world and of sin—which is opposed to the way of Christ. If the words of the Lord, " He who is not with me is against me " demand from even ordinary Christians more than the merely superficial, workaday fidelity of a follower, this is still more true of the priestly servants of the Lord.

III. The Mission in the Church Which He Has Received From God. Now, the priest has received his powers for the building up of the Church as a community of *the saints* (Eph. 4:12). How shall he be able to establish holiness successfully in others if he does not love it and strive after it himself? Where shall the faithful kindle their will to salvation if they do not see it burning in the heart of the priest who exhorts them to it? For this reason the indifferent and, still more, the sinful priest fails in his mission, in spite of his powers, as long as he has not got in him the aspiration towards priestly self-sanctification. Therefore, of all the things which the Church rightly demands in the personal mode of living of the priest, her first requirement is self-sanctification, for she says: " *Clerici debent sanctiorem prae laicis vitam interiorem et exteriorem* *ducere eisque virtute et recte factis in exemplum excellere*" (Canon 124, *De obligationibus clericum*).

Reading : Apoc. 3:1-6.

THE SPIRIT OF CHRIST

THE MEASURE OF OUR SELF-SANCTIFICATION

34th Consideration

Ordination creates the actual priesthood, but it is *the priestly spirit* which makes a *worthy* priesthood. What is this spirit? Who defines its features? The Church; perhaps, with her ordinances, contained in her book of canon law: " *De obligationibus clericorum* "? Or this or that exemplary priest of the past? No! The standard of the priestly spirit is none other than the spirit of the High Priest Jesus Christ Himself, who wills to continue His life and His action in us. Those words of the Epistle to the Romans—" But if anyone does not have the Spirit of Christ, he does not belong to Christ " (Rom. 8:9), are more applicable to us priests than to lay Christians.

Let us therefore meditate upon the fact that *the Spirit of Christ is the measure of our priestly spirit.*

I. What Is the Priestly Spirit of Jesus Christ? It is that basic attitude of the Most Sacred Heart of Jesus which, from the moment of the Incarnation until Its last beat on the cross, sought not the satisfaction of His own wishes but the glory of the eternal Father and the salvation of mankind. In other words, that spirit in which Christ, without any reservation due to self-love, gave Himself up to the task of mediator which the heavenly Father had set Him. The Epistle to the Hebrews describes how our Lord realized in His life this fundamentally priestly attitude. " For Jesus, in the days of his earthly life, with a loud cry and tears, offered up prayers and supplications to him who was able to save him from death, and was heard because of his reverent submission. And he, Son (of God) though he was, learned obedience from the things that he suffered; and when perfected, he became to all who obey him the cause of eternal salvation, called by God a high priest according to the order of Melchisedech " (Hebr. 5:7 ff.). This mediatory will to self-oblation of the Heart of Jesus is the priestly spirit of our High Priest.

II. The Priestly Spirit of the Heart of Jesus Will and Must Live on in His Apostles and Priests. They are indeed to be witnesses of this spirit of their Master: " For God, who commanded light to shine out of darkness, has shone in our hearts, to give enlightenment concerning the knowledge of the glory of God, shining on the face of Christ Jesus " (2 Cor. 4:6). Paul is speaking here of the apostolic mission. If we are to make the " light of the gospel of the glory of Christ " shine, Christ, who is united to us in His being in the *character sacerdotalis,* must also " shine in our hearts " in His spirit, that is, in His redemptive love as Priest and Victim. In his encyclical to the bishops of Germany of December 9, 1921, Pope Benedict XV expressed this obligation in the words: " *Primum omnium illud curandum est, ut Christus formetur in iis qui formando in ceteris Christo destinantur officio muneris.*" " For," he continued, "the priest bears within himself the image of Jesus Christ, the Eternal High Priest, and he must therefore live the life of Christ as if he were another Christ, not alone by participation in His power, *but also by conformity with His disposition.*"

III. How Does the Spirit of Christ Form in the Good Priest? The same Holy Spirit who imprinted the priestly character on us at ordination, also gives us the priestly spirit, though to be sure not without our own co-operation. For just as He continually inspired the spirit of Christ with His high-priestly sentiments from the moment of the Incarnation, so too does He inspire us to strive for inner conformity with the spirit of Jesus. In His discourse at the Last Supper (Jn. 16:8 ff.) our Lord Himself states this unambiguously when He assures the Apostles of the assistance of the Holy Spirit not merely for the *outward* witness which they are to bear of Him in the world, but also of the *inner* witness in their own hearts by which they will at last really be able to recognize Jesus for what He is. "In that day (when the Holy Spirit shall come) you will know that I am in my Father, and you in me, and I in you" (Jn. 14:20). But the priestly soul must daily open itself anew by meditation and prayer to this working of the Holy Spirit. If we do this we shall perceive what the Lord has promised us concerning Him: "He will receive of what is mine, and will declare it to you" (Jn 16:14), for He *is* the light that shines forth in our hearts, "to give enlightenment concerning the knowledge of the glory of God, shining on the face of Christ Jesus" (2 Cor. 4:6).

Reading: Rom. 8:28-37.

SOUND PIETY THE ROOT OF OUR SELF-SANCTIFICATION

35th Consideration

The priest is "appointed for men in the things pertaining to God" (Hebr. 5:1). Therefore he must cherish a firm determination to get into contact with God, to have intercourse with Him. This striving for contact with God is what we call priestly piety. It is the core of the priestly spirit. From it all the other dispositions and abilities suited to a priest must develop if they are to be sound and supernaturally strong. For if they do not come from the sound core of *pietas sacerdotalis* they are deceptive and unfruitful even if they appear magnificent in the eyes of men.

Let us therefore consider that: *the root of the priestly spirit is a sound piety.*

I. In the High Priest Jesus Christ All Virtues Have Their Root, including His love for souls and His union in being and in spirit with His heavenly Father. He expresses this last often, and in the clearest terms: "Amen, amen, I say to you, the Son can do nothing of himself, but only what he sees the Father doing. For whatever he does, this the Son also does in like manner. For the Father loves the Son, and shows Him all that He Himself does" (Jn. 5:19 ff.). In the context of the Gospel these words refer to the cure which Jesus has just effected, of the man who had been thirty-eight years an invalid; it initiates His renewal of healings on the Sabbath. From this spiritual union with the Father His pastoral activity develops as from its root; not merely in intermittent contacts with the Father but in an abiding spiritual unity with Him. This is the priestly piety of the Heart of Jesus. The Epistle to the Hebrews does not tire of emphasizing the fact that the union of our High Priest with the Father, which constitutes His priesthood's superiority over that of the priesthood of the Old Testament, was not merely a union of being but also one of soul and disposition, namely, due to the *constant prayerful piety* of our Mediator (Hebr. 5:7, 7:25, 9:14, 10:5 ff., etc.).

II. The Sound Piety of the Good Priest Is Nothing Other Than the Continuation of That Piety With Which His Lord and Master remained continually turned towards the heavenly Father. The apostolic disciple of Christ knows that he must also be Christ's instrument in his constant loving and adoring union with the Father. Just as he treads the selfsame path with Jesus to reach and bring salvation to man, as His instrument, so also does he approach, in union, Him, the Father " in whom all live." Hence, all his pastoral activity takes its prayerful beginning from the Father, and in the Father finds its prayerful end. All activity for the salvation of man which does not spring from priestly piety may be social; but it is not priestly. Sound priestly piety is, therefore, none other than the spirit of the Apostle of the Gentiles which makes him say at the beginning of his Epistles and again at the end of them: " Blessed be the God and Father of our Lord Jesus Christ, who has blessed us with every spiritual blessing on high in Christ " (Eph. 1:3; Rom. 1:7; 2 Cor. 1:3).

III. The Cultivation of Priestly Piety. The living piety of the priest is shown in *the priest's prayer*. Hence the Church lays upon her priests the obligation to recite numerous prayers each day. She combines each dispensation of the sacramental mysteries, including the celebration of the Eucharist, with a corresponding order of prayers, and though these liturgical prayers are the prayers of the whole Church, the priest is the spokesman and advocate in the "we" of the Church. Daily she places in our hands the Divine Office; in it our mouths and our souls are to be the functional organs of the whole Mystical Body of Christ at prayer. Moreover, the bishops instruct us to take care that: "*ut clerici omnes . . . quotidie orationi mentali per aliquod tempus incumbant, sanctissimum Sacramentum visitent, Deiparam Virginem mariano rosario colant, conscientiam suam discutiant*" (Canon 125). But as first of *all* the obligations of the priest's life she places the cultivation of that union with God which shows itself in the good priest's habit of prayer. How little understanding of the essential nature of his calling does that priest show who despises prayer or contents himself with a mere outward and mechanical performance of his obligations in this regard, and considers outward works which can be seen by the eyes of men of more importance than going before the face of the Lord.

Reading: Jn. 14:12-14.

THE SPIRIT OF FAITH

36th Consideration

If the priest's spirit is inspired by the piety of his Master, this will be shown in the first place by his attitude of mind. To be sure, piety is not merely disposition, but it cannot be realized in practice without disposition. The priest who strives to sanctify himself, sanctifies his thinking by opening his mind to the thoughts of God; in other words, he lives by faith. Who should be the just man who lives by faith if not the man who preaches the faith?

Let us consider, then, that: *the priestly spirit lives on faith.*

I. The Soul of the Most Sacred Humanity of our Lord did not live *from faith,* it is true, for it had the vision of God all the time; but it was precisely its insight into the decree of the Father which determined all its thoughts and strivings in the fulfilment of Christ's mission of mediation. The joyful tidings were the announcement of the intentions of the heavenly Father of our Lord. At the Feast of Tabernacles, when the Jews asked, in astonished admiration: " How does this man come by learning, since he has not studied?" he answered: " My teaching is not *my own,* but His who sent me " (Jn. 7:14 ff.). So firmly united to God were His thoughts and words that He could say: " He who believes in me, believes not in me but in Him who sent me " (Jn. 12:44, 14:9). He does not demand a blind faith in this testimony of His concerning the origin of His words in the bosom of the Father; each can prove it for himself: " If anyone desires to do His will, he will know of the teaching whether it is from God, or whether I speak on my own authority " (Jn. 7:17).

II. The Good Priest Acquires by the Apostolic Spirit of Faith Union with God in thought and word. This spirit makes him, like his model and Master, refrain from proclaiming himself, and makes him speak " not a wisdom of this world nor of the rulers of this world," but rely instead on " the wisdom of God, mysterious, hidden, which God foreordained before the world unto our glory " (1 Cor. 2:7). For naturally it is impossible that our priestly work which has no other aim than to realize among men the saving wisdom of God, should be founded on mere worldly wisdom. The Apostle says of the preacher who nevertheless preaches his own wisdom: " *Adulterat verbum Dei* ". He abuses the word of salvation in an adulterous fashion, as Israel abused the covenant of God. But when the priest speaks to men out of a true spirit of faith, he too may dare to apply to himself those words of His Master: " If any-one desires to do His will, he will know of the teaching whether it is from God, or whether I speak on my own authority " (Jn. 7:17; cf. 1 Cor. 4:16).

III. The Cor Sapiens Sacerdotale Fosters and Cultivates This Spirit of Faith. It distrusts the natural inclination to over-value one's own wisdom and the wisdom of the world, but loves all the more the saving wisdom of God. The good priest *meditates* on it and *studies* it.

He meditates on and prays for the wisdom of faith, because He knows that the teacher of this wisdom is none other than the Holy Spirit, of whom the Lord said to the Apostles: " When he, the Spirit of truth, has come, he will teach you all the truth. For he will not speak on his own authority. . . . He will glorify me, because he will receive of what is *mine* and declare it to you " (Jn. 16: 13-14). Hence in this respect, too, it is the Holy Spirit who forms within us the spirit of Christ.

He studies it because the Church, who in her teaching office is the mouthpiece of the Holy Spirit and at the same time His external instrument in the formation of the priestly spirit, wishes that he should do so. She therefore ordains that *even after ordination* her clergy shall not cease to study, particularly the sacred sciences, in which study they shall strive after that sound doctrine which has been handed down from ancient times and been approved by the Church. And in their studies they shall avoid worldly fashions in expression and outlook (*profanas*—not sacred—*vocum novitates*), and all merely spurious science (Canon 129). Hence, the priestly spirit of faith expresses itself in a constant effort to be " in Christ Jesus, who has become for us *God-given wisdom,* and justice, and sanctification, and redemption " (1 Cor. 1:30).

Reading: 1 Cor. 1:26-31.

APOSTOLIC TRUST IN GOD

37th Consideration

" Now faith is the substance of things to be *hoped for* " (Hebr. 11:1). Priestly piety must fill the thoughts of the apostle with divine wisdom, and priestly action animate the priest's thought with supernatural hope. " For God has not given us the spirit of fear," writes St. Paul to his disciple Timothy (2 Tim. 1:7). From his sound piety the priest draws the strength for his apostolic trust in God. Trust in God is a fundamental feature of the priestly spirit.

Let us therefore meditate on this fact: *that apostolic trust in God is the strength of the priestly spirit.*

I. The Trust in God of Jesus Christ. This trust animated His whole life, suffering and death. In the darkest hours of His sufferings, on the Mount of Olives and the Way of the Cross: in the midst of His sense of dereliction, He does not lose this trust. For as the prophet puts in His mouth: " He is near that justifieth me. . . . The Lord God is my helper, therefore am I not confounded: therefore have I set my face as a most hard rock and I know that I shall not be confounded " (Isa. 50:8, 7). He Himself tells all who are scandalized by the lowliness of His appearance, that His strength lies in the nearness of the heavenly Father: " And He who sent me is with me; He has not left me alone, because I do always the things that are pleasing to Him " (Jn. 8:29).

II. The Good Priest's Trust in God. It consists of conformity with Christ in the matter of confidence in the *nearness and help of the heavenly Father,* and this " through Christ our Lord." Again and again Christ demands this trust from His Apostles. At one time He says to them: " Take courage . . . do not be afraid "; and at another: " Why are you fearful? Are you still without faith?" (Mt. 14:27; Mk. 4:40). This trust in God has always been the great strength of all outstanding priests from the Apostles down to Don Bosco. By it, Peter set the man born lame on his feet again " in the name of Jesus "; in it Paul saw the source and justification of all apostolic power, for he writes: " Such is the assurance [i.e., apostolic trust] I have through Christ towards God. Not that we are sufficient of ourselves to think anything [salutary], as from ourselves, but our sufficiency is from God. He also it is who has made us fit ministers of the new covenant " (2 Cor. 3:4 ff.). " Discharging, therefore, this ministry in accordance with the mercy shown us, we do not lose heart " (2 Cor. 4:1).

III. The Cultivation of a Priestly Trust in God.

This is achieved in the course of our daily exercise of defending and building up. For we must *defend* our priestly spirit against the natural enemy of all trust in God, namely, inordinate self-confidence—that natural inclination to rely on ourselves alone, which easily asserts itself even in the exercise of our priestly office and causes us to lose heart and become dispirited when we see how inadequate we are. This spirit can only be overcome by humility. But as we do not willingly humble ourselves, the good priest is generally humbled by God until he becomes distrustful of his own abilities. That is why our Lord allowed the prince of the Apostles to fall into the ignominy of the denial, and took Paul into the school of humility: " And lest the greatness of the revelations should puff me up, there was given me a thorn for the flesh, a messenger of Satan, to buffet me . . ." (2 Cor. 12:7 ff.). There are many inward and outward crosses in our priestly life, given us " lest we should be puffed up " and designed to lead us from false self-confidence to priestly trust in God. But we must build up our trust in God *constructively*, in the first place by " testing " its strength, that is to say, by setting about mastering our tasks and difficulties by trust in God. Anyone who has once experienced the power of trust in God will always seek it. Then we must pray trustfully. The lengthy instructions on prayer which our Lord gave the Apostles had the same fundamental idea that all the blessing of apostolic work was to come from trust in God and in His Son as expressed in the formula of the prayer of petition, " in the name of Jesus." " Amen, Amen, I say to you, he who believes in me the works I do he also shall do and greater than these he shall do, because I am going to the Father. And whatever you ask in my name that I will do, in order that the Father may be glorified in the Son. If you ask me anything in my name, I will do it " (Jn. 14:12 ff.).

Reading: 2 Cor. 4:1-6, 16-18.

ZEAL FOR THE GLORY OF GOD

38th Consideration

In the Old Testament we repeatedly meet priests who lack joy in their calling; God and the divine service have become burdensome to them. It is to these priests that the Lord says: " Behold, I will cast the shoulder to you, and I will scatter upon your face the dung of your solemnities, and it shall take you away with it " (Mal. 2:3). This is God's judgment on priests in whom the flame of zeal for the glory of God has become extinguished.

Let us consider that: *The priestly spirit is zealous for the glory of God.*

I. Zeal for the Glory of the Heavenly Father Burns Like a Flame in the Heart of Jesus. From the moment of the Incarnation, when the Holy Spirit kindles this zeal, the Lord continually yearns to drink the cup which the Father has given Him (Jn. 18:11). In following this urge He renounces His own glory (Jn. 8:50); the vindication of His own good name He leaves entirely to the Father (Jn. 18:54). Therefore He can say to the heavenly Father at the end of His life: " I have glorified thee on earth; I have accomplished the work that thou hast given me to do " (Jn. 17:4). This zeal is the fire of His heart, which He has come to cast upon the earth, and of which He says: " And what will I but that it be kindled? " (Lk. 12:49.)

II. The Fire of This Zeal of Christ Burns in the Heart of the Good Priest. This zeal is truly the flower of priestly piety, in which the spirit of faith and trust in God opens up into *an active love of God*—an " *amor effectivus.*" It is this zeal which turns the apostle into the good servant, who does the most with the talents of his priestly powers; who watches for the coming of his Master, whatever the hour of that coming may be; and gives bread in due course to the other servants of the Lord, over whom he has been placed. This zeal breaks the fetters of selfish nature; it enables Peter to break away from the narrow traditions of his Jewish blood and make room in the Church for the pagan Cornelius and his whole household. This zeal for the glory of God is the motive force behind the leaven of Christ by which the Church will continue to work its way forward until the whole world is leavened. But if the priest lacks this zeal, he will be like the angel of the church at Laodicea, who said to himself " I am rich and have grown wealthy and have need of nothing," whereas in reality he was "wretched and miserable and poor and blind and naked," so much so that the Lord threatened him: "But because thou art *lukewarm,* and neither cold nor hot, I am about to vomit thee out of my mouth" (Apoc. 3:14 ff.).

III The Cultivation of Zeal for the Glory of God. The Lord speaks the following mysterious words to the angel of the church at Laodicea: "I counsel thee to buy of me gold refined by fire, that thou mayest become rich" (Apoc. 3:18). The Lord offers the lukewarm priest the gold of His own zeal for the glory of His heavenly Father. Now, our zeal is not only too weak and ineffective, but also too impure. It is *weak and ineffective* if we are poor in supernatural love of God; for the person who does not live is not zealous. True devotion to the Most Sacred Heart of Jesus is the great school of love of the heavenly Father. For in the Sacred Heart we contemplate the love of Jesus for the Father, and before the Tabernacle we beg for this strengthening love. For all who venture into the "*fornax ardens caritatis*" are set afire by it. And this fire also purifies us; for our zeal is *impure* as long as we resemble in any way those apostolic colleagues of St. Paul of whom he wrote those bitter words: "For they all seek their own interests, not those of Jesus Christ" (Phil. 2:21); that is to say, as long as we try more or less, in our priestly works, to reserve to ourselves the honour due to God alone. Unfortunately, it is precisely the active, zealous priest who succumbs most easily to the danger of love of power and pride of achievement, and thereby " seeks his own interests." When the disciples returned jubilant from their first mission, our Lord invited them to rest in Him and find refreshment: " Learn from me, for I am meek and humble of heart " (Mt. 11:28 ff.). When the fire of the Heart of Jesus purifies the priest's zeal, it loses all self-interest and love of power and becomes transformed into the selfless, patient, and pure zeal of the Good Shepherd which the Father loves (Jn. 10:17).

Reading: Apoc. 3:14-21.

" He who abides in me, and I in him, he bears much fruit " (Jn. 15:5). In the Christian mind these words of our Lord apply to all the works of the baptized which are conducive to salvation, but they were spoken to the Apostles with reference to their apostolic mission. They mean, in effect, that apostolic work can only be really successful when it proceeds from a soul which is rooted in Christ. Now, everything which lessens, hinders, or actually destroys the close union of the priest's soul with God, is a threat to the priestly spirit; for it loosens his roots from the divine, life-giving soil and so causes wilting and sterility. This loosening out from the fertile soil of the divine is the result of dispositions and attachments which estrange the priest's heart from God and leave it open to those things of which the Apostle says that: " They who do such things will not attain the kingdom of God " (Gal. 5:21). It is therefore part of the " *sapientia cordis* " to fear sin and preserve " faith and a good conscience." This wise mode of living gives to the priestly spirit certain specific characteristics. These shall form the subject of the following Considerations (39 to 42).

WALKING IN THE FEAR OF THE LORD

39th Consideration

In his anxiety to preserve inviolate his union with
God the good priest cherishes in his heart a constant
distrust of himself. Let us consider, then, that: *The
priestly spirit is best preserved by a salutary fear of sin.*

I. Two Utterances of Our Lord are especially apt
reminders to those priests who believe that they can
dispense with the *timor peccati*. The first is: " Do not
be afraid of those who kill the body, and after that have
nothing more that they can do. But I will show you
whom you shall be afraid of; be afraid of him who,
after he has killed, has power to cast into hell " (Lk.
12:4-5). Our Lord spoke these words to His Apostles
just as He was about to send them out on their first
trial-mission. If even the Apostles had to arm themselves with a wholesome *timor peccati*, can we afford to
dispense with it? The other text is: " Not everyone
who says to me, ' Lord, Lord,' shall enter the kingdom
of heaven; but he who does the will of my Father in
heaven shall enter the kingdom of heaven. Many will
say to me in that day, ' Lord, Lord, did we not
prophesy in Thy name, and cast out devils in Thy
name, and work many miracles in Thy name?' And then
I will declare to them ' I never knew you. Depart from
me, you workers of iniquity!' " (Mt. 7:21 f.) All
external priestly work, even if it appears wonderful in
the eyes of men (because the priest has succeeded in
prophesying, driving out devils and working miracles),
is rejected if it does not come from one who maintains

his conscience in harmony with the will of the Father who is in heaven.

II. Therefore the Good Priest Cultivates Timor Peccati. "And in this I too strive always to have a clear conscience before God and before men." With these words the Apostle of the Gentiles concludes his self-defence before the Roman Governor Felix (Acts 24:16). He lets us see in his anxious admission (1 Cor. 9:26) how earnest he was in his endeavour: "I therefore so run as not without a purpose; I so fight as not beating the air; but I chastise my body and bring it into subjection, lest perhaps after preaching to others *I myself should be rejected*!" The great reformers of the Church have always begun their work, not by proclaiming new pastoral methods but by purifying her clergy from unworthy ways, and sanctifying them by means of that scrupulous fear of the Lord with which they themselves were animated.

St. Charles Borromeo and St. Francis de Sales are striking examples of this.

III. How Does the Priest Keep Himself in This Salutary Timor Peccati? Watchfulness is the first condition. Our Lord was tireless in recommending this " Vigilate " to His Apostles. The Church repeats the Lord's warning when she admonishes priests in Canon 125: *Quotidie (clerici) . . . conscientiam suam discutiant.*" Fidelity to the daily examination of conscience will not only keep us watchful, but when, despite watchfulness, we fail to prevent completely our conscience becoming sullied, it will move us to purify it quickly again, and make us use willingly and well that other means recommended in the same canon: " *Poenitentiae sacramento frequenter conscientiae maculas eluant.*" Daily examination of conscience and frequent good confession are the best proved means of preserving a salutary *timor peccati.* They will help the priest who uses them diligently to restore quickly the union of his soul with God when he sins, so that the vital contact between the priestly spirit and the divine nourishment of its roots is never mortally interrupted, or at least never for long. And so the faithful and loving use of these two well-tried means will help us to remain, as St. Paul says, always watchful and ready in our missionary warfare, " holding the mystery of faith in a pure conscience " (1 Tim. 3:9).

Reading: Gal. 5:16-26.

DETACHMENT FROM THE PLEASANT THINGS OF LIFE

40th Consideration

Timor peccati is an essential of the priestly spirit, for without it the priest sooner or later succumbs to the allurements of sin; that is why Holy Scripture calls it " the beginning of wisdom." But the good priest cuts out far more effectively the danger of his good heart being corrupted if he combines with the wholesome fear of sin a *clear-sighted and aggressive spirit* in regard to those forces in his nature which, while not being sinful in themselves, predispose him to sin if he does not carry on a ceaseless warfare against his sensual appetites. The priestly spirit cannot thrive in us unless we carry on a methodical warfare against the desires of the flesh; but it thrives on voluntary mortification of the flesh. " *Ut carne mortificati facilius caelestia capiamus,*" the Church bids us pray on October 19, the feast of St. Peter of Alcantara.

This clear-sighted and aggressive fighting spirit must be directed in the first place against that inclination of our nature which Scripture calls the concupiscence of the eyes.

Let us therefore meditate on the fact that: *The priestly spirit manifests a spirit of detachment from the Pleasant Things of Life.*

I. The Master Demanded This of the Apostles Both by Word and Example.

True, Jesus did not live the austere life of John the Baptist. On the contrary, He ate and drank and dressed like other people. But He was just as indifferent as the Baptist was to providing for His bodily needs. He Himself wished to keep free of the care and management of temporal goods and comforts, and He demanded that His Apostles too should do the same. When He was sending them out for the first time, the only proviso He made regarding their mode of life was this: "Do not keep gold, or silver, or money in your girdles, nor wallet for your journey, nor two tunics, nor sandals, nor staff; for the labourer deserves his living" (Mt. 10:9 f.). And when someone, carried away by enthusiasm, once said to Him: "Lord, I will follow thee wherever thou goest," Jesus replied: "The foxes have dens, and the birds of the air have nests, but the Son of Man has nowhere to lay his head" (Lk. 9:57 f.). A priest who is idealistic, yet hankers after possessions and worldly pleasures, does not get much farther than fine words and futile wishes. His impetus and energy disappear as soon as the Lord stops "breaking bread".

II. Why Is This Spirit of Mortification Necessary to the Priest? As we see by the example of the Lord who " ate and drank with publicans and sinners," the pleasures and joys of the world are not always bad in themselves or to be avoided in all circumstances. But, as they awaken the sensual appetites; the more they are desired and enjoyed (Gregory the Great); the craving for them robs the Apostle of his *interior freedom,* and frequently of his *exterior freedom* too. He is unhappy if he has to suffer poverty and want; and he allows himself to be too greatly influenced by people who can give him the comforts which he misses. How can such a priest remain firm if he meets with persecution and privation? It is otherwise with the Apostle of Christ who has deliberately and consciously schooled himself to doing without, in accordance with the example of his divine Master. He can say, with the Apostle of the Gentiles: " For I have learned to be self-sufficing in whatever circumstances I am. I know how to live humbly, and I know how to live in abundance (I have been schooled to every place and every condition), to be filled and to be hungry, to have abundance and to suffer want. I can do all things in him who strengthens me " (Phil. 4:11 ff.).

III. We Cannot Acquire This Apostolic Spirit of Mortification, unless we systematically accustom ourselves to renounce the enjoyments which are not forbidden to us. In food, drink, smoking: in attire and habits of living: in the choice of recreation and social intercourse: and in the provision for his temporal needs the good priest will not allow himself to be influenced by consideration of the enjoyment which is bound up with these things, but only by their practical utility and necessity *for his calling.* If they hinder his devotion to his mission, he will refrain from their use, or at least restrict it to the right degree. The cultivation of a joyous generosity and charity towards the poor is a most salutary means for a priest to curb his own natural desire for possessions and enjoyments.

Whenever his heart begins to seek the goods and pleasures of the world, he will know that it is probably time for him to subject the law of his members to the law of the spirit, in order that he may " use this world as though not using it " (1 Cor. 7:31). He must not let the *sapientia cordis sacerdotalis* be deluded by the *prudentia carnis.*

Reading: Phil. 4:10-20.

CULTIVATED VIRGINITY

41st Consideration

Celibacy, which is obligatory on all those in Major Orders in the Latin Church, and at least on those holding episcopal rank in the Greek Uniate Church, gives a special stamp to the priestly spirit. For it is, after all, but the outward expression of an *inner disposition* which seems practically indispensable to that spirit of union with God which we have recognized to be the core of the priestly spirit. We call this inner disposition sacerdotal virginity.

Let us then, consider the fact that: *The priestly spirit grows strong in cultivated virginity.*

I. Christ Himself Fulfilled His Priestly Mission in a Life of Voluntary Virginity. As a true human being

He was a real man and possessed within Himself all the powers and rights of ordered, normal man's estate. If these powers of His did not come to the use proper to them, and these rights to their proper fulfilment in the foundation of a family according to the flesh, this was, firstly, because the will of the Father did not bind him to the satisfaction of these demands of nature, and secondly, because our Lord Himself desired to dedicate to the children of Adam all the devotion of His most holy humanity. Hence the *mediatory* will of Christ embraced the surrender of His right to a posterity according to the flesh. Thus, our Lord freely chose His virgin way of life in order to transform from children of God's anger to children of God those whom fallen Adam had begotten according to the will of man and of the flesh. In order to transform the " *massa damnata* " into a " *plebs acceptabilis Deo* ", the high-priestly King made Himself an eunuch for the sake of the kingdom of heaven.

The virginity of Christ is *a fruit of His redemptive love*.

II. This Virginity of Christ Must Be the Soul of Our Priestly Celibacy. The urges and rights of physical man's estate are renounced by the good priest, not in a spirit of compulsion but in *freely chosen* following of Christ, in which we, like Him, desire to dedicate all the strength of our devotion, whole and undivided, to the building up of the kingdom of God from the children of Adam. But as " not all can accept this," but only " those to whom it has been given " (Mt. 19:11), it was a sign of special vocation when as youths we conceived a desire for this conformity with the virginal

Christ, and opened our hearts to the Apostle's advice: "I would have you free from care. He who is unmarried is concerned about the things of the Lord, how he may please God. Whereas he who is married is concerned about the things of the world, how he may please his wife; and he is divided" (1 Cor. 7:32 f.). If our celibacy is animated by this spirit it will become part and parcel of our priestly disposition; a continued operation of the priestly spirit of Jesus Christ in us; an oblation more precious in the sight of God than the sacrifice of his own son Isaac which Abraham was ready to make. Our priestly celibacy will then acquire the character of the religious vow.

III. How Must We Live Our Celibate Lives So That Our Celibacy Strengthens Our Priestly Spirit? If we are to live our celibate lives joyously and fruitfully, *the same spirit* which decided Christ to choose the life of virginity must also animate us: the spirit which makes us "eunuchs for the sake of the kingdom of God." If this motive fails the priest may come to regard his celibacy as a compulsion and restrict its observance to the degree necessary to avoid giving scandal while disdaining or rejecting the *inner chastity,* the *virginal disposition.* When this happens clerical celibacy becomes that ill-concealed Pharisaism of which the world is so ready to accuse us. But the ideal conception of apostolic celibacy can only be acquired and preserved by the priest who regards celibacy prayerfully—particularly in relation to the Eucharistic mystery; and accepts it in a joyful spirit of sacrifice. Devout idealism in the matter of motive must be combined, moreover, with *sober realism in the choice and use of means* for the practical preservation of celibacy. For the firm establishment of the inner chastity of the heart is not possible without sober watchfulness over our senses and instincts, our imagination and our feelings. It requires a discreet distance in the face of all efforts of creatures to win our love, and quick recognition of danger if the undividedness of our devotion to Christ and His interests is threatened. It demands an outward and inward reserve which forbids any dangerous intimacy with the opposite sex, yet does not make us embarrassed or gauche with women. And finally, it calls for a striving towards union with God by a life of prayer which awakens so strongly in the soul the *desideria caelestia* that the *amor mundanus* gives way before it as the darkness gives way to light.

Thus the priest who is a celibate for the sake of the kingdom of God, lives among men like a being from another world, and brings into time a ray of that radiance which will envelop all the children of God in eternity: " For at the resurrection they will neither marry nor be given in marriage, but are as angels of God in heaven " (Mt. 22:30; *cf.* Lk. 20:34 f.)

Reading: 1 Cor. 7:29-35.

HUMILITY OF HEART

42nd Consideration

The human desire for authority and honour is a further threat to the priest's union with God. It can easily seduce the heart of the priest and make him misuse his priestly powers, office and mission for the satisfaction of his own love of power. There is no vice more often and more mercilessly denounced by our Lord in the Gospels than the love of power and honour of the Temple priesthood of His day: " All their works they do in order to be seen by men " (Mt. 23 : 5).

What protection has the priestly spirit against this danger? None other than *true humility*.

Let us, then, consider the fact that: *The priestly spirit serves in humility.*

I. Our Divine Master's Own Priestly Life and Work Were Marked by Humility.

" Christ Jesus . . . emptied himself, taking the nature of a slave . . . therefore God also has exalted him " (Phil. 2 : 5 ff.). If we wish to attain to the glory of heaven with Him, we must tread with Him the path of humility. When the ambitious sons of Zebedee asked, through their mother, for the first places in the kingdom of God, and the other Apostles were annoyed at this, our Lord said to them: " You know that the rulers of the Gentiles lord it over them and their great men exercise authority over them. Not so is it among you. On the contrary, whoever wishes to become great among you shall be your servant; and whoever wishes to be first among you shall be your slave; even as the Son of Man has not come to be served but to serve, and to give his life as a ransom for many " (Mt. 20 : 25 ff.). To teach him humility, our Lord allowed Simon Peter, the future head of his Church, to fall into the ignominy of denying Him. This experience was to prevent him later on from self-complacently misusing the great power of the primacy.

II. Why Must the Priest Fulfil His Mission in Humility? For two reasons. Firstly, because only the humble priest leaves to God the place due to Him in his work—the position of real and effective cause of all the works of salvation, while contenting himself with the role of an instrument in the hand of the Lord. The priest without humility, on the contrary, ascribes to himself an importance which he has not got and which God refuses to recognise by withdrawing His co-operation from the proud priest. Hence, the haughty priest is really ineffectual however impressive he may seem in the eyes of men. His self-complacency merits the reproach: "What hast thou that thou hast not received?" (1 Cor. 4:7). Secondly, because only the humble priest preserves that delicacy of conscience which makes him give to God *the gains of his priestly work* and keep nothing back for himself—the gratitude of the faithful for his good offices with all those effects so seductive for the heart of the priest—honour, influence, and worldly rewards. Even St. Paul had to say of his otherwise so zealous fellow workers in the mission: "For they all seek their own interests, not those of Jesus Christ" (Phil. 2:21). Hence, the proud priest cuts God out of his work in a twofold sense—as the effective cause of the works of salvation and as the beneficiary of the same. Therefore, God leaves his side as He once left the proud Temple priests whom our Lord denounced: "Woe to you, Scribes and Pharisees, hypocrites! because you shut the kingdom of heaven against men. For you yourselves do not enter in, nor do you let those entering pass in " (Mt. 23:13).

III. How Do We Acquire True Priestly Humility?
For one thing, by fighting vain self-complacency in a
carefully fostered *spirit of gratitude* towards God for
deigning to use us for His saving work. This gratitude
is not the false thanksgiving of the Pharisee in the
Temple, but the true gratitude of the Apostle, which
expresses itself in a canticle in praise of the power of
the divine grace, manifest in his work (2 Cor. 12:9 f.).

A second powerful safeguard of apostolic humility is
true love and kindness towards our priestly colleagues.
The proud priest may easily come to regard his colleagues as rivals and potential opponents: feel jealous
of them: spy out their weaknesses: rejoice when he
finds some; and he can seldom resist the temptation to
show them up before others. The humble priest, on
the other hand, enjoys his intercourse with his colleagues, sees their good points at least as well as their
weaknesses, appreciates and helps them. He is obedient
and willing towards his ecclesiastical superiors, not
because he wants to win them to his views, but because
he wants to serve the cause of Christ. And he can do all
this because he is a true disciple of his humble Lord
and Master.

Reading : 1 Cor. 4:6-13.

Union with God and self-denial release the priest
from the slavery in which " the elements of this world "
involve a man; they make him an " otherworldly "
person who is above the world while yet in the midst of
it. We must love this other-worldliness as our homeland
and refuge. The contemplative monk seeks it by withdrawing from the world; the walls of his monastery are

the outward sign of that detachment to which he has bound himself by his vows. But the priest engaged in pastoral work cannot preserve his detachment from the world by material walls. He cannot flee the world; on the contrary, he has to go into it because he has received the power and the mission of the priesthood precisely in order to *sanctify the world.* For this reason union with God and self-denial do not suffice completely for the formation of the priestly spirit; they must be supplemented by a pure and eager *will to sanctify the world.* This priestly will to sanctify the world is called by the Church " zeal for souls " (*zelus apostolicus*). It differs from zeal for the glory of God (38th Consideration) in being directed specifically on man, on saving man from the " corruption of the world " and bringing him safely home into the family of the heavenly Father. The following Considerations (Nos. 43 to 47) will deal with zeal for souls as the third constituent of the priestly spirit.

The measure of sound zeal for souls is, again, nothing other than the spirit of Christ, the *Cor Jesu flagrans amore nostri.* Our Lord Himself never tires of emphasising this; He says it to His Apostles (Jn. 12:26, 17:17 f.); He says it to the Temple priests of His time. whom He denounces precisely because of their false zeal (Mt. 23).

TRUE ZEAL FOR SOULS HAS ITS ORIGIN IN CHRIST

43rd Consideration

Since sound zeal for souls is a reflection of Christ's zeal for souls, it must proceed in the first place from Christ.

I. The Master Demands This in the most detailed description which He has given of His own zeal for souls, namely, in the great parable of the Good Shepherd, in which He says: "He who enters not by the door into the sheepfold, but climbs up another way, is a thief and a robber. But he who enters by the door is shepherd of the sheep. . . . *I am* the door " (Jn. 10:1, 9). Because the Father has entrusted the flock to Him alone, a zeal which has its origin, not in Christ but in one's own will, however well intentioned it may be (for instance, because of humanitarian motives out of social conscience, or a human joy in youth, or out of sheer desire for achievement), is wrong from the start and has no prospect of being blessed by God. Of such exertions our Lord says: "Every plant that my heavenly Father has not planted will be rooted up " (Mt. 15:13). The priestly zeal which starts out from Christ, on the contrary, is rooted like that of the Good Shepherd in the will of the heavenly Father, and receives from it its impulse, measure, and blessing.

II. What Blessing Rests Upon a Zeal That Comes From Christ? Our Lord makes two promises to the shepherd who goes to God's flock through Him. First, *he will be recognised by the sheep as the right shepherd.* " He who enters by the door . . . the sheep hear his voice . . . and follow him because they know his voice. But a stranger [who does not enter through Christ] they will not follow, but will flee from him, because they do not know the voice of strangers " (Jn. 10:3 ff.). Neither the natural ability for leadership of an educated and strong-willed priest, nor his possession of the sacerdotal powers, nor the Church's mission, suffice of themselves to open the hearts of the faithful to the grace of Redemption. But Christ gives the key to the priest who can confess sincerely, with St. Paul: " Knowing therefore the fear of the Lord, we try to persuade men. . . . For the love of Christ impels us " (2 Cor. 5:11, 14). The second promise is: " If anyone enter by me he shall be safe, and shall go in and out, and shall *find pastures* " (Jn. 10:9). If the priest is not bound to Christ by the warm bonds of love, how can he give that love to his flock? True, he can administer the sacramental means of salvation, but he cannot dispense them in such a way as to make the faithful eager for them. But if the priest knows from personal experience the meaning of those words of Jesus: " My Father gives you the true bread from heaven. For the bread of God is that which comes down from heaven and gives life to the world. . . . I am the bread of life " (Jn. 6:32 ff.), he knows how to offer this heavenly food to his flock in such a way as to make it love to live and thrive on it. Hence, the true spiritual union of the priest with Christ is the secret of all successful zeal for souls. That is what St. Paul means when he says: " For other foundation no one can lay [for apostolic work], but that which has been laid, which is Christ Jesus " (1 Cor. 3:11).

III. How Do we Ensure That Our Zeal for Souls Starts Out From Christ? To do this we must *examine the motives* in which we approach the faithful. Since Paul had to complain of his fellow workers, who were so zealous in external missionary work: " For they all seek their own interests, not those of Jesus Christ " (Phil. 2:21), must we not be distrustful of the purity of our own zeal? If we allow our priestly work to be determined only by external requirements, or by the chance inspiration of our own hearts, we do not " enter by the door." But we enter through Christ when we lay our undertakings before Him and beg His blessing. If we do this, Christ will meet us daily in many ways—in our meditations, in our devout celebration of Holy Mass, and in our visits to the Blessed Sacrament as commanded in Canon 125, a. 2. If we commend our tasks to our Lord on these occasions in the words of the saintly Pope, Clement XI: " *Offero tibi, Domine, cogitanda, ut sint, de te— facienda, ut sint secundum te—farenda, ut sint dicenda ut sint propter te,*" our zeal can never fail to have good results.

Reading : Jn. 10:1-9.

THE GOOD SHEPHERD'S VIEW OF MAN

44th Consideration

True zeal for souls starts out from Christ, but its object is man. " For every high priest taken from among men is appointed for men " (Hebr. 5:1). But what he is to do among men is something which the apostle does not know of himself; it has to be shown him " from above." True apostolic zeal has *its own special view of man,* namely, the view of our Lord and Mediator, Jesus Christ. If it has not got this view, it goes astray and leads others astray. The Evangelist speaks of our Lord's view of man in these remarkable words: " But Jesus . . . knew all men, and . . . had no need that anyone should bear witness concerning man, for he himself knew what was in man " (Jn. 2:24 f.).

Let us consider, then: *That true zeal for souls must have as its basis the Good Shepherd's view of man.*

In the first place, the Good Shepherd has no idea of His own concerning man; His idea of man is that of the heavenly Father. He knows that it is the truth about man; but because He is "the word of the Father," by whom all things, even man, have been made, he knows, Himself, with divine and infallible wisdom, "what is in man." His view of man is therefore the only right view. That is why He has "no need that anyone should bear witness concerning man." The Good Shepherd sees man through the eyes of the Father:

I. As Something Belonging to God Which Is in Danger of Being Lost Forever. Man is in danger because he is liable to be carried away by "the world"; and the world is lost by having become the domain of the prince of darkness who at the same time is the prince of death. Therefore in the eyes of Jesus, man is a being who "sits in darkness and in the shadow of death"; indeed, so much has man fallen into the power of the world that he loves the darkness rather than the light (Jn. 3:19).

If the priest has not got his Master's view of man he fails to see the lost condition of humanity deeply and truly enough, and he is complacently trustful of "the world," blind to the seductive snares of the prince of this world; and he only sees the wolf which kills the sheep when it is far too late. Therefore, true zeal for souls calls for the Good Shepherd's wise awareness of the forlorn condition of man.

II. As Something Belonging to God Which Can Be Won Back. It can be won back because it has in it a point of contact for the redemptive will of God. This point of contact is man's craving for eternity, which the world can never satisfy because it is essentially transitory. Every human being is the prodigal son, capable of being homesick for his father's house. Because the Good Shepherd knows this, he begins to court man's love by telling him that the Kingdom of God is within his reach and he pictures the nature of the heavenly Father so attractively as to awaken even in publicans and sinners their true nature, born for eternity; and the world, in which they have hitherto loved the darkness rather than the light, ceases to hold them. The true lover of souls must have the Master's eye for the saving grace in human nature, which is always present even in the most reprobate sinner, and which is nothing else than the craving for eternal life, for which every human heart has been created. But the priest who does not have this Christlike knowledge of human nature easily despairs of man and leaves him to the mercy of the prince of darkness. Therefore, the Good Shepherd's wise conviction of the essential redeemability of lost humanity is a vital constituent of true zeal for souls.

III. As Something Belonging to God Which the Heavenly Father Wills to Win Back at a Great Price. " For God so loved the world that he gave his only-begotten Son, that those who believe in him may not perish, but may have life everlasting " (Jn. 3:16). What must be man's value in the eyes of Jesus if he is worth being ransomed at so great a price, according to the decree of the heavenly Father? No philosophy of the wise ones of this world can rouse us to strive and struggle for man and his lost soul as can Jesus, who alone knows how lovable and precious man is.

Only when the apostle of Christ is enlightened with Jesus' knowledge of man will his zeal for souls become free of the narrowness of the hireling. When this happens he will exclaim in astonishment with St. Paul: " Who shall make accusation against the elect of God? It is God who justifies! Who shall condemn? It is Christ who died; yes, and rose again, He who is at the right hand of God, who also intercedes for us!" (Rom. 8 : 33 f.).

This is the Good Shepherd's view of man. It is one of those mysteries of God " which no one knows but the Spirit of God," and those to whom " God has revealed them through his spirit (1 Cor. 2 : 11, 10; cf. Mt. 11 : 27). The Holy Spirit has been sent by the Lord to impart it to His Apostles (Jn. 14 : 17), and He gives it to us all the more abundantly the more we try to see our own selves and our own value with the eyes of God. The priest who values and cherishes his own soul, remembering that it has been ransomed with the Blood of Christ, knows best what his priestly zeal has to seek in the souls entrusted to him.

Reading : 1 Jn. 3 : 1-3.

LARGENESS OF HEART

45th Consideration

The Father has given the Son power over all flesh. Therefore, the zeal of the Good Shepherd reaches out

to everyone "that he may give everlasting life" to all.
His will to save excludes no one who does not shut
himself out from it. This all-embracing redemptive will
of Christ must also characterise us, priestly apostles
of Christ, within the measure of our competence. That
is to say, our zeal for souls must embrace all those who
are entrusted to our care; it must be large-hearted.

Let us consider, then, that: *True zeal for souls is
large-hearted.*

I. The Good Shepherd's Zeal for Souls Tolerates No Narrowness.

True, according to the will of the
Father, it must be directed first and foremost "to the
lost sheep of the house of Israel." With what zeal Jesus
fulfilled this mission, wandering from town to town
and village to village, preaching the glad tidings to just
and sinners alike; to the masses and to the teachers of
the Law. He schooled a little group of elite, His
Apostles, and devoted His time to individual souls who
sought Him, such as Nicodemus, the Samaritan woman
at Jacob's Well, and the sisters Martha and Mary. But
when people tried to make Him confine His zeal to
Israel according to the flesh, He replied: "Other sheep
I have that are not of this fold [Israel]. Them also I
must bring" (Jn. 10:16). He welcomed every sincere
helper, even if the latter went his own way in outward
things. One day the Apostle John said to Him:
"Master, we saw a man casting out devils in Thy
name, and we forbade him, because he does not follow
with us." Jesus replied: "Do not forbid him; for he
who is not against you is for you" (Lk. 9:49 f.). The
will of the Father was the foundation of Jesus' broad-
mindedness, for He said: "All that the Father gives

to me shall come to me, and him who comes to me I will not cast out . . . for this is the will of Him who sent me, the Father, that I should lose nothing of what he has given me " (Jn. 6:37 ff.).

II. The Largeness of Heart of Jesus Must Live On in the Priest's Zeal for Souls. It is the way of human nature to wish to reserve the good things for oneself and one's friends. Even in the *dispensatio mysteriorum Dei* this instinct can make itself felt in the hearts of us priests, and cause us to prefer those among our parishioners who demand less self-sacrifice from us or who satisfy our self-love more than others. It may so happen that we are so intent on serving the pious that we forget the sinners, or that we favour the rich, neglect the poor, and pay such attention to the " elite " that we come to regard the *plebs sancta* of the rest of the faithful as *profanum vulgus*. But if the priest is animated with the spirit of the Good Shepherd, he will strive to regard with the same devotion all whom the Lord has entrusted to him, " Jew and Gentile, slave and free, male and female," rich and poor, worker and employer, fellow countryman and foreign refugee, priest and layman, religious, secular clergy, communities and individuals, for to him all are one in Jesus Christ— *omnia in omnibus Christus* (Gal. 3:28; Col. 3:11).

III. What Must We Do to Give Our Zeal This Apostolic Liberality? In the first place, we must *find out* about those for whom we are responsible, *their number and their needs*. In doing this we shall come to a useful examination of the relation between our pastoral achievement and the needs of our parish. The words in Ezechiel 33 : 7, that God will require from our hand all the souls whom he has given us, will reawaken our sense of responsibility for those overlooked and neglected.

Secondly, we must examine ourselves for any hidden self-interest which may have made us seek to please ourselves rather than God in our quest for souls. For self-seeking makes us narrow-minded.

Thirdly, we must include all in our prayers, but more especially those in the parish who tend to avoid us or whom we feel inclined to avoid.

Reading : Acts 10:34-48.

COMPASSION

46th Consideration

The priest will feel naturally drawn to those who love the kingdom of God : to " the just," as Holy Scripture calls them. It would be a bad sign of our priestly spirit if they were not our " joy and our crown." But this complacency in the thriving portion of our flock can be harmful to our zeal for souls, if it obscures our view of the other elements whom we cannot, unfortunately, reckon among the " just." According to John 7 : 49, the Temple priests in the time of our Lord, referring to the masses who were not very open to their teachings, said : " But this crowd, which does not know the Law, is accursed!" How easily the shepherd of the flock of Christ can develop the same outlook if some of his parishioners resist his efforts! But if he does so, he scatters his flock instead of gathering it together. We avoid this danger of

aversion and hardness of heart if we deliberately cultivate a spirit of patient love towards the weak and
sinners—the spirit of priestly compassion.

Let us consider, then, that: *A sound zeal for souls
is best preserved by a spirit of compassion towards the
weak and sinners.*

I. The Master Has Revealed This by His Own Example.

He did not repulse the pious, indeed he rejoiced when he came across one of them (Jn. 1:47);
but from the very beginning of His public life He paid
so much attention to sinners that those who considered
themselves good were scandalised (Lk. 15:2). "He eats
with publicans and sinners," they said angrily. But He
justified Himself by reminding them of a judgment on
their conceit and self-righteousness which the heavenly
Father had already passed through the mouth of the
prophet Osee (6:6): "It is not the healthy who need
a physician, but they who are sick. But go, and learn
what this means: 'I desire mercy, and not sacrifice.'
For I have come to call sinners, not the just" (Mt.
9:9 ff.). In this way Jesus established that trust of
sinners in His merciful heart, which has never failed
since. Yes, He even tolerated being called "the friend
of sinners."

II. The Good Shepherd's Compassionate Zeal for Souls Must Continue in Us, Priests.

For God wills
to fulfil not only in His only-begotten Son but also in
Christ's priests the promise which He announced
through Ezechiel: "I will feed my sheep: and I will
cause them to lie down, saith the Lord God. I will
seek that which was lost: and that which was driven

away I will bring back again: and I will bind up that which was broken, and I will strengthen that which was weak, and that which was fat and strong I will preserve" (Ezech. 34:15 f.). Compassion for the weak and the erring is the characteristic which distinguishes the Good Shepherd from the hireling who "has no concern for the sheep." In the ages of faith people used to like to ask themselves why it was that God made men and not angels the servants of His order of salvation (*Summa* 3, q. 64, 7). The Epistle to the Hebrews gives the answer: "For every high priest taken from among men is . . . *able to have compassion on the ignorant and erring, because he himself also is beset with weakness* . . . " (Hebr. 5:1 f.). Paul was not freed from the thorn of his humiliating weakness that God's grace might show itself the more strongly in the compassion which the suffering Apostle was able to give to the ignorant and erring.

III. How Does the Priest Acquire the Quality of Selfless Compassion? In the parable of the Good Samaritan, the first Person to come across the half-dead Jew was "a certain priest . . . and when he saw him, he passed by" (Lk. 10:31). What could and would have preserved that priest from his hardness of heart? What can and must save us from hardness of heart towards the sinners and weaklings of our parish?

First, the *sense of responsibility* which we must bear towards all entrusted to us. "So thou, Oh son of man, I have made thee a watchman to the house of Israel: therefore thou shalt hear the word from the mouth, and shalt tell it them from me. When I say to the wicked: Oh wicked man, thou shalt surely die: if thou dost not speak to warn the wicked man from his way: that wicked man shall die in his iniquity, but I will require his blood at thy hand. But if thou tell the wicked man, that he may be converted from his ways, and he be not converted from his way: he shall die in his iniquity: but thou hast delivered thy soul" (Ezech. 33:7 ff.).

Second, *by gratitude for all the mercy which God has shown to us.* St. Paul expresses this gratitude: "I give thanks to Christ Jesus our Lord, who has strengthened me, because he counted me trustworthy in making me his minister. For I was formerly a blasphemer, a persecutor and a bitter adversary . . . Jesus Christ came into the world to save sinners, of which I am the chief. But for this reason I obtained mercy, that in me first Christ Jesus might show forth all patience, as an example to those who shall believe in him for the attainment of life everlasting" (1 Tim. 1:12 ff.). Impelled by this gratitude, a Francis Xavier thought no place too far away, a Vincent de Paul thought no place too sordid, in which to seek erring souls and lead them home to the flock of the Good Shepherd.

Reading: Mt. 18:11-14.

THE SPIRIT OF JOYOUS SELF-SACRIFICE

47th Consideration

Largeness of heart and compassion are necessary dispositions for us priests, but they would be of little avail for the welfare of those for whom we have been appointed shepherds if they were not combined with the energy of will to make them effective. The Samaritan did not become the rescuer of the half-dead Jew merely by "having compassion" on him—though to be sure, Holy Scripture reckons this in his favour, in contrast to the uncharitable priest—but because "he went up to him and bound up his wounds, pouring on oil and wine. And setting him on his own beast, he brought him to an inn and took care of him" (Lk. 10:34). The largeheartedness and compassion in our zeal for souls only become fruitful for the salvation of souls when they are combined with active selflessness and eager self-sacrifice.

Let us consider, then, that: *True zeal for souls is animated by an eager spirit of self-sacrifice.*

I. The Good Shepherd Has a Noble Spirit of Self-Sacrifice.

"I am the good shepherd. The good shepherd lays down his life for his sheep. But the hireling, who is not a shepherd, whose own the sheep are not, sees the wolf coming and leaves the sheep and flees. And the wolf snatches and scatters the sheep; but the hireling flees because he is a hireling, and has no concern for the sheep. I am the good shepherd. . . . For this reason the Father loves me, because I lay down my life" (Jn 10:11 ff.). What our Lord says here in parable He fulfilled in His high-priestly Passion and death. And in order to go to the utmost limit ("*in finem*") with this noble spirit of self-sacrifice, He continues it in the mystery of the Eucharist, because the flock which He redeemed with His Blood is in constant need of His selfless devotion. And to us priests He has given the power to render Him present on the altar in this Sacrifice of love. (Compare Considerations 6 and 7.)

II. A Noble Spirit of Self-Sacrifice Is a Necessary Condition of the Success of Our Apostolic Work. A condition, not a cause. For the cause is the omnipotent grace of the Lord. But grace comes, not through the self-seeking priest, but through the selfless one; not through the proud and obstinate priest, but through the humble and self-sacrificing one. This spirit of self-sacrifice is the mysterious but indispensable condition for all growth and fruitfulness in the Kingdom of God. " Amen, amen, I say to you, unless the grain of wheat fall into the ground and die, *it remains alone. But if it die, it brings forth much fruit.*" These words refer in the first place to the Redeemer Jesus Christ. But He straightaway declared it to be the general law governing the development of the Kingdom of God and of all apostolic life for He continued: " He who loves his life, loses it; and he who hates his life in this world, keeps it unto life everlasting. If anyone serve me, let him follow me; and where I am there also shall my servant be ". (Jn. 12:24 ff.) Out of his knowledge of this law and his own extensive experience of its effect on his own apostolic life, Paul writes to all his fellow workers of all times: " For I think God has set forth us the apostles last of all, as men doomed to death, seeing that we have been made a spectacle to the world, and to angels, and to men " (1 Cor. 4:9).

III. How Does the Priest Acquire This Noble Spirit of Self-Sacrifice? Its source does not lie in ourselves. Even the words and example of our Lord failed to awaken it in the souls of His disciples during His earthly life. In spite of good dispositions, they fell again and again into that petty and timid selfishness which so unfits a man for apostleship. Only when the fiery baptism of the Holy Spirit came over them were their hearts transformed by that generosity which Paul tells us animates himself and his fellow Apostles, when he writes: "We give no offence to anyone, that our ministry may not be blamed. On the contrary, let us conduct ourselves in all circumstances as God's ministers, in much patience . . . in labours, in sleepless nights, in fastings . . . in long-sufferings, in kindness . . . in honour and dishonour . . . as deceivers and yet truthful . . . as having nothing yet possessing all things " (2 Cor. 6:3 ff.). We too have received this baptism of fire at our ordination. By ordination the Holy Spirit was given to us as a divine power, not only for the operation of the divine mysteries of salvation, but also for the fruitful administration of them. But as this cannot be accomplished without self-sacrificing and energetic action, the Holy Spirit gives the grace of apostolic self-sacrifice to each of us in the measure that the souls entrusted to our care require it of us. That is to say, an apostolic spirit of self-sacrifice is a *charism of our state in life,* which the Holy Spirit will awaken in every priest who does not offer positive resistance to it. Now, this positive resistance consists in permitting ourselves to give way to the inclination of our natures for the pleasant things of life and the approval of the world. The more the priest goes against these weaknesses of his nature, the more the spirit of divine love produces in him that noble spirit of self-sacrifice which will make his zeal for souls fruitful in apostolic works.

Reading : Acts 20:17-38.

The Good Shepherd follows up each individual soul. Those whom the Father has given him (Jn 6:39 ; Lk. 15:3 ff.) He gathers together, with great trouble, in order to make up the ninety-nine who form the flock, because " there shall be but one fold and one shepherd " (Jn. 10:16, 17:22 ff.). For the salvation of the individual is too greatly endangered if he is not incorporated into and does not live in the community of the children of God.

Now, the community of the children of God is what Christ calls His Church. It is the organization ordained by God for the salvation of the individual soul.

Therefore every priest is also a minister of Christ for the building up of the Church or, as St. Paul puts it, " for building up the body of Christ " (Eph. 4:12; cf. 19th Consideration). In order to cope with this task the priest needs certain dispositions and abilities; all these have their root in his understanding of and zeal for the welfare of the community of the faithful. We usually call this quality " *sentire cum ecclesia*," or ecclesiastical spirit.

The following Considerations (Nos. 48 to 53) will deal with the ecclesiastical spirit as a necessary evidence of the true priestly spirit.

LOVE OF THE CHURCH

48th Consideration

" In this manner therefore you shall pray: Our Father . . . Thy kingdom come!" (Mt. 6:9-10). The words " Thy kingdom " definitely embrace all that God is. But anyone who has the spirit of Christ knows that the kingdom of God which is to come to man is that community of the disciples of Christ to which Our Lord committed His mission in the world and entrusted the entire fullness of His redeeming grace, namely, His Church. It is nothing other than the people of God and God's order of the new covenant. *The coming of the Church* must therefore be the basic object of the prayer and loving solicitude of every disciple of Christ, but above all, of the apostolically-minded priest. For he is the appointed herald of this kingdom of God.

Let us consider, then, that: *Love of God's Kingdom, the Church, is essential to the priestly spirit.*

I. **"Christ Also Loved the Church, and Delivered Himself Up for Her, That He Might Sanctify Her"** (Eph. 5:25 f.). In these few words Paul expresses everything which Christ did in His earthly life because He loves His Church. Now, what He does and will continue to do for her from His throne of glory to the end of time, is described for us throughout the whole Book of Revelation. In his visions the seer of Patmos shows us the Lamb that was slain triumphantly bringing the Church to man in a continual fight against the powers of Antichrist, and forming that commonwealth, the New Jerusalem, which will be presented to Him as a bride. With all her members she sings a continual canticle of praise of the Lamb: "Thou wast slain and hast redeemed us for God with thy blood, out of every tribe and tongue and people and nation, and hast made them for our God a kingdom and priests, and they shall reign over the earth" (Apoc. 5:9 f.). This commonwealth of those who confess Him, suffering in time, but rising triumphant in the day of the Second Coming of the Son of Man, is loved as His bride by the glorified

Christ. In order to purify her from every stain and blemish He delivers Himself, as He had once done in His Passion and death, but now continually and in an unbloody manner on our altars, until the day when He shall conduct her home as the immaculate *Sponsa Agni*.

II. Christ's Love of His Church Must Live On in His Apostles and Priests. Because they were convinced of this, the Apostles were not content with " saving from this perverse generation " (Acts 2:40) those who believed their words. They were equally eager to add them to the " community of the faithful," and with them to build up, on the cornerstone that is Christ, " as living stones, built thereon into a spiritual house, a holy priesthood, to offer spiritual sacrifices acceptable to God through Jesus Christ " (1 Pet. 2:5). Unity in faith and love of Christ are the inner bonds by which this organism is held together, but the holders of the ecclesiastical offices are the *visible workers* who carry out this spiritual building of the divine edifice (Eph. 4:7 ff.) All the spiritual powers which they have received have been given them to be used for the building up of this house of God. And the more strongly the love of the Master lives in them, the more joyfully will the workers apply themselves to the work which has been given them in the great task of building up the Church of God.

This love is nothing else than the active and self-sacrificing *eccleciastical spirit of the good priest*.

III. How Does the Priestly Spirit Foster Its Love for the Church ? Pope Pius XII has dealt with and answered this question in detail in the third part of his encyclical,

Mystici Corporis Christi. The father of Christianity expects us to be actuated with a love of the Church which sees Christ Himself in her, and imitates Him in the breadth and energy of His love for her, in constant prayer for all her members and in filling up what is lacking of the sufferings of Christ (Col. 1:24). Should we not check up on our *sensus ecclesiasticus* once more, taking this exalted model as our standard?

To see and love the *Universal Church* in the spirit of the Encyclical is certainly something very exalted, yet not difficult to accomplish. But to love in this spirit that part of the Church which has been allotted to *us* as God's vineyard may sometimes demand a high courage and spirit of sacrifice. But we shall succeed in achieving both if we try to see and love the part of the Church entrusted to us with the eyes and heart with which Christ sees and loves both the whole and the part.

Reading : Apoc. 21:2-5.

DEVOTION TO THE SUCCESSORS OF PETER

49th Consideration

In his first Epistle St. Peter describes the Church of Christ as an ordered organization in which the well-disciplined building force builds up the many-shaped building stones—the baptized—to form one single " spiritual house " in which " spiritual sacrifices accept-able to God " are offered to God through Jesus Christ (1 Pet. 2:5 ff.). The inmost core of this building force, indeed its source, is Christ Himself, "For from him the whole body (being closely joined and knit together through every joint of the system . . .) derives its increase to the building up of itself in love " (Eph. 4 : 16). But Christ works *invisibly* in the Church; therefore a *perceptible* revelation of His unifying and ordering will is necessary. Now, this is given to us in the Pope, the " Representative of Christ on earth." If our priestly work among the faithful is to serve to build up the spiritual temple of God, it must seek to be in perfect harmony in all its undertakings with the principles and instructions of the visible representative of Christ on earth.

Let us consider, then, that: *Those who possess the true priestly spirit are amenable in all matters to the instructions of the Apostolic See.*

I. Three Utterances of Christ Justify Our Fidelity to the Pope.

The first is: " Feed my lambs . . . feed my sheep " (Jn. 21 : 15 ff.). These words give Peter and his successors authority over all the faithful. Hence, if I too have some authority over the faithful, that authority has been given me by Peter and I am answerable to him for it. The second text is: " And I will give thee the keys of the kingdom of heaven; and whatever thou shalt bind on earth shall be bound in heaven and whatever thou shalt loose on earth shall be loosed in heaven " (Mt. 16 : 19). These words assign to the representative of Christ a power of disposal and authority which reaches up into heaven itself. If I follow the decisions of Peter in matters of faith and morals, I have infallible directions for my work in the building up of the Church, and any departure from these inevitably causes errors and malformations in the divine structure of the Church. The third text is our Lord's words to Peter: " But I have prayed for thee, that thy faith may not fail; and do thou . . . strengthen thy brethren " (Lk. 22:32). These words guarantee to the visible Head of the Church a special help from Christ which will enable him to break the power of Satan that is prone to sow discord and disunity among his " brethren." In and by the pope, Christ unites not only the building stones but also the builders, not only the faithful but also their pastors. Hence no salutary building up of an ecclesiastical communion is possible except in union with and subordination to the supreme visible Head of the Church. For such is the will of Christ.

II.   Christ Has Made the Weal or Woe of the Priesthood of the New Covenant Dependent on This Law of Fidelity to the Pope.   What would have become of the priesthood if the Roman Pontiffs had not concerned themselves for its maintenance and its dignity? Not only the heretics of the sixteenth century, but also all heretical bodies have lost their devout understanding for the priesthood shortly after parting from the Roman Church, and even if they did not dispute it, they very soon fell away from it. In the schismatical churches the priesthood has sunk, for the most part, to a humdrum professional body no longer capable of animating the faithful. In the Roman Church, on the contrary, Peter in his successors has never ceased, down the centuries, to repeat his exhortation: " Now I exhort the presbyters among you—I, your fellow presbyter and witness of the sufferings of Christ, the partaker also of the glory that is to be revealed in time to come—tend the flock of God which is among you, governing not under constraint, but willingly, according to God; nor yet for the sake of base gain, but eagerly; nor yet as lording it over your charges, but becoming from the heart a pattern to the flock. And when the Prince of the shepherds appears, you will receive the unfading crown of glory " (1 Pet. 5:1 ff.). Where outside the Roman Church is a voice to be heard which proclaims the essential character and the dignity of the sacred priesthood as Pius XI has done in his Encyclical, *Ad Catholici Sacerdotii*? It is the Magna Charta of our profession in our days. Am I familiar with it?

III. How Does the Priest Cultivate the Spirit of Submission to the Apostolic See? The Acts of the Apostles contain two texts which may answer this question for us. The first is: " On hearing this they held their peace " (Acts 11:18). The Primitive Church, which had got so very excited over the conflict regarding permitting the uncircumcised to be baptized, calmed down when Peter, in virtue of his mission as Supreme Head, defined his own position in the matter. In our days, too, there are questions of Christian doctrine and Christian principles which agitate and divide the faithful. There are questions of tremendous range and importance such as the workers' voice in industry; or of the most delicate kind, such as the bodily assumption of the Virgin Mary into heaven. Only he who has to confirm his brethren in the faith, as representative of Christ on earth, can decide such questions with certainty. " On hearing this [his decision] they held their peace."

The other text is: " But prayer was being made to God for him by the Church without ceasing " (Acts

12:5). Only when the pope makes a decision concerning faith or morals binding upon the whole Church is he in a state of divine, infallible certainty; otherwise he is fallible in his guidance of the Church and capable of being defeated by the malice of the enemies of Christ. Hence he needs our prayers. Therefore: *Oremus pro beatissimo Papa nostro! Dominus conservet eum et vivicet eum et beatum faciat eum et non tradat eum in animam inimicorum ejus.*

Reading : Mt. 16:17-20.

REVERENCE AND OBEDIENCE TOWARDS THE BISHOP

50th Consideration

Peter had to lead the flock of his Master in union and agreement with " his brethren "; Peter's successor guides the Church in union and agreement with the " bishops "; the Holy Spirit has appointed them to rule the Church of God (Acts 20:28). Now, according to Canon 329 the bishops are " the successors " of the Apostles and in virtue of divine ordinance have jurisdiction over certain territories of the Church, which they rule with due power under the authority of the Bishop of Rome.

Hence, in the structure of the Church of God, the bishop is, within his diocese and subject to the supreme power of the pope, not merely the lawful possessor of the full power of the priesthood, but also the holder of all authority necessary for the administration of his diocese. Consequently, no priest can co-operate lawfully in the building up of the Church except on the instructions and under the supervision of the bishop responsible for the area in which he works. The same principle holds good regarding priests not under diocesan rule but answerable to their superiors.

Let us consider, then, that: *The priest serves the Church in reverence and obedience to the authorized bishop.*

I. Paul Has in Mind this co-ordination of the priest's work under the rule of a bishop when he writes to Titus, the youthful Bishop of Crete: "For this reason I left thee in Crete, that thou shouldst set right anything that is defective and shouldst appoint presbyters in every city, as I myself directed thee to do" (Tit. 1:5). Not on their own, but under the watchful supervision of Titus, these presbyters are to preach the Gospel, deal with falsifiers of the same, and introduce the evangelical way of life among all classes. The Apostle of the Gentiles has similar things to say of the authority of Timothy over the priests working in his diocese of Ephesus, and he concludes his remarks concerning the relations between bishop and presbyter with the emphatic warning: "I charge thee before God and Christ Jesus and the elect angels that thou observe these things impartially, in no way favouring either side" (1 Tim. 5:21). Enlightened by these directions of the Apostle of the Gentiles, the Church prays over us on the day of our ordination: "Pour down, Lord, on these thy servants whom we are dedicating to the honourable office of the priesthood, the gift of thy blessing. May they by the dignity of their behaviour and the pattern of their lives show themselves true elders, moulded by the teaching that Paul gave to Titus and Timothy."

II. This Basic Relationship Between Bishop and Priest shows clearly that the latter is essentially the servant of the bishop responsible for the region in which he works. Therefore he is not competent to deal with the work given him according to his own judgment but only according to the wishes of the bishop. He has bound himself to this in the " *Promitto reverentiam et obedientiam* " which he made at ordination. Therefore he tries to earn the approval accorded to the " faithful and prudent stewards " by the care with which he dispenses to the household committed to his care the spiritual foods from the storehouse of the Master which the bishop has placed in his keeping (Lk. 12:42). For he has received ordination in order to be made " a prudent helper of his bishop " (Rite of Ordination).

III. The Priest Shows Due Reverence and Active Obedience to His Bishop. Firstly, by carrying out his instructions, whether of a general nature or relating specially to his pastoral domain, even if in doing so he has to sacrifice his own views and wishes. This is not always easy, but the Good Shepherd has made His blessing on our pastoral work conditional upon this co-ordination and subordination. Insubordination, on the other hand, brings its own revenge, for the saying that " Disloyalty hits its own master " is also true in the life of the priest. Secondly, by refraining from criticism, either in thought or word, of the bishop's ordinances. Such criticism robs ourselves and others of our joy in work and often wastes a lot of time besides. Many times the bishop's instructions could be carried out in the time thus spent in futile criticism of them. Would we not do better to bear in mind the words spoken at the consecration of the bishop: "*Qui maledixerit ei, sit ille maledictus, et qui benedixerit illi, benedictionibus repleatur*"? And thirdly, by striving to preserve his apostolic zeal and his charity of heart even if the bishop and his administrators treat him unreasonably or unjustly. For that too may sometimes happen. In such cases the saints have replied according to the instructions of the Sermon on the Mount (Mt. 5:40-42), and this has brought them more blessing than if they had won a lawsuit.

Reading : The Bishop's Charge in the Rite of Ordination.

LOVE OF ONE'S FELLOW PRIESTS

51st Consideration

When our Lord sent out the Twelve, and a little later the Seventy-two, to preach the Kingdom of God, He sent them two by two (Mk. 6:7; Lk. 10:1). Elsewhere, too, He seldom gave His orders to one individual alone (Mk. 11:1, 14:13, 33, 16:12; Lk. 9:51). For He wished to form the heralds of His Kingdom into a body and to give their successors for all time to understand that: *The priest must regard his apostolic colleague with brotherly love.*

I. For This Is Definitely His Will. "This is my commandment, that you love one another as I have loved you" (Jn. 15:12). In the scene of the washing of the feet, He tried to impress indelibly on the minds of the Twelve this commandment: "If, therefore, I the Lord and Master have washed your feet, you also ought to wash the feet of *one another*" (not the feet of some unknown old men who will have disappeared from view tomorrow, but one another's). "For I have given you an example, that as I have done to you, so you also should do" (Jn. 13:14 f.). When the Apostles failed in brotherly love towards each other, He always made this the occasion for emphasizing His commandment anew. "Now there arose also a dispute among them, which of them was reputed to be the greatest. But he said to them, 'The kings of the Gentiles lord it over them, and they who exercise authority over them are called Benefactors. But not so with you. On the contrary, let him who is greatest among you become as the youngest, and him who is the chief, as the servant. . . . But I am in your midst as he who serves'" (Lk. 22:24 ff.). "A new commandment I give you, that you love one another: that as I have loved you, you also love one another. *By this will all men know that you are my disciples,* if you have love for one another" (Jn. 13:34 f.).

II. The Lord Commands His Messengers to Have Brotherly Love Because This Is Necessary for the Building Up of His Church, for

(*a*) the community of believers which is to be formed is to be *a realm of unity and love*. For this He has come into the world and He gathers together those who through the words of the Apostles are to believe in Him, "that all may be one" (Jn. 17:20 f.). But how are the baptized to form a community united in love if their shepherds are divided among themselves? In Micheas 3:5, God denounces "prophets . . . that bite with their teeth, and preach peace." Paul seems to have this text in mind when he writes to the quarrelsome leaders of the Church in Galatia: " By charity serve one another. For the whole Law is fulfilled in one word: Thou shalt love thy neighbour as thyself. But if you bite and devour one another, take heed or you will be consumed by one another " (Gal. 5:13 ff.). For the basic principle of the Kingdom of Christ is: " *Qui caritatem erga alterum non habet, praedicationis officium nullatenus suscipere debet* " (St. Gregory the Martyr).

(*b*) But the apostolic worker *also needs* marks of brotherly love for *himself*. If he is to persevere in his difficult calling, he must have someone with whom he can find understanding, sympathy, advice, and encouragement. Where should he expect to find this if not among his professional colleagues? For this reason the Church desires that her priests should live a *vita communis* as far as possible: " consuetudo vitae communis inter clericos laudanda et suadenda est, eaque, ubi viget, quantum fieri potest, servanda " (Canon 134). The strength of the apostolic orders, such as the Dominicans and Jesuits, is largely due to the fact that they foster a spiritually deep community life in which the individual priests find encouragement and help. The same help and encouragement should also be found in the community of the parish presbytery where several priests live together.

III. How Does the Priest Show His Caritas Fraterna?

The twelfth chapter of the Epistle to the Romans contains a description of Christian charity from which we can take some points as headlines for true fraternal charity among priests:

(*a*) Invicem diligentes in *dilectione sine simulatione* (9):

Love never thrives where it is not rooted in mutual sincerity. Insincerity and sham are a corrosive poison destructive of the *unitas clericalis* in the communal life of priests. St. Paul regarded being obliged to work with "false brethren" (Gal. 2:4; cf. 2 Cor. 11:20) as one of the specific trials of our calling.

(b) Singuli *honore invicem praevenientes* (10). Is it not a curious fact that zeal in our calling should often be the cause of dissension, when one cleric grudges the other success and recognition? "For since there are jealousy and strife among you, are you not carnal, and walking as mere men?" (1 Cor. 3:3). Every priest merits honour because of his ordination, by which God has picked him out from the crowd, and because of the authority with which the Church invests him. What the individual may have over and above in the way of personal charm, position, and importance hardly matters one way or another in comparison with this. We are acting *secundum hominem* and not *secundum Dominum Christum,* if we behave towards each other, not as brothers, but as superiors and inferiors (cf. Mt. 23:8 ff).

(c) (Fratrum) *necessitatibus communicantes* (13): Helpful in material necessities, for instance in case of a colleague's illness or on days when he is unusually busy with his sacred duties. In times of spiritual stress, to encourage a colleague when he is oppressed by failure and disappointment; to protect his good name if he is slandered or judged unjustly; to pray for him and give him a brotherly reproof if he takes to ways dangerous to his happiness as a priest; to receive him kindly and help him when he turns back.

Reading : Epistle to the Romans 12:3-16.

UNION WITH DECEASED AND SAINTED COLLEAGUES

52nd Consideration

Fraternal charity among the envoys of Christ is an indispensable element in the building up of the kingdom of God in the *earthly* domain. But it extends even *beyond* this earthly world, and continues to give and receive there. Fraternal charity goes to the needy brethren in purgatory and even goes up to the members of our calling among the blessed in heaven.

Let us consider, then, that: *The priest shows his love for the Communio Confratrum by praying for the dead and by honouring the blessed colleagues in heaven.*

I. Mementote Fratrum Vestrorum Defunctorum: for

(a) *Our deceased colleagues need our help.* How God judges the priest in eternity, whether more sternly than the lay Christian or not, who can know? We do know, however, that the priest generally speaking recognizes more clearly the malice of sin and is given more grace to avoid it. Because God and His means of salvation were so near to him, he may have been frivolous and presumptuous in relying upon them, and been less repentant for his sins and atoned less for them than the layman. Holy priests have thought with fear of the purification which awaits the priest in purgatory (Lk. 12:48).

(b) *We have ample opportunities of being helpful to our fellow priests.* Every day the Church exhorts us, in the Memento for the Dead, to offer the sacrificial death of Christ, the most effective possible help for the suffering souls in purgatory, for the relief of the souls of priests too. The *preces pro defunctis* in our Breviary likewise remind us daily of this act of charity. Warm fraternal charity will also move the faithful to remember their deceased clergy in their prayers and good works. Reverent care of the graves of former priests of our diocese also comes under this heading. The saying that those who show charity will also have charity shown them is true of the clergy, too.

II. Mementote Fratrum Vestrorum Glorificatorum !

for

(*a*) We belong to a body of men of holy calling. Is it not an encouraging thought that the majority of canonized saints were priests? The great number of holy popes and bishops, and of regular and secular clergy, of missionaries of the faith and heroes of charity reveals the fact that the message of salvation has found among those who announce it the most fertile soil in which to bear fruit, thirty, sixty, and a hundredfold. Our Lord promised to the Apostles and their successors that signs and wonders would follow their work; in His name they would drive out evil spirits, speak in new tongues, take up serpents, and if they drank something deadly, it would not hurt them. They would lay hands upon the sick and they would get well (Mk. 16:17 f.). Have not these things been fulfilled to the letter right up to our own days in holy priests (Don Bosco, for instance); in some cases, already in their lifetime, in others after their death?

(*b*) It becomes the priest to have intercourse with his sainted Brethren in the priesthood. How often the Church herself presents these saintly figures to our eyes in the second nocturn of the Divine Office! How well we could overcome our tepidity and discouragement if we read these passages with due thought! But the power which our confreres in heaven wield over the heart of our High Priest, and the love with which they can join with those on earth who are continuing the struggle for the edification of the Kingdom of God which they had carried on unceasingly in their earthly life, should move us, still more than their example, to have recourse to them.

Reading : Apoc. 14:13.

COMMUNION WITH MARY, THE MOTHER OF THE LORD

53rd Consideration

Among the popes, bishops, and priests whom the Church has canonized because of their meritorious work in the building up of the mystical Body of Christ, one can find hardly one who was not distinguished for a specially great devotion to the Mother of the Lord. In their sermons and writings they invariably turn to the priests of their time, urging them to place their work for the Kingdom under the patronage and protection of the Mother of Christendom.

As docile pupils of these holy models let us therefore consider: *That the good priest seeks union with Mary, the Mother of the Lord, in his apostolic work.*

I. The Mind of the Church Teaches Him to Do This, that mind of the Primitive Church, in which the Apostles awaited the Holy Spirit, the divinely creative force for the edification of the Church: " All these with one mind continued steadfastly in prayer with the women and Mary, the mother of Jesus, and with his brethren " (Acts 1:14); that mind of the Church which sees in the words of our Lord on the cross: "Woman, behold thy son " and " son, behold thy mother!" (Jn. 19:26 f.) the last will of the Lawgiver of the new Kingdom, by virtue of which not only the beloved disciple John but also every witness and servant of the New Covenant should be bound in the closest possible manner to the end of time to the mother of Him who is at once Priest and Victim of the New Covenant, and through whom Mary is the mother of the New Covenant. The Gospel tells us that "from that hour the disciple took her into his home " (Jn. 19:27). Hence the orthodox mind of Christendom expects every servant of Christ and dispenser of the mysteries of the New Covenant to take Mary into the priestly plans, tasks, and works.

II. This Immemorial Christian Belief Can Be Well Justified in the Light of an Intelligent Christian Faith.

In his encyclical on the Mystical Body of Christ, 29 July, 1943, Pope Pious XII also deals with the question of the relationship in which the Blessed Virgin stands to the Mystical Body of Christ. Here it is shown that even in her earthly life Mary was always present and participating in those events in the earthly life of her Son which were particularly significant for His life mystically continued in the Church. " Upon the mystical Body of Christ, born of the broken Heart of the Saviour," the encyclical concludes, " she bestows that same motherly care and fervent love with which she fostered and nurtured the infant Jesus in the cradle." Until the last day the Mystical Body of Christ will continue to be an organism continually growing and maturing in the world as in the hidden womb, until it is born into the clear day of the eternal glory of the Head, Christ. It remains continually in that stage of childhood in which it needs the warm mother love and care with which Mary fostered and nurtured the Child Jesus in the crib and on her breast. This train of thought is in no wise new. Father Olier, the founder of St. Sulpice, proceeded from it to his conception of the Church as the *Jesus vivens in Maria,* a conception which has such a formative influence on the theology of today.

III. How Does the Good Priest Seek Communion With Mary in His Apostolic Work?

(*a*) *Christ* is and remains the whole origin, object, and purpose of His apostolic work; for the words: " I am the door " (Jn. 10:9; cf. 42nd Consideration) still hold good. But the door is easier to find if Mary leads us to it by the hand, and it opens more readily if we knock on it with Mary.

(*b*) Mary knows the good pastures, on which the flock of the Lord thrives; for in her is " all grace of the way and of the truth, . . . all hope of life, and of virtue " (Ecclus. 24:25). The *sensus ecclesiasticus* approves a pastoral practice founded upon the principles of the Children of Mary congregation and makes use of it, particularly in the guidance of souls who show a genuine desire for perfection.

(*c*) Mary is clear-sighted and *strong against all the enemies of the apostolic work*. She treads upon the serpent's head even before we have perceived it. Therefore, the enlightened priest seeks her co-operation in order that through her he may recognize the dangers which threaten his flock and overcome them with her powerful aid.

Reading: Apoc. 12:1-7, 13-17.

THE PRIESTLY SPIRIT: FRUIT OF THE HOLY SPIRIT

54th Consideration

The priestly spirit is the disposition in which the good priest makes use of the sacred powers which have been given him in the Sacrament of Holy Orders for the salvation of souls. Experience teaches us that this disposition has to be acquired with much effort. To grow continually in it and finally to become mature in it, must be the aim of every priest. But the establishment and growth of this spirit are not a mere matter of self-discipline or ascetical endeavour, and it would be quite erroneous to assume that the *degree* of priestly spirit acquired corresponds exactly to the *degree of our efforts* to acquire it. For of course our effort does not cause it; it is only one of the conditions upon which it is given us from above. The originator of the priestly disposition within us is, on the contrary, *the Holy Spirit*. He gives it to every man who receives the commission to build up the Mystical Body of Christ; moreover, He "divides [it] to everyone according as he will" (1 Cor. 12:11).

We will therefore conclude our meditations on the priestly spirit with the consideration that: *The priestly spirit is the fruit of the Holy Spirit in the priest who serves his flock faithfully.*

I. The Priestly Spirit Was the Fruit of the Holy Spirit Even in Our High Priest Jesus Christ. For did not our Lord Himself say in His discourse to the inhabitants of his native town, Nazareth: " The Spirit of the Lord is upon me because he has anointed me ..." (Lk. 4:14 ff.) The Evangelist concludes his enthusiastic account of the emergence of Jesus and His activities in the region of Lake Genesareth with the remark that God had fulfilled in Jesus the prophecy: " I have given my Spirit upon him, and he will bring forth judgment to the Gentiles " (Isa. 42:1 f.; Mt. 12:18). When Peter, in his discourse in front of the house of Cornelius, was describing the life and work of our Lord, he epitomized the impression of the Primitive Church saying that they knew " how God anointed Jesus of Nazareth with the Holy Spirit " (Acts 10:38). So we see that Holy Scripture bears witness to the fact that the high-priestly spirit of Jesus is *the fruit of the Holy Spirit*. But our Lord opened His heart to the Holy Spirit by prayer and sacrifice, although He was already united to the Holy Spirit by the mystery of the hypostatic union and the intertrinitarian relation of His person to that of the Holy Spirit.

II. Hence the Priestly Spirit Is Likewise Fruit of the Holy Spirit in the Dispenser of the Mysteries of Christ. St. Paul goes into this very thoroughly in the twelfth and thirteenth chapters of the First Epistle to the Corinthians. In the twelfth chapter (verses 27-30) he speaks of the charismatically gifted members of the Church in Corinth and those who hold offices in it, and he impresses upon them that all their various gifts and merits originate from the same Holy Spirit: " Now there are varieties of gifts, but the same Spirit; and there are varieties of ministries, but the same Lord; and there are varieties of workings, but the same God, who works all things in all" (12:4 ff.). But in the thirteenth chapter, in the "Canticle of Love," the Apostle speaks of the only condition on which the possession and use of these particular gifts will be effective for the salvation of those who possess them. And that condition is—*love*. "If I should speak with the tongues of men and angels . . . and if I have prophecy . . . and if I have all faith . . . and if I distribute all my goods to feed the poor, and if [as testimony of my preaching] I deliver my body to be burned, yet do not have charity, *it profits me nothing*. For this charity is patient, is kind, does not envy, is not self-seeking, is not provoked . . . bears with all things, believes all things, hopes all things, endures all things" (1 Cor. 13:4 ff.). Now, the characteristics of this love are those of the disposition which Paul has already described in the Epistle to the Galatians and which he calls explicitly "the fruit of the Spirit" there. "But the fruit of the Spirit is: charity, joy, peace, patience, kindness, goodness, faith, modesty, continency" (Gal. 5:22 f.). The *power* of all offices and the *spirit* behind the exercise of these offices must proceed from the Holy Spirit both in the community as a whole and in the holders of the various offices and gifts, if they are to build up the Kingdom of Christ; for "No one can say 'Jesus is Lord' except in the Holy Spirit" (1 Cor. 12:3).

III. The Holy Spirit Implants His Fruits in the Soul of Every Priest Who Serves His Flock Faithfully. This is in the nature of the priestly office. Since his powers are given to him as *manifestatio Spiritus ad utilitatem* [Ecclesiae] (1 Cor. 12:7), the Holy Spirit moves and enlightens only the priest who uses the precious gifts of the Spirit in zealous service of his parish, but not the priest who buries them as the lazy steward of the Gospel buried his talents. For the graces of ordination must bring in dividends, and to do this they must be used. But when the priest proves himself a faithful steward of his Master's goods, the Holy Spirit is at his side and in his heart. Despite all the limitations and shortcomings of his work, such a priest may confidently hope for what the Church prayed for him on the day of his ordination: " In the day of God's just and irrevocable judgment may they rise again, *filled with the Holy Spirit,* with conscience undefiled, in faith undimmed, and unfailing charity " (The bishop's prayer after the delivery of the chasuble).

Reading : 1 Cor. 12:1-11, 28-31.

The Perfect Man Equipped for Every Good Work

55th Consideration

The Holy Spirit equips the Catholic priesthood with the sacramental powers conferred at ordination and the spirit of priestly charity, so that it may be able to fulfil its mission of building up the kingdom of God in the world. But that is not all. All these gifts are only *effects* of the Holy Spirit; they are not *the Holy Spirit Himself.* The equipment of the Catholic priesthood for the fulfilment of its mission reaches its perfection in the fact that the Holy Spirit Himself unites Himself to the priest in such a manner that the priest becomes the actual organ of the Divine Spirit of love in His efforts to sanctify the world.

Let us consider, then, that: *The equipment of the holy priesthood for its task reaches its perfection in the priest's organic relation to the Holy Spirit.*

I. The Sacred Priesthood Is the Normal Instrument of the Holy Spirit for the Sanctification of the World.

This truth is the basic theme of the discourses of our Lord at the Last Supper. Just after He had appointed the eleven priests of the New Covenant by His order: "Do this in commemoration of me," He spoke to them of the witness they were to bear of Him in a hostile world. When He saw how timid and discouraged His words had made them, He said: "Let not your heart be troubled. . . . I will ask the Father and he will give you another Advocate to dwell with you forever, the Spirit of truth whom the world cannot receive, because it neither sees him nor knows him. But you shall know him, because *he will dwell with you, and be in you*" (Jn. 14:1 and 16 f.). "He will bear witness concerning me. And you also bear witness, because from the beginning you are with me" (Jn. 15:26 f.). Here the Lord speaks of a co-ordination of the Holy Spirit with the Eleven who have been chosen for the apostolate which, firstly, continues to exist in eternity, that is to say, does not end with temporal death; secondly, is the actual cause of the witness which they are to bear to Christ in the world; thirdly, will eliminate in the Apostles that well-justified consciousness of their own inadequacy, which was the cause of their discouragement and faintheartedness in that hour. Hence, from the hour on the feast of Pentecost in which the Lord's promise was fulfilled, the

Apostles regarded themselves as *organs of the Holy Spirit,* and found in their co-ordination with Him the source of the courage which conquered the world, and the strength which no obstacles could break. As they were aware that they themselves would have to leave the earthly battlefield on their death, they consecrated well-tried brothers in the faith, by placing these, by the imposition of hands and by prayer, in the service of the Holy Spirit, who alone is able to change those who are not always suitable into "fit ministers of the new covenant," which is a covenant " not of the letter but of the spirit " (2 Cor. 3:6). In such fellow workers the aged prince of the Apostle sees "those who *preached the gospel . . . by the Holy Spirit sent from heaven.* Into these things angels desire to look " (1 Pet. 1:12).

II. The Mystery of the Organic Relationship Which Exists Between the Catholic Priesthood and the Holy Spirit has been little explored as yet. Doubtless, the formal effect of this relationship consists in the constant impetus which the Holy Spirit gives to the Incarnate High Priest to accomplish in us those actions by which He makes us ministers of His mission (see Considerations 12 to 15) and to stand by us according to His promise in all our exertions in the service of that ministry (Mt. 28:18). Scheeben views this mystery from a different angle; he sees it in the impetus which ceaselessly comes forth from the Holy Spirit and duly encompasses the Catholic priesthood, enabling it to exercise its ministry in the building up of the Mystical Body: " The Catholic priesthood shall bear Christ Himself anew in the womb of the Church . . . by the power of the Spirit of Christ reigning in the Church, and thereby organically build up His mystical Body, as Mary, by the power of the same Holy Spirit bore the Word (of the Father), born in His own humanity, and gave Him His true, i.e., His real, human body" (Scheeben, *Mysterien des Christentums*, Herder-Rademacher, p. 466 f.).

III. Through This Organic Relationship to the Holy Spirit the Ordained Priest Is "The Man of God . . . Perfect, Equipped for Every Good Work" (2 Tim. 3:17). Paul applies this description of "the man of God, perfect, equipped for every good work" to Timothy in as much as the latter possesses a knowledge of the Sacred Scriptures which are inspired by God. The context leaves no doubt, however, that the Bishop of Ephesus is the "perfect man of God" in the eyes of Paul not because he possesses a good knowledge of the letter of the Scriptures but because he possesses the Holy Spirit, who manifests Himself in the letter of the Scriptures and "equips" the apostolic minister, by the imposition of hands, for every good pastoral work. It is therefore the Holy Spirit, united to the ordained in Ordination, who in the final resort, makes the priest a "man of God, perfect, equipped for every good work." The more completely and submissively the priest permits himself to be used as the instrument of the Holy Spirit, the more valuable he is in the eyes of God, and the more "the spirit of love and of power and of prudence" manifests itself in him, while "the spirit of fear," which is natural to human nature in the proximity of the kingdom of God, is more and more eliminated. The good priest knows this, and this knowledge gives him a confidence in the success of his mission which seems inexplicable, in fact foolish, to the natural man. The priest who is weak in faith and who trusts to his own strength lacks this confidence because he lacks sufficient knowledge of his organic relation to the Holy Spirit, and does not put this relation to the test.

With these thoughts we conclude our considerations on the equipment of the Catholic priesthood. God is not like the great ones of this world, who so often entrust their servants with tasks beyond their strength. We are equipped with the power and strength of God Himself. It is the fire from the *fornax ardens caritatis*, the high-priestly heart of Christ, which the Holy Spirit hid in our hearts for the salvation of the world on the day of our ordination. It cannot be lost, but its driving, illuminating and warming force can be hindered by the ashes of worldliness, and the dull, becalmed inaction of sloth and discouragement. Therefore, it must be set ablaze again and again. Every priest who fans the apostolic gifts to a flame within him can say with the Apostle of the Gentiles: " Discharging therefore this ministry [the sacred priesthood] in accordance with the mercy shown us, we do not lose heart " (2 Cor. 4:1). " Not that we are sufficient of ourselves to think anything [conducive to salvation] as from ourselves, but our sufficiency is from God. He also it is who has made us fit ministers of the new covenant, not of the letter, but of the spirit " (3:5 f.).

Reading : 2 Tim. 1:6-14.

PART FOUR

THE BLESSINGS OF THE PRIESTHOOD

"I have appointed you that you should
go and bear fruit, and that your fruit
should remain" (Jn. 15: 16).

THE BLESSINGS OF THE PRIESTHOOD:

1. FOR THE WORLD AND THE CHURCH

Preface

In our previous meditations on the Catholic priesthood we have examined its relation to the priesthood of Christ, its sacred duties and the supernatural powers with which it is equipped, and which give it its character. For the consideration of these characteristics is well calculated to induce us not to allow our priestly zeal to flag. Now, there is another angle from which to view the Christian priesthood, and one which may well awaken in us a profound joy in our priestly calling: *namely, a consideration of the blessings which flow from the Catholic priesthood.*

We shall therefore devote the last section of our exposition of the " *Resuscites gratiam* " of the Apostle to a consideration of the blessings of the Catholic priesthood. We turn our attention only now to this attractive subject because the previous considerations were necessary to a just recognition of it. For only one who comprehends the essential nature, mission, and equipment of the sacred priesthood with the eyes of faith, can rightly assess its beneficent power; the person not enlightened by faith cannot do so.

The blessings which flow from the Catholic priesthood benefit *two worlds,* so to speak—the one is the world outside of the priest, the part of the kingdom of God which has been allotted to him *in the world and the Church* as his outward sphere of action; the other is the world within the priest, the kingdom of God *in his own heart*. In these two worlds the blessed gift of priesthood effects its beneficent and saving work in a completely different ways. Hence our series of considerations falls into one group concerning the blessed effects of the sacred priesthood in the outward Kingdom of God, namely, the building up of the same in the hearts of men and their community, the Church (Considerations 56 to 65); and another group concerning the beneficent effects of the priesthood on the hidden Kingdom of God in the soul of the priest himself (Considerations 66 to 79).

We do not need to expend many words on the practical utility of such considerations. The justification of our efforts is to be found in the exhortation of Pius XII's *Menti Nostrae*, September 23, 1950, where he says that, in order to interest the faithful in the Catholic priesthood and particularly to inspire suitable young men to seek admission to it, " the ministers of God, in their sermons and catechetical instructions and also in private conversations should zealously strive to refute the prejudices and false ideas so prevalent nowadays concerning the priesthood, and *set in their true light* its exalted dignity, its value and its merits " (CTS edition, p. 31).

We trust that the following Considerations may serve in some measure towards fulfilling the intentions of our Supreme Pastor.

By Its Share in the Building Up of the Church

56th Consideration

When we speak of the blessing which the sacred priesthood effects in the world, we mean *Christ's blessing of salvation in as much as it is mediated through the office of the priesthood.* That is to say, we do not mean the good works which various individual priests have effected in the course of the history of the Church for the good of mankind, for these may have arisen from individual gifts of a natural or a charismatic nature. On the contrary, we shall now proceed to examine the results which flow to the world and mankind from the priesthood, as such, as a result of its essential nature; and which flow from it, not intermittently, but continually.

Now, the whole treasure of the redemptive grace of Christ has been given over, in the first place, to the administration of the Church. She is the woman who takes the leaven of Christ and buries it in the three measures of flour, " until all of it is leavened." *Extra Ecclesiam nulla salus.* Therefore, the Catholic priesthood cannot effect any blessing in the world other than the blessing which is entrusted to the Church and which the Church dispenses. The whole redemptive action of the sacred priesthood is therefore carried out as *a service of the Church* (1 Cor. 12).

This priestly service of the Church does not consist, however, in the mere dispensing of gifts which the Church has lying ready in her treasure chambers; the priest is more than a messenger in the Kingdom of God; he is a builder in the Kingdom of God, and he is this, in the first place, in that he is the instrument of Him who

Himself has instituted the Church as the treasure chamber of all His blessings in the world.

Let us therefore consider that: *The sacred priesthood is a constant source of blessing for the world by reason of its part in the building up of the Church.*

I. For the Church of Christ Has Yet to Be Built Up in the World. True, as He hung on the Cross, our Lord brought forth the Church from his wounded side like a new Eve or mother of all the living, animated by the Holy Spirit (*Mystici Corporis Christi*, par. 27), replete with all that she needed for the fulfilment of her destiny: the salvation of mankind. But she was still, in outward appearance, weak and undeveloped, a creature born on Good Friday, only—so it seemed—to be immediately trodden in the dust. This vehicle of divine mercy was capable of development, however; she was destined to grow and develop until the end of time, in order, finally, to become the perfect bride of the Lamb in all her glory, " not having spot or wrinkle or any such thing, but that she might be holy and without blemish " (Eph. 5:27). For this growing process, which, like all earthly life, has its relapses and periods of weakness, the Church needs to have at her command *special building forces and their services.* She possesses these in the two fundamental gifts designed for her growth: the gift of the divinely ordained procreation of people to whom she has to apply the leaven of Christ—she has this in the mystery of lawful and fruitful marriage; and in the gift of bringing down from heaven the leaven of Christ, and burying it in the world and in man; she has this in the *sacred priesthood.* Christian marriage and the sacramental priesthood are the two organisations which the Holy Spirit uses to build up the Church to be the perfect bride of the Lamb. Therefore, theology calls these two mysteries of salvation simply "the Sacraments for the edification of the Church" ("*Sacramenta Ecclesiae*" in contrast to the "*sacramenta personalia*").

II. The Particular Contribution of the Holy Priesthood to the Building Up of the Church to Be the Perfect Bride of Christ.

Since the foundation of the New Covenant, marriage has had the essential purpose of bearing for the Church and bringing to her the children who are born into their natural life through it. The task of the priesthood is to incorporate into the Church (so that she grows *into* them and they *into* her), the children who, though born for the Church, are not yet set on the right road of life in her by their mere birth in her. To be sure, every believer in Christ has a part in this task in as much as everyone is capable of carrying out the basic act of incorporation, namely, of administering Baptism, and of confirming its effects by works of lay-priestly charity, in particular by prayer of petition. But the most effective acts in life, by which mankind and the Church are bound together to a powerful unity of life, can be carried out only by the consecrated priest through that dispensation of the mysteries of Christ (1 Cor. 4:1) which is reserved to him alone. What these consist of individually is the subject of the following meditations. In the faithful accomplishment of this "*dispensatio*" the Catholic priesthood carries out its particular part in the building up of the Church of Christ. It takes up the call which went out to man way back in the days of the Primitive Church: "Draw near to him [Christ], a living stone, rejected indeed by

men but chosen and honoured by God. Be you yourselves as living stones, built thereon into a spiritual
house, a holy priesthood, to offer spiritual sacrifices
acceptable to God through Jesus Christ " (1 Pet. 2:4 f.).
The Catholic priesthood takes all those who heed the
cry and incorporates them into the mysterious divine
structure which is the Church.

**III. " Behold the Dwelling of God With Men, and
He Will Dwell With them "** (Apoc. 21:3). All the joy
of devout Christendom in its possession of the Church
and its enjoyment of its blessings implies a debt of
gratitude towards the sacred priesthood, because it is the
instrument of the Holy Spirit which He uses for the
building of this tabernacle among men, and because it
is the instrument of the divine Fatherhood, from which
the Bride of the Lamb comes forth. It is, so to speak,
the divirely appointed provider and foster father of the
Mystical Body of Christ. Every zealous priest has a
share in that relationship of builder of the Church in
which the Apostle of the Gentiles exulted in his words
to the Church of Ephesus: " Therefore, you are now
no longer strangers and foreigners [in the Kingdom of
God], but you are citizens with the saints and members
of God's household: you are built upon the foundation
of the apostles and prophets, with Jesus Christ Himself
as the chief corner stone. In Him the whole structure is
closely fitted together and grows into a temple holy in
the Lord; in Him you, too, are being built together into
a dwelling place for God in the Spirit " (Eph. 2:19 ff.).
The Church, knowing this, sees in the " Apostles and
prophets " and their successors and co-operators in the
world, those who lay the foundations of her existence in

the world; for this reason she loves her bishops and priests as fathers to whom the child owes its existence and its welfare.

Reading : Eph. 4:11-13.

By Its Service in Preaching the Message of Salvation

57th Consideration

God's redemptive will turns to man by revealing Himself to him in the *message of salvation.* If this is *accepted* in faith, the grace of salvation can mature and bear the *fruit of salvation.* But "without faith [in the message of salvation] it is impossible to please God" (Hebr. 11:6). Therefore, mankind needs to have the message of salvation announced to it. For this reason Christ has entrusted His Church with a permanent and real *ministerium Verbi Salutis,* and given the accomplishment of this task essentially to the apostolic and priestly office, just as He had combined His own priesthood with the office of teaching. By doing this he has instituted the priesthood to be the herald of salvation to mankind.

Let us consider, then, that: the Catholic priesthood shows itself a source of blessing for humanity *by its service as herald of the divine words of salvation.*

I. This Service Is Obligatory on the Priesthood (cf. 20th Consideration). True, every Christian assumes by Baptism and Confirmation the duty of bearing witness to God's will for the salvation of mankind and so of being a herald of the divine message of salvation (1 Pet.

2:9). But Christ has commissioned the Apostles with the actual proclamation of the joyful tidings of His Father and promised and sent them the Holy Spirit as a continual official support in this (Jn. 14:17; Acts 10:42 ff.). Now, the latter did not pass on their office of teaching to everyone, but only to those whom they appointed to it by the imposition of hands and by prayer. Even when the Holy Spirit commanded the Church of Antioch: " Set apart for me Saul and Barnabas unto the work to which I have called them " (namely, the preaching of the Gospel to the Gentiles), the leaders of the Church deemed it first necessary to pray over them and lay their hands on them. Only then did they allow them to set out on their first missionary journey (Acts 13:1 ff.). The orthodox Catholic Church has never wavered in her conviction that the *office* of teaching the way of salvation is a *priestly* office.

II. The Sacred Priesthood Fulfils the Ministerium Verbi Salutis With True Devotion. The history of the preaching of the faith since the days of the Apostles bears witness to the fact that the hero of missionary enterprise and selfless zeal in the service of the Gospel is and always has been the priest. In the priestly herald of salvation Christ goes not only to those who are still sitting " in darkness and in the shadow of death "; in teaching the Catechism and in preaching he also breaks the bread of God's word for the children of His Church. The history of Christian preaching and catechising is a demonstration of the priesthood's zeal in the service of the *Verbum Salutis*. Finally, the Good Shepherd possesses in the priesthood the watchful guardian of the unadulterated purity of His Gospel. It is true that heresies and sects have often originated from holders of holy orders, but on the whole a good priesthood and more especially a good episcopate has always been the firm pillar of orthodoxy. What persecutions and sufferings popes, bishops, and simple priests have endured in order to preserve inviolate the treasure of the truths of salvation! How easily, in contrast to these, have lay Christians (as, for instance, the Byzantine Emperors during the period of christological strife, or the Emperor Charles V in the confusion of the sixteenth century) tended to compromise as regards the falsification of the truths of salvation! It is plain that this difference is due to the fact that the Holy Spirit is co-ordinated in an especial way with the priest as the official herald of the truths of salvation, to help him "for the good of the Church." But this help would remain unfruitful if it were not accepted, and indeed prayed for, with loving responsiveness by the individual good priest.

III. It Is Therefore True and Correct to Apply to the Catholic Priesthood the Words : " You Are the Light of the World ! " (Mt. 5:14). Christ and Christ alone is the light of the world (Jn. 8:12). But the radiance of His light, with which He wills to enlighten every man who comes into the world (Jn. 1:4, 9) is so very much bound up with the preaching office of His Apostles and their successors and priestly helpers, that He calls them, precisely as He calls Himself, *" the light of the world."* The Church has explained the thoughts of her heavenly Bridegroom very beautifully through one of her great servants of the words of salvation: " For Christ, as a truly watchful and faithful father, desired that such servants and ministers, after fire had fallen on them from heaven, should light the evangelical fire and not hide it under a bushel but set it up on a lampstand, so that its radiance should pour out far and wide and drive away all the darkness and errors which lay upon heathen and Jew " (Homily on the Feast of St. Peter Canisius).

Hence the Church, in gratitude for the blessing which the holy Catholic priesthood gives to the world in its service of the words of salvation, prays daily in the Canon of the Mass for " all orthodox believers and professors of the Catholic and Apostolic Faith."

Reading : 1 Tim. 2:1-7 (Second Epistle of the Votive Mass " *Pro Fidei Propagatione* ").

By the Administration of the Sacramental Mysteries

58th Consideration

By the ministry of the word the Catholic priesthood, as organ of the Holy Spirit, prevents the Incarnate Logos from being forgotten in the world and His joyful tidings from being falsified, and ensures that the Church shows herself to be " the pillar and mainstay of the truth." The apostolic word of the Logos is only a sign for Him, however; it is not *the Word Incarnate Himself*. But the world can only be redeemed *by Him Himself*, and the Church can only grow from and in Him Himself (Eph. 4:15 f.).

Therefore, God in His wisdom has thought of and put into operation a means by which all those who believe in the Incarnate Word can actually, tangibly,

have Him, for their salvation. This means consists in
the *Sacramental System* of the New Covenant. By this
system the Church is equipped with the power so to
unite her Head, Jesus Christ, to her members, that what
she promises in her proclamation of the words of salvation becomes the most real of realities in the sacrament;
for the Incarnate Word gives His own life to the believer
who receives the sacrament.

But the Founder of the Church has not given the
sacramental power to all the members of the Church
in the same measure. Baptism is the only sacrament
which all can administer, because it is the most
necessary of all the sacraments; and the Sacrament of
Matrimony is naturally dependent on the will to marry
of those eligible for marriage. The administration of
the other sacraments, on the contrary, is reserved to the
sacred priesthood. In the dispensation of these sacraments the beneficent power of the priesthood for the
Church and for the world is revealed in a might and
depth of which even the devout Christian can only have
the faintest conception.

Let us therefore consider that: The Catholic priesthood is an inexhaustible source of divine blessings for
humanity and the Church *by reason of its dispensation
of the sacramental mysteries*.

**I. The Administration of the Sacramental Mysteries of
the New Covenant Is Entrusted to the Sacred Priesthood.** The Eucharist, Holy Orders, Confirmation, the
sacramental remission of sin, and the administration of
Extreme Unction are reserved entirely to the dispensation (*dispensatio*) of the sacred priesthood. And even
for Baptism, too, the priest is the *minister ordinarius*

(Canons 738, 741, 742). The Sacrament of Matrimony would quickly degenerate if the priests did not proclaim this " mystery " and watch over its preservation. Finally, the sacramental system is placed in the care of the priesthood not only in order that it may be administered, but also that its administration may be not only *valida,* but also *digna.* Therefore all priests engaged in the sacramental service within the unity of the Church can say with Paul: " Let a man so account us, as servants of Christ and stewards of the mysteries of God " (1 Cor. 4:1).

II. By Administration of the Sacramental Mysteries the Holy Priesthood Conveys to Believers the Certain Enjoyment of the Fruits of Salvation. To be sure, the faith which develops into perfect love of God is capable of itself of bringing man to salvation. But how difficult it is to achieve this love without the sacramental graces, and how much more difficult to persevere in it even unto death! But where the sacraments are received from the anointed hand of the priest, the mysteries of the Incarnation and the redeeming death of Christ work their saving effect on the human soul with certainty provided they are validly administered and worthily received. For when the priest, by the exercise of his sacred powers, causes the Lord to work the wonders of His grace in the soul of the believer, Christ enters like radiant day into the soul which until then had been in the twilight of the uncertainty of salvation. For in the sacrament the divine Master keeps His word to His priestly servant so absolutely literally that it seems hyperbole, in view of our extrasacramental experience of prayer, that: " Whatever you ask in my name, that I will do, in order that the Father may be glorified in the Son. If you ask me anything in my name, I will do it" (Jn. 14:11 ff.). In the priestly *ministratio sacramentorum* these words are verified without reserve. They must therefore apply in the first place to the sacramental power of the priesthood.

III. Therefore Everyone Should Respect the Priest Because He Is the Servant of Christ and Steward of the Mysteries of God. Everyone should reverence the Catholic priest, but only those who have the spirit of Christ can do so. The Church, animated by the spirit of Christ, is herself the model of sound reverence for the priesthood, and at the same time, as a wise mother, she educates her children in this reverence. From the very hour in which the Holy Spirit ordained her sons to the priesthood she does this. In the first place, by the devout wisdom and childlike gratitude towards God expressed by word and ceremony in the Rite of Ordination, she shows the faithful what a great gift God has given her in a newly ordained priest. She does it, too, in all the definitions of doctrine in which she protects the mystery of the priesthood against all the denials and denigrations of its character and beneficence; and in her code of Canon Law, in which she directs the " steward of the mysteries of God" to administer the treasures of salvation, not negligently and sparingly, but in such a manner that the Master's household receive " their ration of grain in due time," and that he himself, if the Master comes " on a day he does not expect, and in an hour he does not know," shall be found so doing, and receive a glorious reward (Lk. 12:42 ff.).

Reading : 1 Cor. 4:1-5.

BY THE EUCHARISTIC MYSTERY

59th Consideration

Of all the gifts of salvation entrusted to the steward-ship of the Catholic priesthood, the mystery of the *Most Holy Eucharist* is the fundamental one. For in It the other sacraments are embraced, just as the fruit of a plant is inherent in its root. For does It not contain the originator (*realiter*) of salvation Himself, and not merely the gifts of His dispensation? Christendom therefore rightly calls the Most Holy Eucharist " the Supreme Good," which Christ, of His great love, left to His own. But as the Lord applies this gift of love to man only through His ordained priests, the priesthood is daily, from the rising of the sun to the going down thereof, the mediator of blessing for humanity and for the Church *through its Ministerium Eucharisticum*.

I. For This Ministry Is Reserved Exclusively to the Sacred Priesthood. When the Lord said " Do this in remembrance of me " at the first celebration of the Eucharist, He definitely thereby commanded the whole community of believers to celebrate the commemoration of His death in the manner in which He had just done it; for all were to partake of the supper at which He gave His own flesh and blood to be their food and drink as He had promised in the synagogue at Capharnaum (Jn. 6 : 58 ff.). He did not, however, give to all *the power* to render present the gifts of the Last Supper by changing the bread and wine into the substance of His most holy Flesh and Blood. This power was reserved from the very beginning to the Apostles and to those who were ordained by them " to the breaking of bread " by the imposition of hands and by prayer. This has been the conviction of the Church since the days of the Apostles. Because of this conviction she has refused any compromise with the false doctrine initiated in the sixteenth century and heralded afresh in our own day, that " the commandment which Jesus gave to the Apostles at the Last Supper, to do what He Himself had done, refers to *the whole community* of believers,"; and that, consequently, the people possess the true priestly power, but that " *the priest,* on the other hand, acts only by virtue of the orders received from the community " (in Encyclical, *Mediator Dei*). Against this conception the Church proclaims as the clear doctrine of tradition: that the priest it is " whose voice alone renders the Immaculate Lamb present on the altar " (Encyclical, *Mystici Corporis Christi*).

II. In the Mysterium Eucharisticum the Catholic Priest Brings Inexpressible Blessings on the World, by causing his high-priestly Master, Jesus Christ, by the outward visible rite, to incorporate into His unique Sacrifice on Calvary the whole Church and through Her all creation, and to apply to us the fruits of that unique Sacrifice. The priest adds nothing more to the redemptive act of Christ; this act is perfect in itself in every respect, for " Jesus, having offered one sacrifice for sins, has taken his seat forever at the right hand of God . . . For by one offering he has perfected forever those who are sanctified " (Hebr. 10:12 ff.). If the ordained priest nevertheless " renders present " again, at the Lord's command, the redemptive act of Christ, in the *ministerium Eucharisticum,* he does so in order to offer the Author of salvation and His work to the human beings who are drawn out of nothingness into existence, down the ages. He does this, however, not in a mere commemorative ceremony which refers back to the work of Redemption as to a past event, the effects of which the believer can make of benefit to himself, but in a *reality* (*realitas*) which he is able to render present by the celebration of the visible Eucharistic Sacrifice. Hence, the individual believer, or a community of believers, or finally the Church as the sum of her members, allow themselves to be incorporated into that sacrifice which our Head, Christ, offered once and for all, in order to offer to the Father not only Himself but also " those who are sanctified " and with them, everything which is given him to offer from the universe of created things and forces. But the priest has it in his power to offer or not to offer this holy *mysterium* of sacrifice. If he uses his power, he becomes for the world the living sign of that love which the Most Holy Trinity bears the world, that love in which Father, Son, and Holy Spirit, through the priestly Mediator Jesus Christ, accept as a pleasing oblation the endless stream of humanity, in so far as it does not withdraw itself from purification and redemption through the blood of Christ. By this Eucharistic ministry the ordained priest becomes the visible symbol of the redemption of the world by the Triune God.

III. The Church and the World Owe the Catholic Priesthood Endless Thanks for the Ministerium Eucharisticum. The Church is conscious of this. She loves the priest with the love of the Bride of Christ;

for she sees in him the trusted servant of her Bridegroom, who alone is able to obtain for her that communion with Him in which He gives Himself to her
already here below in mystical sacrifice, in the divine,
sacrificial banquet and in the silent presence in the
Tabernacle. Hence, she rejoices in the power which her
priests have over her Bridegroom. But she also rejoices
in the *spirit* which leads her priests to the altar, for she
knows very well that in this mystery " the flesh profits
nothing," but that the divine spirit by which the Father
draws to His Son all who grasp the Eucharistic mystery
(Jn. 6:45) is the spirit which animates the priest when
he goes to offer the Eucharist with faith and devotion.

Since the world, of itself, is only " flesh," it cannot
conjure up any genuine and salutary understanding of
the blessings which flow to it through the Eucharistic
ministry of the priesthood. At most it admires the
visible manifestations of it—the aesthetically impressive
outward form of the liturgy; but the hidden events of
salvation remain closed to it. Nevertheless, the Church
does not cease to pray to the heavenly Father, not only
for her own sake but for the sake of the world, " May
they [the priests] change by a holy benediction bread
and wine into the body and blood of Thy Son for the
service of Thy people " (the Bishop's prayer after
delivery of the chasuble to the Ordinand in the Rite of
Ordination).

Reading : Jn. 6:60-71; *Imitation of Christ,* Book IV,
Chap. 5.

BY ITS ZEAL IN THE ACCOMPLISHMENT
OF CHRIST'S ORDER TO BAPTISE

60th Consideration

In the discourse in which our Lord promised the Eucharistic Mystery He said that the fruitful reception of this sacrament depends on one condition, which He expressed in the words: " Whoever beholds the Son, and believes in Him, shall have everlasting life " (through the Bread of Life) (Jn. 6:40). But the believer shows his faith in the first place by being *baptised*. " He who believes *and* is baptised shall be saved " (Mk. 16:16). Without Baptism there is no admission to reception of the Eucharist, and therefore the order to the sacred priesthood to celebrate the Eucharist has the most intimate connection with the command to bring the human race to Baptism. Hence, the beneficent power of the Catholic priesthood is also demonstrated in its ministry of baptising.

Let us therefore consider that: *The sacred priesthood opens the founts of salvation to mankind* (Jn. 7:37-39) *by its zeal in accomplishing Christ's order to baptise.*

I. The Priesthood Bears the Main Burden of the Commandment to Baptise. The Lord's command to baptise (Mk. 16:16; Mt. 28:18) is accomplished in three phases. In the first phase, the aspirant must be prepared for the reception of Baptism; the joyful tidings must be announced to him and the laws of the Kingdom of God brought home to him. The non-ordained Christian can do this in case of necessity; but even in the days of the primitive Church the Apostles reserved to themselves and to those appointed by them for the purpose, the office of preparing converts for Baptism (Acts 2:38, 6:2). The second phase of the ministry of baptising consists *in the administration of the Sacrament of Baptism itself*. This office too can be fulfilled by all orthodox believers, if they do it according to Christ's ordinance. But already in the primitive Church the actual administration of Baptism was the right and duty of the bishop, according to Tertullian; and the Church of today declares emphatically that the ordinary minister of solemn Baptism is the priest alone. In fulfilment of this duty the priest is, moreover, charged by the Church with the duty of watching carefully to see that the orthodox doctrine regarding the essential character of the Sacrament of Baptism and its correct administration is preserved from all falsification. The third phase in the fulfilment of the office of baptist consists in all those endeavours by which the effects of the Sacrament of Baptism are preserved from error and corruption in the baptised person, and are brought to full maturity by the provision of favourable conditions of growth. This phase lasts the longest, for it covers the whole life of the Christian. In this phase too the ministry of Baptism is not a matter for the priest alone—parents and teachers and, not least, the baptised person himself, must co-operate in carrying out these tasks. But the duty of preserving the grace of Baptism demands from the priest the onerous pastoral work of preserving the life of grace in the children of God by the administration of the Sacrament of Penance, nourishing it with the Eucharistic Bread, confirming it through the Holy Spirit in Confirmation, and strengthening it against the invisible enemy of salvation at the hour of death by the Sacrament of Extreme Unction. Hence, the ordained priesthood truly bears the main burden of Christ's commandment to baptise.

II. By This Office of Baptist the Priest Transforms Mankind Into the People of God; for in this office he is the willing instrument of the heavenly Father, who wills to communicate His own life to those who accept His message of salvation (1 Jn. 3:1 f.); the instrument of the Divine vinedresser, who, in each baptised person raises and fosters a new branch on the vinestalk which is Christ; the servant of the Holy Spirit in that work of divine love whereby the human race is changed from "a people . . . who had not obtained mercy" to "a chosen race, a royal priesthood, a holy nation, a purchased people", who "proclaim the perfections of him who had called you out of darkness into his marvellous light" (1 Pet. 2:9). Finally, in his office of baptist, the priest is the "friend of the bridegroom" (Jn. 3:29), and the baptised represent the bride whom he presents to Him. He wins for Him a race of children whom He can present to the heavenly Father at the Eucharistic Sacrifice with the joyful words: "Behold, I and my children whom God has given me" (Hebr. 2:13). By their office of baptising priests become fathers of the children of God.

III. May God Preserve to Humanity the Blessings of the Priest's Ministry of Baptism. In the Vespers of the third feria after Passion Sunday, which was the vigil of the day of the *Scrutinium* of Catechumens in the Early Church, we pray to this day: "*Da nobis, quaesumus, Domine, perseverantem in tua voluntate famulatum; ut in diebus nostris et merito et numero populus tibi serviens augeatur.*" This is a prayer for the gift of the priestly office of baptist. If the knowledge of Christ has died out in the once so flourishing Christian lands of the Near East and the altars once built to His honour are now deserted and in ruins, it is solely because there is no longer a priesthood to exercise in its three phases the office of baptist in those countries. Only in exceptional cases, such as in Japan, have lay Christians persevered without a priesthood in carrying out Christ's command to baptise. That is why the Church prays for the grace of a priesthood zealous in the office of baptising. It has pleased God at times to respond to this prayer in a manner which has astonished the Church, when He has given her servants of holy Baptism with the strength and zeal of the Apostle Paul, St. Boniface and Francis Xavier. May He also, *in diebus nostris*, strengthen the priests of the Church in the apostolic zeal which will make them tireless in the *famulatus baptismatis perseverans* for the salvation of the peoples of the present day!

Reading : I Pet. 3:18-22.

BY ITS CARE FOR THE PRESERVATION OF CHRISTIAN MARRIAGE AND THE FAMILY

61st Consideration

In his office of baptist (60th Consideration), the priest fulfills his primary task in relation to man, namely, that of transforming him from a child of God's anger to a child of God. But this direct service in relation to the individual is preceded by an indirect one, the priestly service towards the source whence the individual comes, namely, the service of *marriage and the family*. Although the Catholic priest renounces the foundation and building up of a family by a marriage of his own, he is called to serve the basic institution for the propagation and upbringing of mankind, the divinely ordained marriage and family.

Let us consider, then, the blessing which the sacred priesthood brings to human society *by its care for the preservation of Christian marriage and family life*.

I. The Vocation to This Service is inherent in the apostolic office itself, in as much as this binds the priest to teach all, and to carry out in the Kingdom of Christ what Jesus taught and ordained, " teaching them to observe all that I have commanded you " (Mt. 28:20). Now, one of the things which Jesus commanded was that marriage should be restored to what it had originally been when given to man by the heavenly Father (Mt. 19:3 ff. and 5:27 f.), and that family life should be subject to the Fourth Commandment and receive the blessing promised to the observance of that commandment (Mk. 7:10, and elsewhere). Conscious of this call, Paul discloses in his Epistle to the Ephesians the new view of marriage as " a great mystery—I mean in reference to Christ and to the Church " (Eph. 5:32)— and the Apostles require the faithful to sanctify their marriages and their family life. It is from the same awareness of its being part of his vocation that the priest of today derives his sense of responsibility for the preservation of the divine order in marriage and family life, defends it against all denials and attacks, and endeavours as far as possible to ensure that it is carried out in the area for which he is responsible by the the *missio* *canonica* (Canons 1019-1143, but particularly 1020, 1031, 1033, 1095).

II. The Solicitude of the Catholic Priesthood for Marriage and the Family has been manifest throughout the history of Christianity. Whenever the *bonum prolis* or the *firmitas ligaminis* or the *aestimatio sacramenti* of marriage is threatened, it is always the pastor of the parish in question who strives to combat the destructive spirit of selfishness and proclaims the law of God, even if he has to make himself unpopular with his parishioners in doing so. In the Sacrament of Penance he appeals to the conscience of man and wife, lest they abuse the sacrament and destroy the fruit of their love. The encyclicals of the popes and the pastorals of the bishops, in which they call upon the Christian people to observe the right order in marriage and family life, are necessary to prevent the general terms of this order from fading from the consciousness of Christendom. But the accomplishment of this order in the practical life of the faithful depends on the zeal with which the pastoral clergy *help* married persons and parents to stick to these principles. The blessing which the high-priestly King of Christendom wills to confer upon human society by His ordinances stands or falls according to the degree of zeal which the clergy bring to that care of marriage and the family which is incumbent on them under the marriage laws of the Church (CJC 1019-1143; 1335; 1372, etc.).

III. The Recognition Which the Catholic Priesthood Receives for Its Solicitude for the Christian Family finds its most beautiful expression in the friendly terms which usually exist between the married and their priests, whose advice they seek in all the perplexities and troubles which they meet with in bringing up their families.

These cordial relations are most valuable for the formation of a sound Christian public opinion. Where priest and people are united in a relationship of unbroken confidence, the anti-Christian spirit has little chance of gaining much foothold. A particularly salutary effect of the priesthood's care and sympathy for the family is the eagerness with which so many Christian parents themselves encourage one or several of their children to enter the priesthood.

Reading : Eph. 5:21-6:9.

By Its Contribution to the Blessing of Christian Culture

62nd Consideration

" And he who was sitting on the throne said: ' Behold, I make all things new!' " (Apoc. 21:5). When time is at an end and the Lord takes over at the last day all things in the world which He has " reconciled to himself " the radiance of eternal life will shine forth, and there will be perpetual youth, and inviolable freshness. But the saving power of the redeeming Blood of Christ will not remain imperceptible and hidden in the midst of the things of this world until the Last Day. On the contrary, it reveals itself already in this world, acting—in a process of healing perceptible only to the eyes of faith, upon the things which the author of sin has wounded and infected, not only within the human soul but also in the outward ordinances of human society. To be sure, the world will not be changed into an earthly paradise by this healing power of the Blood of Christ, but it will receive from it those vital forces and impetuses which enable that better pattern of life which we call *Christian culture* or *the Christian order,* to be built up. The whole Church of Christ is the mediator of these vital forces, and she is this, in the first place, through her sacred priesthood. One cannot say, it is true, that the priesthood is the primary creator of the riches of the Christian way of life and culture; in this it is excelled by Christian laity in many domains: in fertility of gifts and energy. Its merits in fostering Christian culture lie, rather, in the fact that it *creates the conditions* from which the Christian order of life and Christian culture must arise.

In view of this achievement let us consider, then, *the part played by the priesthood in achieving the blessing of Christian culture.*

I. The Holy Priesthood Preaches the Order of Christian Culture in the World.

From the words of Jesus: " All power in heaven and on earth has been given to me. Go, therefore . . ." (Mt. 28:18 f.), already the Apostles inferred not merely the duty of a world-embracing ministry of Baptism (60th Consideration), but also the right of the baptized to *a new order to " subdue the earth"* (Gen. 1:28). At all times and in all places popes, bishops, and priests have consistently urged the faithful, in the first place to free themselves from all slavery to " the elements of the world " but then to rouse themselves to a consciousness of a new lordship over creation rooted in Christ, as Paul once urged the Corinthians: " Therefore let no one take pride in men. For all things are yours, whether Paul, or Apollo, or Cephas; or the world, or life, or death; or things present, or things to come—all are yours, and you are Christ's, and Christ is God's " (1 Cor. 3:21 ff.). But this lordship of the members of Christ, which originates from the kingly Head, demands not only a noble inner supremacy over the elements of the world, but also *a new love for the world* and its order. Paul calls us to this with the words: " For the rest, brethren, whatever things are true, whatever honourable, whatever just, whatever holy, whatever lovable, whatever of good repute, if there be any virtue, if anything worthy of praise, think upon these things " (Phil. 4:8; cf. 1 Tim. 4:4). To their credit, the clergy have always regarded the preaching of this cultural commandment as their duty. Wherever it has been neglected Christendom has been rapidly and disastrously enslaved under the humiliating thraldom of " the elements of this world."

II. The Holy Priesthood Mediates the Creative Force for the Accomplishment of This Order. This force is the living spirit of Christ. For as we know, culture is always the fruit of the spirit. When the spirit takes nature into its service, it creates culture. Hence, a culture becomes Christian when its inner pattern of life and its outward works are no longer formed by the mere human spirit, or by the human spirit ruled by the prince of darkness, but by the human spirit which has " put on Christ." *To form this spirit in the heart of man is the priesthood's particular task and specific contribution to culture.* It performs it both by the preach-

ing of the wisdom of the Gospel and by the sacramental imparting of the Holy Spirit to those who possess the ability and the vocation to form the Christian way of life and Christian culture. But since the deepest meaning and final end of all Christian effort for the order and good of the world is not its effect on the earthly welfare of humanity, but rather to make man acceptable to God, the Church orders her priests to " bless " all human work in the world in so far as it is worthy of the blessing of Christ. She anoints the hands of priests and bishops in order that everything which they bless may be blessed by heaven, and she gives them her special formula of blessing for every work which is established for the good of humanity. For only when the priest places the human work in the high-priestly hands of Christ does it receive that consecration which relegates it among the " all things " which He who sits upon the throne will " make new " on the Last Day.

III. Therefore, the Priest and the World Are Not Always Opposed : for instance, when they meet in striving for the spirit and the power of Christ. When the Apostle of the Gentiles deals in the Epistle to the Galatians with the question of how the Christian must stand in relation to " the elements of this world," he concludes with the words : " But as for me, God forbid that I should glory save in the cross of our Lord Jesus Christ, through whom the world is crucified to me and I to the world " (Gal. 6:14). With these words he is not pronouncing a sentence of damnation on the world; rather, he is indicating the place where the world and the apostle must meet, if this meeting is to be profitable to their mutual salvation. And this one and only place is by the cross of Christ. Therefore, there is no Christian culture and way of life, except the one which has its origin in the cross of Christ; for it is there that the blood of Christ flows, in which God will make all things new, in heaven and on earth.

Reading: Eph. 4:17-24.

By Administration of the Power to Forgive Sins

63rd Consideration

The Church consists of the baptized; as the sum total of the baptized she is the Body of Christ, of which the individual baptized persons are the members. But the members of this body are sinners. Hence, the Church is the " Church of sinners "; the Church *for* sinners because she frees her members from sin by the baptismal ministry of her priests. But since the baptized fall into sin again in spite of Baptism, she is also a Church made up of sinners, a Church *in* sin. That sins are committed in the Church accounts for the fact that she has " spots and wrinkles "; that she is a Church whose members can be sick, disabled, spiritually dead, in fact displeasing, indeed detestable in the eyes of God. But because in her Head, Christ, she is whole and pure and inaccessible to everything ungodly, God does not reject her, and she is the constant object of that fatherly love and mercy by which He wills to bring healing to the sick. And through His Son he has created the holy priesthood as the normal instrument of His will to save, in that He has given to this priesthood the power to forgive the sins of the children of the Church. Hence, the priesthood assumes an immensely important and benign relationship to the Church *by its administration of the power to forgive sins.*

I. Christ Transmitted This Power to the Holders of the Apostolic Office. When he sent out the Twelve, and later the Seventy-two, for the first time, He commissioned them to drive out devils and to heal all kinds of sickness as He Himself did. Now, He Himself drove out devils and cured sickness by removing from souls the deepest cause of these sufferings, namely, sin. He restored to the children of God the image of God which had been distorted in them by sickness and diabolical possession, by saying to them: " Take courage, son; thy sins are forgiven thee " (Mt. 9:2). Now, He willed to give to His Church for all time, as a remedy for the sinfulness of her members, this power to forgive sins. Therefore, when He appeared to the assembled ten Apostles in the hall in Jerusalem on the day He rose from the dead, He greeted them with the words: " Peace be to you! As the Father has sent me, I also send you." Then he breathed on them and said: " Receive the Holy Spirit; whose sins you shall forgive, they are forgiven them; and whose sins you shall retain, they are retained " (Jn. 20:19 ff.). With these words our Lord founded a health service to last till the end of time *for His Bride suffering in the sinfulness of her members.* And He combined the administration of this service with the apostolic priestly office.

II. The Fruit of This Foundation Is the Penitential Organization of the Church in as much as this owes its origin and beneficent effect to the priesthood's administration of the power to forgive sins. For as we know, there is no remission of sin without penance for the sin: even under the covenant of expiation the holiness of God demands this. Hence, the office of forgiving sin includes the duty of leading the sinner to penitence and to acts of penance. It lays upon the priest, first, the task of warning against sin, and then that of exhorting the sinner to turn away from sin. From generation to generation the Catholic priesthood has shown itself to be " the salt of the earth " in its accomplishment of this service. By its preaching of penance it provokes the disintegrating forces within the Body of Christ to resistance and precisely thereby makes them reveal themselves. This angry opposition on the part of sinful Christians may bring great trials and sufferings to the zealous priest. It may in fact bring him finally to share the lot of John the Baptist, the great preacher of penance. But if the sinner who has been exhorted does not shut his soul against grace, the long and often so weary task of healing the spiritually sick person—a task which demands much patience, intelligence, and love— now begins. This task is more or less concluded, it is true, with the pronouncement of the words of sacramental absolution. But the penitent may need much long, and often arduous, attention even after this if the cure is to last. Is not this healing service of the priesthood on the Mystical Body of Christ the core of all the sound fruit of penance which the vinestalk of Christ produces from generation to generation, to the joy of the merciful Father in heaven? A healthy state of the

Church depends on holiness in her members. With the exception of a few unsullied souls, the holiness of her members is the fruit of their penance for past sins. To produce this fruit, souls need the priestly healer.

III.   In the Eyes of the Church the Priest, With His Power to Cure Sin, Is the Messenger Through Whom God Fulfils the Prophecy once made known through the prophet Ezechiel: " Behold, I myself will seek my sheep, and will visit them. As the shepherd visiteth his flock, in the day when he shall be in the midst of his sheep that were scattered, so will I visit my sheep, and will deliver them out of all the places where they have been scattered in the cloudy and dark day. . . . I will seek that which was lost: and that which was driven away, I will bring again: and I will bind up that which was broken, and I will strengthen that which was weak: and that which was fat and strong I will preserve: and I will feed them in judgment " (Ezech. 34:11 ff., 16). The Church sees God's faithful fulfilment of His promise in the priest who carries out the *ministerium reconciliationis* with the zeal of the Curé of Ars. Therefore, she loves her priests and prays for them: " May they have power and authority to drive out evil spirits by the imposition of their hands and the words of their mouth: and be proved physicians of Thy Church, endowed with the blessed gift of healing and with heavenly strength " (Second Oration after the bestowal of the Order of Exorcist).

Reading : Jn. 20:19-23; James 5:14, 15.

IN THE WORK OF SELF-RENEWAL

64th Consideration

Certain essential powers in the order of salvation have been so transmitted to the Church that none but a priest can dispense them to the faithful. Hence the human race and the Church would have to do without necessary means of salvation if the priesthood were not sufficiently maintained. The care for the renewal and education of the priesthood is the concern of the whole Church in the first place, but the most effective instrument she can use for this purpose is the holy priesthood itself. In this important matter, too, the Church, both Head and members, is dependent upon the wisdom and zeal with which the priesthood of the time makes this intention—" For the provision of good priests "—its own.

Let us consider that: the Catholic priesthood also proves itself a source of blessing for the world and the Church by *constantly renewing itself for the salvation of the world.*

I. In This Effort It Accomplishes the Will of Its High Priestly Master. For Christ must bring into the barns of His heavenly Father the harvest which ripens in the world from the seed of His message of salvation; and to do this He uses human harvesters. The Apostles whom the Father " gave " Him, He Himself trained to be such helpers during His earthly life; and He already bade these pray " the Lord of the harvest " to increase their numbers, for " The harvest indeed is abundant, but the labourers are few. Pray therefore the Lord of the harvest to send forth labourers into his harvest " (Mt. 9:37 f.). Hence the Eleven, immediately after the Ascension of our Lord, set about making up their full number once more by electing Matthias. So, too, the Apostle of the Gentiles writes to his disciple Titus: " For this reason I left thee in Crete, that thou shouldst set right anything that is defective and shouldst appoint presbyters in every city, as I myself directed thee to do " (Tit. 1:5). And so the mystical Christ continues to provide for priestly mediators of His graces of salvation, just as, according to the Apocalypse, He appointed, supervised, tried, and purified the pastors of the Seven Churches of Asia (Apoc. 2 and 3).

II. The Most Effectual Helpers of the Church in the Provision of Priests Are the Clergy Themselves. Admittedly, the Christian people have also shared at all times and in many ways in the efforts of the Church to recruit and sanctify servants for the altar. Christian parents above all have joyfully given their best sons for the apostolic service, and in devout communities eager self-sacrifice enables even the poorest son of the parish to rise to the altar if he proves suitable for the priestly state. Religious and laity vie with each other in praying for vocations to the priesthood, for so our Lord has commanded. But enthusiasm for the priesthood would soon grow lame among the faithful if the shepherds of the flock did not preserve it and reanimate it by word and example. And above all, the actual production of the stewards of the mysteries of God by the conferring of Holy Orders and the formation of candidates in the priestly spirit is the work of the existing holders of Holy Orders, namely, the bishops, and the teachers and professors appointed by them. In every age of the Church the eternal High Priest inspires some great and striking priestly figures such as St. John Chrysostom, St. Gregory the Great, St. Dominic the founder of the Order of Preachers, St. Ignatius Loyola, Bishop Ketteler, St. Pius X, to renew and further, with enlightened minds and burning love and in accordance with the needs of their time, the great work of educating the priesthood.

III. In the Work of Forming the Priesthood We Are in the Mysterious Service of Divine Promise. The heavenly Father makes use of us to fulfil His promise to the Messianic King in Psalm 88: "Forever will I confirm your posterity" (v. 5) and "His Posterity shall continue forever" (v. 37). In Isaias 53:11 f. the Lord says: "Because his soul hath laboured, he [my servant] shall see and be filled. . . . Therefore will I distribute to him very many, and he shall divide the spoils of the strong, because he hath delivered his soul unto death . . . and hath prayed for the transgressors." Is not this prophecy fulfilled in an especially beautiful sense in the work of the constant renewal of our ministry? The efforts of the priesthood to maintain and renew itself fulfil, furthermore, the mysterious words of the Psalmists to the bride of the Messianic King: "The place of your fathers your sons shall have; you shall make them princes through all the land " (Ps. 44:17). In the constant renewal of the priesthood, which has already prepared its successors before it leaves the earthly battleground, God fulfils with wonderful fidelity the promise which He made to the royal Bride of His Son in the words quoted above.

Reading: Tit. 1:5-9.

THE PRICE AT WHICH THE HOLY PRIESTHOOD PURCHASES THESE BLESSINGS

65th Consideration

" He went about doing good." Into these words (Acts 10:38) the Early Church compressed its account of the earthly life of our Lord. If redeemed humanity ever looks back at the life of the world from the shores of eternity, it must see that even after His earthly life Christ has continued to " go about doing good " down the ages, and that He has done so and continues to do so most perceptibly in His holy priesthood. For despite all its limitations and failings, and within the limits indicated in the foregoing Considerations, it is the continuously active " *Salvator Mundi* " or, if these words should scandalize, then the visible organ, which serves the Saviour with generous devotion in the world.

Now, the *individual priest's* share in the work of the priesthood for the redemption of the world is commensurate with the degree to which he dedicates his person, powers, and time to applying the divine merits of salvation to the portion of the world to which he has been assigned. This personal devotion to the dispensation of the merits of the Redemption is *his contribution* to the salvation of the world and the building up of the Church in it. It is therefore fitting that we should consider very particularly this personal contribution of the individual priest to the priesthood's beneficent work for the world and the Church. It is the price, so to speak, at which the apostolic servant of Christ must purchase for mankind the saving redemptive work of his Master. This application is the same in *kind* in all priests, but in *power* it is not the same in all. For how much of this " price " he will devote to the salvation of the part of the world entrusted to him, is left to the choice of each individual priest.

We shall consider, then, *what the individual priest must stake* in order to bring the salutary fruits of the priesthood to the Church and the world. It is

I. The Application of Tireless Service. When Jesus made Himself the servant of His Apostles, He also demanded that they should be the servants of His disciples; they must apply themselves to giving the people of God " their ration of grain " in due time; they must be watchful so that the Lord, at whatever time He comes, " shall find His servant so doing " (Lk. 12:42 f.). " *Talem enim pastorem decet esse in Ecclesia, qui more Pauli, omnibus omnia fiat, ut in illo reperiat aeger curationem, moestus laetitiam, desperans fiduciam, imperitus doctrinam, dubius consilium, poenitens veniam atque solatium, et quidquid tandem ad salutem est cuique necessarium*" (St. Peter Canisius, in the Homily on his Feast). This service must be carried out without any claim on recognition or reward; for even when we have done all we can, we should say, nevertheless: " We are unprofitable servants; we have done what it was our duty to do " (Lk. 17:10). The more a priest uses his holy powers in this selfless spirit of service, as did, for instance, Don Bosco, the greater is the blessing which streams down from heaven on his work.

II. The Application of Apostolic Prayer. Although the fundamental duties of the priestly office, namely, the administration of the sacraments and the relevant preaching and teaching, can be accomplished with that minimum of prayer which the form of the sacraments demands, Christ and the Church require almost *constant prayer* from the priest. In His instructions to the Apostles, Christ always encouraged them to this; and in His discourses at the Last Supper He impressed upon them that they must accompany their whole mission in the world with constant prayer in His name: " And whatever you ask in my name, that I will do, in order that the Father may be glorified in the Son. If you ask me anything in my name, I will do it " (Jn. 14:13 f.). But the Church surrounds the administration of the mysteries of salvation with the rich order of prayer of the liturgy, binds the priest to the recital of the formidable Divine Office and expects him, in addition, to animate all his pastoral activity among the faithful with his private prayer. For it is in the order of things, and a fact proved by experience, that the more a priest prays, the more effectual his work is. The blessed fruit of pastoral work grows and ripens in the sunshine of apostolic prayer. If, on the other hand, prayer accompanies outward activity to only a slight degree, the fruit too is but small and without vigour.

III. The Spirit of Willing Renunciation. We have been told: " Freely you have received, freely give " (Mt. 10:8). The priest must do his work, not for his own gain and advantage, but for the benefit of the Church. If he seeks his own satisfaction in honour, power, or the contemptible effort to gain money, experience proves that he hinders the effect of his work. People like to watch with their own eyes the growth and completion of their works; this satisfaction is generally denied to the apostle of Christ, for what he does is in the realm of " the substance of things to be hoped for," something which is done in this life, it is true, but not in a way which can be perceived by us. This brings to the soul of the priest that torturing uncertainty and anxiety in which, with St. Paul, he fears lest perhaps, having preached to others, he himself should be rejected (1 Cor. 9:27). Finally, the priest must carry out his work although the world, which is to be saved by it, does not ask it of him, but on the contrary, is prone to repulse him with hatred: " They will expel you from the synagogues. Yes, the hour is coming for everyone who kills you to think that he is offering worship to God " (Jn. 16:2). The messenger of Christ may experience this so bitterly at times that he feels inclined to say, with Paul: " For I think God has set forth us the apostles last of all, as men doomed to death. . . . We have become as the refuse of this world, the offscouring of all, even until now " (1 Cor. 4:9, 13).

Hence, service, prayer, and patient self-denial are the price at which the priesthood has to purchase the blessings which it is to bring to mankind. But it is precisely in this that the Catholic priesthood is the continuation of Christ who, in the days of His earthly life, went through the world serving, praying, and suffering—*benefaciendo*—and who will continue to do so until the end of the world in individual priests in so far as these are animated by the same spirit which the Apostle of the Gentiles expressed in the beautiful admission: " But I have written to you . . . brethren . . . that I should be a minister of Christ Jesus to the

Gentiles . . . that the offering up of the Gentiles may become acceptable, being sanctified by the Holy Spirit. I have therefore this boast in Christ Jesus as regards the work of God. For I do not make bold to mention anything but what Christ has wrought through me to bring about the obedience of the Gentiles, by word and deed, with mighty signs and wonders, by the power of the Holy Spirit . . ." (Rom. 15:15 ff.).

Reading: 1 Cor. 4:1-13.

THE BLESSINGS OF THE PRIESTHOOD:

2. FOR THE PRIEST HIMSELF

PREFACE

1. The grace of the holy priesthood is a gift of *God to the Church,* that is to say, that to those who receive it, it is given as a *gratia gratis data* for the benefit of the Church and not for the personal advantage of the recipient. Because of this loose and, so to speak, fortuitous connection of the sacred power with the person of the ordained, it can achieve its salutary effect on the Church and the faithful even if the bearer of this power is an unworthy person. Since the grace of ordination is used for the good of the Church by members of Christ, who are instruments of the grace-giving God, through the use of their reason and

their freedom, enlightened by faith, the bearer of the priestly power nevertheless has got a personal share in the work of the sacred ministry. He receives from his priestly actions blessings which enrich, exalt, and sanctify him, personally, if he accepts them. In this sense one can speak of the blessings of the Catholic priesthood for the priest, personally.

2. We know of these blessings partly from revelation and partly from the experiences of the priestly state. Holy Scripture reveals them to us in those passages in which it speaks of proofs of special divine favour given to bearers of the apostolic mission (Lk. 10:17 ff.) and in the discourses at the Last Supper (Jn. 14-17). Both places are rich mines in which we may unearth those hidden movements of life which bind God and the bearer of Apostolic powers, one to the other: and these movements of life are sources of blessing and favour. The Epistles of the Apostles disclose such blessings in all the passages in which the authors reflect on the meaning and value of their apostolic office and work. The Apostle of the Gentiles does this particularly in the two Epistles to the Corinthians, the Epistle to the Philippians, and the Pastoral Epistles. Reading between the lines, one can find these supplemented in the Letters which the Seer of the Book of Revelation had to send to the Bishops of the Seven Churches (Apoc. 2 and 3). Outside of Holy Scripture there is astonishingly little to be found relevant to our subject. Christian literature for priests contains an almost unbroken stream of warnings in which the priesthood of

each generation is reminded of its duty of devotion to the Church (to ' souls '); and its real, or alleged, short-comings are lamented, often very sternly. Demands are made which appear to take an abnormal strength of character for granted in the priest. True, not only the Church (Canon 124), but also the priest's own devout sentiment tells him that he must be a shining example of virtue and rectitude to the faithful—*sanctior prae laicis*. But that he can be this because he is an especial favourite of God and because a flood of divine favours, designed to strengthen and inspire him personally beyond the ordinary degree, streams down on him unceasingly from the grace of ordination—this is a point seldom brought home to us satisfactorily in this edifying literature. Even the commentaries on the above-mentioned Bible passages for the most part pass over these contributions to our subject which would be so important and consoling to the priest. This is because the connection of these texts with the apostolic calling has been lost sight of.

This deficiency in devotional and theological litera-ture on the priesthood is made good to some extent by the revelations of outstanding priests concerning certain graces of their state which fortified them in their apostolic life's work. We find these revelations in the notes on their work and its origins, and in letters and diaries in which they attribute the success of their apostolic efforts to such effects of the graces of their state. Examples of such documents are the letters of St. Francis Xavier or the spiritual journals of Jean Jacques Olier, founder and first rector of St. Sulpice, in as much as these report manifestations of grace, which, they are convinced, are not exceptional personal favours but normal phenomena in the life and struggles of every zealous steward of the mysteries of God.

3. In an effort to classify the testimonies concerning the manifold blessings reported in the above sources, and from this classification to draw up at least an approximately systematic sequence of these blessings, we choose the way which our Lord Himself chose at the return of the seventy-two disciples from their first missionary assignment. For from this report one can co-ordinate everything contained in other parts of the Scriptures and in the revelations of experienced priests.

4. The person called to the priesthood must not make the question, as to what he gains by obedience to this call, the impetus behind his manner of discharging its duties; the decisive motive must be the call of God Himself, which he heard. But God has combined with this call the promise of the blessings which are to distinguish the priestly life. Therefore, the following Considerations are designed to help towards ensuring, that we do not only carry out our ministry merely from a consciousness of inescapable obligation, but do so with the joyous enjoyment of the fruits in the form of blessings which God causes to bloom and mature from it for the priest personally.

THE REPORT OF THE RETURN OF THE
SEVENTY-TWO DISCIPLES

ACCORDING TO MATTHEW

"At that time Jesus spoke and said, 'I praise thee, Father, Lord of heaven and earth, that thou didst hide these things from the wise and prudent, and didst reveal them to little ones. Yes, Father, for such was thy good pleasure.

"'All things have been delivered to me by my father; and no one knows the Son except the Father; nor does anyone know the Father except the Son, and him to whom the Son chooses to reveal him. Come to me, all you who labour and are burdened, and I will give you rest. Take my yoke upon you and learn from me, for I am meek and humble of heart; and you will find rest for your souls. For my yoke is easy, and my

ACCORDING TO LUKE

"Now the seventy-two returned with joy, saying, 'Lord, even the devils are subject to us in thy name.' But he said to them, 'I was watching Satan fall as lightning from heaven. Behold, I have given you power to tread upon serpents and scorpions, and over all the power of the enemy; and nothing shall hurt you. You do not rejoice in this, that the spirits are subject to you; rejoice rather in this, that your names are written in heaven'" (10:17-20).

"In that very hour he rejoiced in the Holy Spirit and said, 'I praise thee, Father, Lord of heaven and earth, that thou didst hide these things from the wise and prudent and didst reveal burden light'" (11:25-30).

"But blessed are your eyes, for they see; and your ears, for they hear. For amen I say to you, many prophets and just men have longed to see what you see, and they have not seen it; and to hear what you hear, and they have not heard it'" (13:16-17).

them to the little ones. Yes, Father, for such was thy good pleasure.

"'All things have been delivered to me by my Father; and no one knows who the Son is except the Father, and who the Father is except the Son, and him to whom the Son chooses to reveal him'" (10:21-22).

"And turning to his disciples he said, 'Blessed are the eyes that see what you see! For I say to you, many prophets and kings have desired to see what you see, and they have not seen it; and to hear what you hear, and they have not heard it'" (10:23-24).

THE APOSTOLIC COMMUNITY OF LIFE WITH CHRIST

66th Consideration

> "Now the seventy-two returned with joy" (*Lk.* 10: 17).

The blessings which come to the Catholic priest from his calling, originate from Jesus Christ, the founder of our priesthood. Therefore, no one can explain them to us as well as our Lord Himself. He speaks of them in many parts of the Gospels, but the Holy Spirit has condensed together everything about them in the reports in Luke 10:17-24, and Matthew 11:25 f., and 13:16 f., of the return of the seventy-two from their first apostolic mission. We shall follow our citation of these reports with Considerations on the blessings which arise for the priest himself from the discharge of the apostolic office.

Luke begins with the words: "Now the seventy-two returned with joy." The returning men had several reasons for being joyful, but the deepest of them was the consciousness of being united with Jesus in a community of life and work. The interests of Jesus were their interests and their interests were Jesus' interests.

In the grace of ordination the good priest possesses an inexhaustible source of holy joy in as much as the grace of his state gives him *the right to the apostolic community of life with Christ*.

I. "That They Might Be With Him" (Mk. 3:14).

With these words the Evangelist indicates *the first reason* for which the Apostles were chosen: their calling was to make them belong to our Lord's company. This membership was to be a distinction and the fulfilment of the deepest craving of their hearts rather than a tie and a burden. For the heart of man cannot satisfy itself; it needs things outside itself to give it objects for its urge to action, and it needs people around it to which it can give itself, and who in their turn can give themselves to enrich its inadequacy. The person who lives for himself alone becomes isolated and dies even before his heart ceases to beat. Now, the more precious and worthy the person to whom we give ourselves, the more richly we feel ourselves endowed by Providence.

To have found in Jesus Someone Whose richness promised to make good the poverty of their own existence—this was the first satisfaction which the Apostles experienced when John the Baptist said to them, " This is he of whom I said, ' After me there comes one who has been set above me, because he was before me.' . . . And I have seen and have borne witness that this is the Son of God " (Jn. 1:29 ff.). Immediately they begin to seek His attention. The fact that He does not rebuff them, but speaks His " follow me " to each one of them (Jn. 1:35, 51), is a heavenly favour, and the more He draws them to Him, the more convinced they become that they have found Someone in Whose service and for whose friendship it is well worth giving one's life. Even in the dark hours of their Master's Passion and death they did not lose the consciousness that their lives and destinies were bound up with His; their consciousness of discipleship was only temporarily overshadowed by their grief because they thought they had lost Him, and by their shame, because they had failed in the hour of trial to stand the test of preserving their union with Him.

II. The Grace of Ordination Gives Every Priest the Permanent Right to This Apostolic Community of Life With Christ. To be sure, every baptized person has a claim to community of life with Christ—the claim of the member who belongs to the Mystical Body. But when one of the multitude of baptized is raised up by

ordination to be a servant of Christ and steward of
the mysteries of God (1 Cor. 4:1)—to transmit to the
people of God the graces of redemption on which the
Mystical Body lives, he enters into a new relationship
to Christ, that of the *servant* to whom the Lord has
entrusted His goods, the *steward* who has to apportion
to the other servants the food which will enable them
to find strength and joy in the kingdom of God. If he
is found faithful in this service, he will receive the
most honourable recognition. " Blessed are those
servants whom the master, on his return, shall find
watching. Amen, I say to you, he will gird himself, and
will make them recline at table, and will come and
serve them " (Lk. 12:37). The experience of our calling confirms that the Lord changes the *servant* relationship into that of *friend* and *confidant* not only in
heaven but already in this life. " You are my friends if
you do the things I command you " (Jn. 15:14). The
longing to be taken into this apostolic relationship of
servant and friend to Christ is one of the most reliable
indications of a true vocation to the priesthood; it
shows the possession to a high degree of the loving
spirit of faith.

**III. Priestly Joy in the Community of Life With
Christ** is the same in its *essential character* in all good
priests, but in its *degree* it is very different. Its
strength depends upon the extent of our supernatural
recognition of the greatness and richness of the person
of our Lord, and of our realization of the dispropor-
tion between our nothingness and His greatness. The
happiness to which those called can attain through the
grace of the apostolic union with Christ was experienced

personally by Paul and epitomized in his avowal: " The things [in my life before meeting with Christ] that were gain to me, these, for the sake of Christ, I have counted loss. Nay more, I count everything loss because of *the excelling knowledge* of Jesus Christ, my Lord. For his sake I have suffered the loss of all things, and I count them as dung that I may gain Christ and be found in him " (Phil. 3:7 f.). If the priest makes good his right to community of life with Christ by prayerful intercourse and apostolic devotion to Christ's interests, he will be able to confess joyfully, like the Apostle: " For to me to live is Christ " (Phil. 1:21).

Reading: Phil. 3:4-15.

THE NOBILITY OF THE PRIESTLY OFFICE

67th Consideration

> " Now the seventy-two returned with joy " (*Lk.* 10: 17).

There are many ways in which a priest returns to the Lord. There is the return from the superficiality of the worldling to a spiritual encounter with Jesus; there is the return of the wayward to the Friend of sinners—including priest sinners; there is the return of the zealous priest from his work in the vineyard of the heavenly Father, to report upon the state and success of his work. The return of the seventy-two was a return of this latter kind. They returned " with joy," and this was partly because the mission on which the master had sent them out had been a success. *Apostolic work achieved* is always a source of joy in the life of a priest.

Let us consider, then, that: The gift of the priest-hood is a source of blessing for its bearer *because of the nobility of the work for which it fits him.*

I. "Even So Let Your Light Shine Before Men, in Order That They May See Your Good Works" (Mt. 5:16). God has so created the human heart, that it is inclined to value itself according to the cause which it has to serve. The noble-minded person suffers if he sees his life going by without his being able to achieve what seems to him worth while, and he envies his brother, whom fate has called to a service which is accounted worthy of esteem and important for the community to which he belongs. When the Lord called the Twelve, they were lured by the greatness of the Person who called them, but they were also lured by the *nobility of the service* to which they were called. Jesus knew how to awaken and intensify the self-esteem of the fishermen's sons of Bethsaida when He called out to them after the miraculous draught of fishes: "Come, follow me, and I will make you fishers of men" (Mk. 1:17). He calculated the power of kindling with which he wished to inflame the hearts of the Twelve when, His eyes fixed on them, He said: "You are the salt of the earth. . . . You are the light of the world. . . . Even so let your light shine before men, in order that they may see your good works and give glory to your Father in Heaven" (Mt. 5:13, 14, 16). To give their life to such a work they will leave father and mother, their nets and the sea; to become eager preachers of the Kingdom of Heaven, and to serve those things "into which the angels desire to look."

II. A Devout Sense of the Nobility of the Priest's Work Is Necessary to preserve our joy in our calling. If this is missing or if it is only poorly developed, then our priestly service is not sufficiently attractive to our hearts. Then we are in danger of satisfying our mere natural urge to action in our priestly ministry; of showing off our power, and of acting out of a desire for recognition and honour, or even for worldly gain. But if we reflect on the nobility of the priest's work in the eyes of God, we grow in the knowledge that, in fulfilling our professional duties, we are permitted to be " God's helpers " in leading man back to his Lord, and then worldly motives will lose their power of attraction more and more, and, if they remain unsatisfied, will cease to be a source of disappointment or of bitterness. We must, therefore, foster our consciousness of the nobility of our calling. We must not allow the eye of faith, with which we see the *inside* of our pastoral action, its origin in God, in whose hand we are only instruments, and its co-ordination with God, for whose glory alone we do it, to grow dim. It is in order that this supernatural view of our work should never be lost but should continually increase, that we have been warned: " Take care, therefore, that the light that is in thee is not darkness " (Lk. 11:35).

III. " We Are God's Helpers." There is a high and noble pride in these words of the Apostle (1 Cor. 3:9). Paul spoke them to counter certain narrownesses and jealousies which were tending to diminish the esteem of the apostolic office in the Church at Corinth (1 Cor. 3:1-9). But this consciousness of nobility is based upon the nobility of our work, as revealed by our Lord

Himself when He promised His Apostles: " Amen, amen, I say to you, he who believes in me, the works that I do he also shall do, and greater than these he shall do " (Jn. 14:12). The priest who is enlightened by faith perceives the fulfilment of this promise of our Lord, particularly and literally in the administration of the sacramental mysteries of salvation. The longer he exerts himself in the priestly office, the more does his heart become filled with that astonished joy which the Apostle of the Gentiles expressed in these words: " Of that gospel I was made a minister by the gift of God's grace . . . to announce among the Gentiles the good tidings of the unfathomable riches of Christ, and to enlighten all men as to what is the dispensation of the mystery which has been hidden from eternity in God " (Eph. 3:7 ff.). The heart of the good priest becomes ennobled by recognition of the nobility of his office.

Reading : Col. 1: (24) 25-2:3.

THE APOSTOLIC POWERS

68th Consideration

> " Now the seventy-two returned with joy, saying: ' Lord, even the devils are subject to us in thy name ' " (Lk. 10: 17).

A person's will to live and joy in life depend on the *feeling of strength* that he has. If it is weak and inconstant he lives in a state of fear and discouragement, and does not venture to undertake tasks which would give meaning to his life and help his fellow men. This is also true in regard to the Kingdom of God. "But from the days of John the Baptist until now, the kingdom of heaven has been enduring violent assault, and the *violent* have been seizing it by force" (Mt. 11:12). If this is true of all who want to get to heaven, then it is especially true of those who should lead in the conquest of it, namely, apostles and priests. They must be strong people, and the consciousness of their strength is one of the real blessings which come from the grace of ordination. Impressed by this perception of their strength, the Seventy-two say to our Lord: "Lord, even the devils are subject to us in thy name."

Let us consider, then, that: With the grace of the priesthood the good priest is also given *the gift of apostolic power*.

I. The Lord Promises This. Our Lord did not disapprove of the consciousness of power of the Seventy-two as expressed in the joyful astonishment of their report that even the devils were subject to them in the name of Jesus. He attributed that power in the first instance to His superiority over the prince of darkness, but then He reinforced their consciousness of it by the assurance: "Behold, I have given you power to tread upon serpents and scorpions, and over all the power of the enemy; and nothing shall hurt you" (Lk. 10:18 f.). According to Mark, our Lord repeated this promise on the day of His Ascension, for the comfort of all who should work in the propagation of the Gospel to the end of time: "And these signs shall attend those who believe: in my name they shall cast out devils; they shall speak in new tongues; they shall take up serpents; and if they drink any deadly thing, it shall not hurt them; they shall lay hands upon the sick and they shall get well " (Mk. 16:17 f.). The promise was fulfilled on the day of Pentecost, so that Mark could conclude his Gospel with the words: " But they went forth and preached everywhere, while the Lord worked with them and confirmed the preaching by the signs that followed " (16:20). The Church sees the proof of this power of Christ in the Apostles and disciples of the Early Church mainly in the visible miracles and signs of the messengers of Christ. But Paul draws our eyes away from the miraculous power to the spiritual power when he writes to his disciple Timothy: " For God has not given us the spirit of fear, but *of power and of love and of prudence*" (2 Tim. 1:7). What Mark and Paul wish to testify is: that the Lord has co-ordinated in His apostolic servants the powers by which they can overcome all the hostile powers in the world, even the demoniacal ones, and the possession of these powers is part of the apostolic and priestly equipment.

II. The Apostolic and Priestly Consciousness of Power Is Based on a Genuine Right to the Power of Christ, the power of the Lord of the Universe, who has said: " All power in heaven and on earth has been given to me " (Mt. 28:18). Because the good priest is the " Minister of Christ " he is also the minister of this irresistible sovereign power of his Master and he therefore knows that he is a match for all the opposing powers which contend with the Kingdom of God, if only Christ deigns to use him as the instrument of His power. It is this consciousness of power which makes Paul say: " I can do all things in Him who strengthens me " (Phil. 4:13). It was this consciousness of power that enabled St. Boniface to lay his axe to the Hessian oak and turned their proud defiance into noble humility. To this day this consciousness of power gives the minister of Christ confidence and perseverance in embarking on and carrying through His pastoral tasks, even if he is weak, timid and oversensitive by nature, and if the difficulties confronting his efforts seem insurmountable.

III. But the Priest Can Only Make Good His Claim to the Power of Christ if He Gives Scope to the Strong Arm of Christ; therefore, there is a second condition necessary, namely, that he *prays* for the assistance of Christ and *renounces all trust in his own strength*. His prayer must come from that spirit of faith " which overcomes the world " and of which our Lord says: " If you have faith like a mustard seed, you will say to this mountain, ' Remove from here '; and it will move. And nothing will be impossible to you " (Mt. 17:19). But confidence in oneself lames the arm of the Lord. Paul believed for a while that he could work better for the Gospel if he were cured of that mysterious weakness which hindered his nature from developing fully in devotion to the apostolic ministry. Therefore he begged the Lord three times to free him from this temptation of the devil. But the Lord replied: " My grace is sufficient for thee, for *strength* is made perfect in *weakness*." From then onwards the full consciousness of power penetrates the soul of the Apostle. He now says: " Gladly therefore I will glory in my infirmities, that the strength of Christ may dwell in me. Wherefore I am satisfied, for Christ's sake, with infirmities, with insults, with hardships, with persecutions, with distresses. For when I am weak, then I am strong" (2 Cor. 12:9 f.). Such ministers of the power of Christ seize the Kingdom of God by force.

Reading : 2 Tim. 1:6-14, 4:14-18.

PREDESTINATION TO ETERNAL LIFE

69th Consideration

> " You do not rejoice in this, that the spirits are subject to you; but rejoice in this, that your names are written in heaven " (Lk. 10: 20).

All apostolic work must be done, in the final resort, " for the greater glory of God." Whether it brings a *reward* to the person who does it, is of no importance in itself. But since it cannot be accomplished without the personal devotion of the apostolic minister, God's goodness and justice do not permit that the reward which the labourer deserves should be withheld (Lk. 10:7).

Now, it is one of the particularly bright sides of the apostolic life that *eternal life* is promised to its ministers as the result of their priestly labours. This the Lord guarantees to the returning Seventy-two with the words : " Do not rejoice in this, that the spirits are subject to you; rejoice rather in this, that *your names are written in heaven*." Therefore, predestination to eternal salvation is bound up with the apostolic office.

Naturally, not the final and irrevocable predestination, for otherwise Judas could not have become the "son of perdition." It is, rather, a temporary and conditional predestination, but yet one far more effective than that of the non-priestly disciple of Christ. We have every reason to ponder deeply upon this mystery of particular election.

Let us consider, then, that: One of the gifts combined with valid ordination is *our (conditional) predestination to eternal life.*

I. The Fact of This Predestination. The Lord speaks of the predestination to election not merely to the Seventy-two; He emphasises it almost every time that He speaks of the calling and destiny of the Apostles and other messengers of His Gospel. Actually, in His first instruction regarding the apostolic ministry, He says: "And you will be hated by all [in the exercise of your office] for my name's sake; but he who has persevered to the end will be saved" (Mt. 10:22; cf. Mt. 10:32, 33; 20:1-16, etc.; Lk. 22:28-30). The reason for this so definite promise lies in the essential character of the priestly calling and its work; it is, in its inmost nature, an acknowledgement of the Son of God, in whom the redemptive will of God has been made manifest to all (Tit. 2:11). He who is the mediator of salvation to others must naturally win it for himself, if he performs his ministry of the Gospel of salvation through inner conviction. Hence, the Apostle of the Gentiles says to each of his fellow workers: "Take heed to thyself and to thy teaching. . . . For in so doing thou wilt save both thyself and those who hear thee" (1 Tim. 4:16).

II. The Condition Necessary to Our Election is none other than that faithful stewardship of the sacred gifts entrusted to us by which we give to our fellow men what they need for their salvation. Our Lord speaks most explicitly of this in the parables of the Watchful Servants, which have been transmitted to us in the greatest detail in Luke 12:35-48. For there the question is under what conditions the "servant" keeps his place safely in the household of his master on the day when the master comes. Jesus tells what this condition is when He says: "Who, dost thou think, is the faithful and prudent steward whom the master will set over his household to give them their ration of grain in due time? Blessed is that servant whom his master, when he comes, shall find so doing. Truly I say to you, he will set him over all his goods. But if that servant says to himself, 'My master delays his coming,' and begins to beat the menservants and the maids, and to eat and drink, and get drunk, the master of that servant will come on a day he does not expect, and in an hour he does not know, and will cut him asunder and make him share the lot of the unfaithful." Hence, only that servant who has neglected his duties and has not given to the souls entrusted to him what the Lord had ordained they should have, will be shut out from the table of the Lord in heaven. But the servant who has exerted himself for the good of the souls entrusted to him, will enter into the joy of the Lord; indeed, even if his stewardship has been deficient he will enter into it. If his deficiency was due to lack of knowledge of the divine will, he will nevertheless be saved, but not without " being beaten with stripes " on account of what he has done wrongly. If his stewardship was deficient despite a good knowledge of his pastoral duties, he will still be saved, but only after " many stripes " (cf. 1 Cor. 3 : 12-13).

III. Hence, the Grace of the Priesthood Definitely Includes Predestination to Eternal Salvation on condition that we do not bury our talent like the lazy servant of the Gospel, but use it well for the welfare of those souls entrusted to us. How much grief of soul, timid, but otherwise zealous priests, would spare themselves if they would only accept with faith and gratitude this generous promise of election which the Lord has made them. They seek to justify their discouragement with the worried admission of the Apostle of the Gentiles, who had done more than any of his fellow Apostles, yet did not feel himself thereby justified (1 Cor. 4:4). But actually, this remark of St. Paul's is no more than a fleeting shadow which sweeps over his sunlit soul and its confidence of salvation. In his heart the Apostle is convinced that " the crown of justice is laid up " for him as the reward for his ceaseless efforts . . . and not only for him but " for those who love his [the Lord's] coming." For every priest who truly serves his calling, devotes his care and labour to preparing for the Lord's coming, may therefore share the Apostle's confidence.

Reading : Lk. 12:35-38, 41-48.

A BLESSING WHICH HAS THREE DISTINCT MARKS

70th Consideration

> " In that very hour he rejoiced in the
> Holy Spirit and said: 'I praise thee,
> Father, Lord of heaven and earth that
> thou . . . didst reveal them to little
> ones. Yes, Father, for such was thy
> good pleasure " (Lk. 10: 21).

With these words the spirit of Jesus proceeds to lead
us into the deepest blessings which arise from the
priestly office for its holders.

According to the Gospel account, our Lord suddenly
turned away from the disciples who were standing
around Him, and His spirit soared up to the Father.
He prayed, and He did so with a visible emotion which
was unusual with Him, " rejoicing in the Holy Spirit."
His prayer was a prayer of thanks for having perceived
the operation of the heavenly Father on the Seventy-
two; this operation is described as a " revelation " to
the disciples; our Lord called the object of this revelation " these things," i.e., words which denoted something present. Now, what this was is not defined and
can only be inferred from the following passages.
Altogether, these words of our Lord strike the hearer
as being extraordinarily mysterious; they speak of a
gift of the Father, but without revealing what it is;
they only give us some clues by which we can find this
out for ourselves if we are attentive. On the other
hand, our gaze is directed to three circumstances in
which the revelation of " these things " happened. They
are given in the peculiar character: first, of the giver

of this revelation; second, of those who receive it, and third, of those who witness it. The peculiarity of these circumstances points to the unusual, supernatural and distinctive character of this revelation. We shall make them the object of our consideration.

Let us consider, then, that: the priest who fulfills his apostolic mission faithfully, as the Seventy-two did, is promised by Christ *a blessing which has three distinguishing marks.*

I. It Is Distinguished by Its Donor. The donor is *the heavenly Father Himself.* "I praise thee, Father, Lord of heaven and earth, that thou . . . didst reveal these things." So the mystery of "these things" comes from the Deity Himself, and its intimation (revelation) proceeds directly by divine action and not through the mediation of any created being. On the contrary, in this proceeding the Father shows His supreme and absolute sovereignty over everything created, and for this reason the Son of Man addresses Him deliberately with the words, "Father, Lord of heaven and earth!" With wonder Jesus perceives this in His heart; therefore He concludes the prayer with the words: "Yes, Father, for such was thy good pleasure!" Hence, the Father reveals Himself where true work for the Kingdom of Christ is done. For apostolic work has its origin, ultimately, in the Father.

II. It Is Distinguished by Its Recipient. This gift is not given to all; it is given to the "simple," the "little ones." Now, the "simple" in the eyes of Jesus are the children of God whose hearts are undivided, who, moreover, give themselves with their *whole* hearts to their Father and place their powers, with simple reverence, in the service of the glory of the Lord of heaven and earth. The Seventy-two were of this kind. They were not like the Temple priests and Scribes in the days of our Lord, who thought themselves so wise and clever, and did not place themselves in the service of the Holy Spirit because they feared they might give themselves away too much. People like that are invariably unsuited to the task of building up the kingdom of Christ. But the simple are suited to this task, because they do not hinder the power of God by conceit, and they rejoice because " the foolish things of the world has God chosen to put to shame the ' wise,' and the weak things of the world has God chosen to put to shame the strong, and the base things of the world, and the despised, has God chosen, and the things that are not, to bring to naught the things that are " (I Co. I : 27 I.). To such as these the Father deigns to reveal His mysteries, but He hides them from the wise and clever.

Whether the words of Jesus are unreservedly applicable to all who are simple in heart, as pious Bible commentators of today like to assert, or whether they apply to the simple who are entrusted with the apostolic mission, still remains indefinite, but it is not of importance for us; for it is certain that the eye of the Lord looks beyond the Seventy-two to all who shall carry out the apostolic mission with the same simple hearts to the end of time, that is to say, to all good priests.

III. Distinguished by Its Witness. Jesus in His most holy humanity is the witness of the revelation. In it

He sees in this hour the revelation of the Father to the disciples; He rejoices because the breath of the Spirit of Love has touched them and He bears testimony to this with an access of joy which astonishes the disciples all the more, because their Master otherwise hid His affective life from those around Him; His deep insight into the purpose of all things preserved it in a certain calmness, in fact, usually overshadowed it with a restrained sadness. But now the joyfulness of the Lord betrayed that in the " revelation " of the eternal Father to the disciples something had happened for which His heart had been longing intensely.

These three circumstances, in which " these things " were revealed, only indicate in the first place, that in them nothing in the least ordinary had been disclosed. The revelation was a distinction. Each of these three circumstances signified such a distinction. The first disciples of our Lord now recalled something which He had said to them at the beginning of His public life. It was at the first meeting of Jesus and Nathanael. The latter was surprised that the Rabbi from Nazareth knew what he, Nathanael, had confided to God alone in prayer shortly before; for this reason he promptly acknowledged Jesus as " the Son of God, the King of Israel." Whereupon Jesus said: " Amen, amen, I say to you, *you shall see heaven opened,* and the angels of God ascending and descending upon the Son of Man " (Jn. 1:45-51). Did Jesus rejoice now because the Father was beginning to make this come true?

Reading: Jn. 16:25-27.

THE REAL MYSTERY OF CHRIST

71st Consideration

> " All things have been delivered to me
> by my Father; and no one knows who
> the Son is except the Father, and who
> the Father is except the Son, and him
> to whom the Son chooses to reveal him "
> (*Lk.* 10: 22).

After His heart had soared up to the Father, our
Lord turned back to His disciples to continue His
explanation of the blessings which rest on the apostolic
office and service. For He had yet to disclose the
mystery of " these things " which the Father hides
from the wise and clever but reveals to the simple. The
words which followed now served this purpose : " All
things have been delivered to me by the Father; and
no one knows who the Son is except the Father, and
who the Father is except the Son, and him to whom
the Son chooses to reveal him."

This discourse of the Lord must be understood, in
the first place, in the light of the situation in which
it was spoken; one must seek its relation to " these
things " which the Father reveals to the apostolic
servants of His Son. The universality implied in the
statement would seem to show that what has just been
perceptibly effected as *an isolated case* in the Seventy-
Two is a *permanent and continuous law* of the Kingdom
of God.

What, then, is the content of the revelation with
which the heavenly Father honours His simple servants
in the apostolic office? The Lord answers : it is an

interdivine knowledge. It is, in the first place, the knowledge which the Father has of the Son; but it is also the knowledge of the Father concerning the Son which the Father has given to the Son with " all " that He has given Him, and which the Son can pass on to others if He so wills. Hence, " these things " consist of *the mystery of Christ as it is known in the bosom of the Godhead itself.* It is the mystery of the *Logos,* which is present in the person of our Lord and which the Seventy-two have proclaimed in the world in the accomplishment of their apostolic mission.

Let us consider, then, that: of all the blessings which the grace of the apostolic priesthood gives, the most important and exalted is *the supernatural revelation of the true mystery of Christ which is imparted to the priesthood.*

I. Initiation Into the Real Mystery of Christ cannot

follow in any other way, of course, than by a revelation of the Father. That is why the Lord says in His discourse at Capharnaum: " No one can come to me unless the Father who sent me draw him. . . . It is written in the Prophets, ' *And they all shall be taught of God!* ' Everyone who has listened to the Father, and has learned [what I really am and not merely what I look like], comes to me, . . . This is why I have said to you, ' No one can come to me unless he is enabled to do so by my Father ' " (Jn. 6: 44 f., 66). Since this revelation embraces a mystery of the life of the Trinity, it is incomprehensible in itself for the merely human mind, that is to say, for the wise and clever of this world. Therefore, if it is given to the disciples of Christ, this signifies a great honour due to the unimaginable condescension of God to His creature, a proof of the most profound intimacy with the Father and the Son. Hence, we can understand how the Apostle John could write: "He who believes in the Son of God has the testimony of God in himself" (1 Jn. 5:10).

II. The Reason Why Our Lord Rejoiced in the Holy Spirit Was Because the Father Had Initiated the Messengers of the Gospel Into the Mystery of the True Christ. For without apprehension of this fundamental mystery of the Gospel of salvation, the mystery of the "*one* Lord Jesus Christ, the only-begotten Son of God, born of the Father before all ages, God of God, light of light, true God of true God," they cannot accomplish their mission to the world. One who does not know this mystery in the interdivine reality which is known only to the Godhead itself, can also, it is true, speak of Jesus Christ, but only in so far as the mere human mind can perceive Him; he is one of the wise and prudent of this world, whose utterances about Christ must, in the nature of things, be superficial and lacking in objectivity, because the *real* Christ is unknown to him. But the simple, to whom He is revealed, can not only *proclaim* the message of salvation but can even *realise* it; for not only has the true Christ been made known to them, but with Him they have received *the power* which the Father has given to the Son together with "all things." And in view of the fact that this power is at their disposal without limit for their apostolic tasks, one can understand the words which Jesus spoke later to His Apostles: "And whatever you ask in my name, that will *I* do, in order that the Father may be glorified in the Son" (Jn. 14:13). The heart of the Lord rejoices in the Holy Spirit over this.

III. A Growing Comprehension of This "Revelation" Is the Deepest Source of All True Priestly Happiness. Our Lord Himself discussed this truth in His discourses after the Last Supper, particularly as recorded in John 15:15-17. It is a question of the most personal side of His relation with His Apostles, when they shall have begun their great task of preach-'ing His Gospel in the world. They will then no longer be beginners in a relationship of service to their Master, Christ—hired servants who as more or less unenlightened executors of the orders of Christ carry out the external pastoral work, but do not understand the inner meaning which it has in the plan of their Master. Such priests would be like the servant who "does not know what his master is doing." But if, as servants, they are zealous in their service, the Lord changes His relationship to them by accepting them as His friends. "You are my friends if you do the things I command you" (Jn. 15:14). But how does this change from servant to friend take place? Exactly the same way as the "revelation" which was given to the Seventy-two. "But I have called you *friends, because all things that I have heard from my Father I have made known to you.*" They are initiated into the interdivine relationship between the Father and the Son. When the Church sings these words (Jn. 15:15-17) jubilantly at the conclusion of the Rite of Ordination, she is none other than Christ Himself, rejoicing in the Holy Spirit. Christ is rejoicing because He is being given, once more, apostles who are enlightened with the mystery of the true Christ, and are therefore equipped to build up still further the Kingdom of God. The priest's soul too begins to rejoice when he realises what has been done in him: that he has been taken up into a process of divine self-revelation, which will gain in impetus the more and the better the ordinand carries out the task which "his Friend" has laid upon him. He experiences each day anew and with increasing joy what Jesus promised to His priestly friends: "He who has my commandments and keeps them, he it is who loves me. But he who loves me will be loved by my Father, and I will love him and *manifest myself to him*" (Jn. 14:21).

Reading: 2 Cor. 4:1-6.

THE RIGHT OF REFRESHMENT IN THE HEART OF JESUS

72nd Consideration

> "Come to me, all you who labour and are burdened, and I will give you rest. Take my yoke upon you, and learn from me, for I am meek and humble of heart; and you will find rest for your souls. For my yoke is easy, and my burden light" (Mt. 11: 28-30).

As a special proof of His favour, the heavenly Father grants to the simple apostolic servant comprehension of the mystery of the relation in which the

Father and the Son stand to each other within the Godhead—the *true* mystery of Christ as a being privy to all the secrets and possessing all the immeasurable riches of the Godhead, that is, of Christ who is God, one in being with the Father. Jesus knows that if His disciples should grasp this revelation completely they would be overcome with that *fear* of the greatness and sublimity of His being which had once made Peter exclaim: " Depart from me, for I am a sinful man, Oh Lord!" (Lk. 5:8). It is not to awe them that the heavenly Father reveals to the disciples the true secret of His Son, but on the contrary, in order that this knowledge may be a *source of joy and blessing to them.* That is why our Lord immediately followed the revelation of His oneness with the Father by the *invitation* to come to Him and seek from Him refreshment in the difficulties of the apostolic service: "Come to me, all you who labour and are burdened, and I will give you rest. Take my yoke upon you, and learn of me, for I am meek and humble of heart; and you will find rest for your souls. For my yoke is easy, and my burden light."

Let us consider then, that: The zealous fulfilment of the duties of their priestly calling gives the servants of Christ *the right to find refreshment in the heart of Jesus;* for it is to them that the Lord cries:

I. " **Come to Me, All You Who Labour and Are Burdened.**" The more recent Catholic devotional literature tends to extend the circle to those to whom these words are addressed to include all believers in

Christ who feel frustrated in life. But it emerges from Matthew's report that the invitation is directed, if not exclusively, at least primarily to those who, like the Seventy-two, are suffering the trials of the apostolic service—in other words, to those who bear His yoke. They are exhorted to seek refreshment from the exhaustion which the fulfilment of the apostolic mission brings.

II. **"I Will Refresh You . . . and You Will Find Rest."** The apostolic labour of Christ's servant is not, then, to be an uninterrupted consumption of himself, as certain superidealists inside and outside our calling demand that it should be. The law of life, that one must *take* in order to be able to *give,* applies to the priest too; the illuminating flame of witness which Christ kindles in the world, must be nourished by Christ Himself. The apostolic servant, too, must fulfil the meaning of this law in the rhythm of give and take; and there must therefore be a refreshment which corresponds with his labour and anxiety and yoke-bearing, and replace the strength he expends. What does Christ give to His envoy to refresh him? An exegesis from the " letter " which " kills " replies: *His yoke.* Does He not indicate His offer of refreshment when He continues in the same breath: " Take my yoke upon you "? Does He not demand, nevertheless, that His servant should consume himself without interruption in His service, but in such a way that it becomes a source of " rest " by being more meek and humble? On the eve of His Passion, Jesus put this question to the

Apostles: "When I sent you forth without purse or wallet or sandals, did you lack anything?" And they said: "Nothing" (Lk. 22:35 f.). Does He not tell us here in what the refreshment consists to which He invites us? It embraces *everything which the apostolic servant of Christ needs,* even the requirements of his bodily maintenance. For this reason Christ shared His own earthly bread with His disciples. But He gives more; and more essential things than this: He refreshes them with " the bread of God . . . which comes down from heaven and gives life to the world." That is, with Himself, given visibly under the form of the Eucharistic bread, and invisibly in that mysterious exchange of life of which He says to the Apostles: " In that day [of my Ascension] you will know *that I am in my Father, and you in me, and I in you.* He who has my commandments and keeps them, he it is who loves me. But he who loves me will be loved by my Father, and I will love him and manifest myself to him. . . . If anyone loves me, he will keep my word, and my Father will love him, and we will come to him and make our abode with him" (Jn. 15:20-23). In the Apocalpyse, this train of thought of our Lord's is carried to a conclusion, in that the Lord promises the indifferent angel of the Church of Laodicea, if he repents of his lukewarmness: " Behold, I stand at the door and knock. If any man listens to my voice and opens the door to me, I will come in to him *and will sup with him, and he with me*" (Apoc. 3:20). With the grace of the priesthood a mystical exchange of life between Christ and His servants begins. The divine host gives His friends food which cannot be described in human language. If the priest comes to enjoy them in faith, he learns what they contain and how wonderfully they restore his strength.

III. The Enjoyment of These Refreshments Depends on One Condition, However, and that is: *"Take my yoke upon you and learn from me, for I am meek and humble of heart."* The will of the apostolic servant must bow beneath the will of Christ, and his neck must bow to the yoke and take the weight of the divine treasures of salvation in order to convey them to mankind. Must the refreshment be bought at a dear price, then? No, that is not so. For if our eyes are fixed on our Master as we work, we find— that "the yoke is easy and the burden light." For our Employer *is* a meek one, who does no violence: and a humble one, Who bows His own neck with the willingness of a good servant beneath the yoke which is laid upon Him, although the Father has given Him all things. The priest who bears the cares and burdens of apostolic work as Jesus has done, is not overwhelmed with hurry and worry; he finds "rest for his soul."

If we listen to these words without love, we may hear them, to be sure, but they will glance off our hearts as off a stone. But if we listen to them with love, if we find our joy in serving Him to whom the Father has given all things, they will penetrate our souls and free them from everything which fetters and oppresses them.

Reading: Jn. 14:18-25. Psalm 22.

PRECEDENCE OF THE OTHER SERVANTS OF GOD

73rd Consideration

> " And turning to his disciples he said,
> ' Blessed are the eyes that see what you
> see! For I say to you, many prophets
> and kings have desired to see what you
> see, and they have not seen; and to hear
> what you hear, and they have not heard
> it ' " (Lk. 10 : 23-24; cf. Mt. 13 : 16 f.).

The Lord concludes His address to the Seventy-two
with a *beatitude*. This differs from the beatitudes of
the Sermon on the Mount (Mt. 5 : 3 ff.) in that it does
not refer, as those do, to future gifts, which are only
promised conditionally. Here *the gift is already present and unconditional*. To be sure, it is seen in
the first place only by Jesus; for, of course, only He
has seen the " prophets and kings " of whom He speaks.
But as devout Israelites, those present guess to whom
He is referring: to Moses and Elias, David and
Solomon. The Evangelist emphasises the fact that
Jesus spoke this beatitude to the disciples very specially
—that is to say, not to the other people standing
around, in as much as these were not entrusted with an
apostolic mission and exerting themselves in its fulfilment. Hence, here too it is a question of a proof of a
favour which is given on account of the apostolic office.
The holder of this office, the ordained priest, is glorified *because he has a position of priority above the
rest of God's servants by virtue of that office*.

I. **The Reason for This Glorification of the Apostolic
Servant** lies in the fact that the servant of Christ sees
and hears what the prophets and kings longed to see
and hear, but did not. What Moses and Elias, and

Jeremias, and David and Solomon desired to see and to hear was nothing else, in the eyes of the devout Israelite, than the Messianic King of the people of God and His Kingdom. True, they saw Him in proto-types and they heard of Him in prophecies, but they did not see Him Himself; they had to go to their fathers still hoping for Him. But His apostolic ser-vants *do* see and hear Him. And they see and hear more of the Lord than their physical eyes and ears convey to their minds; for of course those others stand-ing around, even the enemies of the Lord, could perceive that much. The macarism emphasises the recognition and the hearing which is specially given to the simple-hearted apostolic servants. It is again *the apprehension of the true mystery* of Christ, as only the Divine Persons know it—the self-revelation of the Father and the Son, which caused the Lord to rejoice in the Holy Spirit. It is the advantage which the Apostles have over the great heralds of the Messianic promise, an advantage which the " kings and the prophets " may well envy them, and which the Lord Himself extols in them. Therefore these words of glorification conclude and epitomise, as it were, the infor-mation conveyed in the Gospels concerning the gifts and blessings which the apostolic office brings to those who carry it out well.

II. The Purpose of This Glorification is to establish in the apostolic servant of Christ the proper and necessary sense of self-esteem which he needs for the fulfilment of his office. For his privileged position in the Kingdom of God is meant to serve him in the fulfilment of the tasks of his mission. The Apostle of the Gentiles draws a far-reaching conclusion from this. In the Second Epistle to the Corinthians (3:6-12), he compares the Apostle of Christ with Moses. Both are in the service of the mystery of Christ. But Moses served in the shadow which emanated from it, the shadow which had to flee as the light approached, and which was to disappear when the light finally rose like a sun over the world. The Apostle, on the contrary, is in the service of the light itself and is illuminated with its radiance, a radiance which in the eyes of heaven outshines the radiance of Moses as he came down from Mount Sinai. For Moses' service was a " ministration that condemned "; the apostolic service, on the contrary, is " the ministration of the spirit . . . that justifies." The Apostle sees the power and the glory of his ministry so firmly rooted in the knowledge and possession of the true mystery of Christ (4:5-6) that there is no longer any question of surreptitiousness or lack of courage in his work. The apostolic servant of Christ must see this as Paul saw it; only then will he realise why he is more privileged than Moses or David; only then will he apprehend the full import of our Lord's words: " He who hears you, hears me; and he who rejects you, rejects me; and he who rejects me, rejects him who sent me " (Lk. 10:16). The glory with which Christ invests His priests is the reflection of the majesty and glory which are His own attributes. We must neither deny nor hide it, because it is the proof, so to speak, of our competence before the people to whom we are sent.

III. The Fruit of This Glorification is the reverence, obedience and love which the whole Church of Christ on earth and her orthodox members show towards the good priest of their Lord. The world is scandalized by this high esteem of the faithful for their priests; that is but natural since it does not know the rank of the priest in the eyes of God. With the Church it is otherwise. Marvelling at the gracious condescension of her Master in raising lowly sons of men from the dust, in lifting up the poor from the dunghill, and placing them with princes, with the princes of His people (Ps. 112:7-8), she exults in the Office of the Apostles: *Nimis honorificati sunt amici tui, Deus; nimis confortatus est principatus eorum* " (Ps. 138:17).

Reading : 1 Pet. 1:10-12.

THE PRIEST'S SHARE IN THE FRUITS OF SALVATION BROUGHT FORTH BY THE FAITHFUL

74th Consideration

> " And he who reaps receives a wage, and gathers fruit unto life everlasting, so that the sower and the reaper may rejoice together " (Jn. 4: 36).

In the account of the return of the Seventy-two disciples, there is no mention, apart from the successful driving out of devils, of any missionary success which the messengers of salvation met with among the children of Israel. That is striking, for surely it is one of the greatest satisfactions of a priest's life to be able to perceive that his efforts have not been fruitless. Now, if the Lord says nothing on this occasion about a *fructus extrinsecus* of apostolic labour, He mentions it all the more emphatically in another place. It was the time that He sat by Jacob's Well at Sichar and saw in a vision the fruit of the words of salvation proclaimed by Him. He saw it as a ripening harvest, awaiting the reaper. As the Apostles returned from the town at the same moment and rejoined Him, He called upon them to get to work on this harvest, and encouraged them with the words: "Well, I say to you, lift up your eyes and behold that the fields are already white for the harvest. And he who reaps receives a wage, and gathers fruit unto life everlasting, so that the sower and reaper may rejoice together" (Jn. 4:35-36). The wage promised here, and the fruit which the apostolic reaper is permitted to gather unto life everlasting, is a share in the harvest which the word of salvation will produce in souls; that is to say, *the results of our pastoral efforts among the people to whom God's call sends us.*

Let us consider, then, that: *The priest's participation in the fruit unto life everlasting which the faithful bring forth* is another source of joy in his calling.

I. The Fruit Unto Life Everlasting Which the Faithful Reap.
This is the thirty, sixty and hundredfold fruit reaped by those "who, with a right and good heart, having heard the word, hold it fast, and bear fruit in patience" (Lk. 8:15). It is the result of *all the good works* which devout souls show forth; in fact it is the fruitbearing *soul* itself, which is so transformed by the divine seed of life that, like the good tree, "it cannot bear bad fruit." It is the "great multitude which no man could number, out of all nations and tribes and peoples and tongues," and the

total treasury of the merits of these, which will be given over to the angel before the throne of God, that he may offer as incense together with the prayers of all the saints, upon the golden altar (Apoc. 7 : 9 and 8 : 3 ff.).

II. The Priest's Share in the Fruits of Salvation Reaped by the Faithful.

Of course, the lord of the harvest, *the heavenly Father*, is the real reaper of this fruit. He has given to redeemed humanity the seed of His word, which can develop so fruitfully; He has also given them the tilled field of a right and good heart in which the seed can take root; and by the sunshine and rain of His helping graces He has given growth, until the fruit was ripe for the heavenly kingdom. But as God's word would not have reached to fulfilment if it had not been accepted willingly by *the soul of the faithful believer,* that soul has, after God, the right to the possessions and enjoyment of the fruits of salvation; and it is God's joy, as Father, to grant the soul this. Only now do *the sower and harvesters* have their turn; what the sower sowed and the apostolic harvesters brought into the barns of heaven belongs primarily to others and not to them. But since it is the will of the " Lord of the harvest " that the fruits of salvation in the temporal kingdom of God cannot be sown without the sower of Christ and cannot be harvested without the apostolic labourers of the harvest, the heavenly Father gives to these too a share in the harvest, a share in the enjoyment and possession of the riches of salvation. Hence, what is won for eternity by the priestly harvest work and saved from destruction by our pastoral care does not belong to us, it is true, and the saying that the priest "wins" many souls is to be understood with many reservations; nevertheless, it presupposes a certain claim in regard to souls whose salvation we are permitted to serve and to the works which they have done at our instigation. It is recognised by God and by these souls in the next world, and sometimes already in this one. Hence, it is to this outcome of apostolic work that our Lord referred when He exhorted the Apostles to harvest-work in the Kingdom of God with the words: "Lift up your eyes and behold that the fields are already white for the harvest. And he who reaps receives a wage, and gathers fruit unto life everlasting, so that the sower and the reaper may rejoice together." In this way He wished to awaken in the hearts of His disciples that hunger to "win souls" and increase the glory of God by their good works; in this way He still awakens that holy passion which made a Francis Xavier pray: "Give me souls and keep the rest!" (Cf. Rom. 1:13-15.)

III. This Share in the Fruits of Redemption Reaped by the Faithful Should Fill the Good Priest With Joyous Confidence—the confidence that the good works of his flock and of the souls saved through him may be reckoned as the gain which the good servant earns by disposing well the talents of the priesthood entrusted to him. To be sure, this confidence must be based on genuine and selfless shepherding of the flock if we are not to think, like the angel of the church of Laodicea, that we are rich and have need of nothing, whereas in reality, as far as the result of our pastoral work is concerned, we are "wretched and miserable and poor and blind and naked." But if the devout priest sees the Gospel progressing in his parish and producing works which have their root in faith and charity, then, like Paul, he may thank God joyfully because the souls entrusted to him, when they heard and received the word of God from him, " welcomed it, not as the word of men, but, as it truly is, the word of God." In such a parish he may well see his hope, his joy, his crown of glory " before our Lord Jesus Christ at his coming " (1 Thess. 2:13, 19). So the reaper may rejoice even here and now at the harvest which he is gathering unto life everlasting. He thinks of it every day when he prays: *Merear, Domine, portare manipulum fletus et doloris: ut cum exsultatione recipiam mercedem laboris* (Ps. 125).

Reading : 1 Thess. 2:13-14, 17-20.

" Quae Apponuntur Vobis " (Lk. 10:8)

75th Consideration

> " And remain in the same house, eating and drinking what they have; for the labourer deserves his wages " (Lk. 10: 7).

When our Lord sent out the Seventy-two, He gave them certain rules of conduct to be observed on the way (Lk. 10: 3-12). They were to take neither purse, nor wallet, nor sandals with them, but when they entered a house, He said, they were to " remain in the same house, eating and drinking what they have; for the labourer deserves his wages." Hence, as regards the needs of their human nature, He does not leave them to go their apostolic ways unprovided for. For of course the messenger of Christ cannot fulfil his task if he does not devote to it the powers of his nature, both physical and spiritual. Therefore, this nature must also be given *from the kingdom of God* what it needs in order to serve the supernatural ends effectively and fruitfully. Thus it is that the grace of ordination also gives to the ordinand the right to the satisfaction of those needs without which our nature could not perform its service in the *ministerium Christi*.

Hence, yet another of the blessings of the grace of ordination is that *it protects the just claims of the priest to the satisfaction of the natural requirements of existence*.

I. Christ Wills It So. Therefore He bases His instruction—that the messengers of His Gospel should eat and drink what they find in the houses of those who receive them, on a principle of the theocratic rule of life: " You shall not muzzle an ox when it is treading out corn " (Deut. 25:4); *cf.* " For the labourer deserves his wages " (Lk. 10:7). When His enemies were scandalized at His disciples for not living the austere life which John the Baptist lived, He always stood up for them against the rigorism of these critics. Times of affliction and hunger, oppression and persecution would come to them, and even their temporal life would not be inviolably ensured to them by the kingdom of God, *but their right to these earthly goods* is never disputed; the injury to these rights will be made good a hundredfold and those who injure them will not escape punishment. Voluntary renunciation of these good things for the sake of the Kingdom of God is not commended to all, but only to those to whom " it is given "; hence it follows that such renunciation is not one of the normal requirements of the Kingdom of God, and therefore requires the help of exceptional graces which are not given in the natural course with the grace of the apostolic office. On the other hand, He demands humility from the messengers of His Gospel all the more emphatically; they are not to seek preferment for themselves, and they are to look upon their colleagues as brothers. Yet He does not condemn the sons of Zebedee for wanting the best places in the Messianic Kingdom. On the contrary, He lets it be known that even in the other world there are to be differences in rank; he reveals, however, that the adjudication of rank is not His concern, but His heavenly Father's. Thus, Jesus protects the requirements of human nature in His disciples, gives them on earth what is necessary for their satisfaction, and promises full satisfaction of their other claims in the next life (Mt. 19:27-30; *cf.* the Homily of Venerable Bede on this text in the Breviary, *Commune conf. non Pontif II* (in Luke 12)).

II. Therefore Only Those Who Do Not Know the Spirit of Christ Make the Excessive Demand That the Priest Should Renounce in Principle the Right to These Natural Possessions. Naturally no one, except perhaps an unbeliever, says that the priest can live on air or that he is without rights. But the fact that he *claims* material support, respect, and recognition of his authority is taken amiss in many quarters nowadays and decried as a transgression against his priestly character. The priest of today is only recognized and acknow-

ledged as the emissary of Christ when he acts like
Paul, who could say to the Christians of his day: " I
will not be a burden to you; for I do not seek yours,
but you " (2 Cor. 12:14 f.). It is the same in our
days: people are inclined to allow " authority " over
those called to the Kingdom of God only to the priest
who commends himself to them by emulating the
Apostle of the Gentiles in making no claim on them.
Paul, however, could do things which not everyone
can do. Even among the Apostles he was pre-eminent
in his gifts of nature and of grace. What he demanded of
himself he did not demand even of his fellow apostles;
and yet he did not find fault with their apostolic teachings because they allowed themselves to be maintained
by the Christian communities. In the 9th chapter of
the First Epistle to the Corinthians, Paul gives us an
illuminating proof that while he demanded of himself
the utmost renunciation of the demands of nature, the
other Apostles did not hold with him in this.

**III. Therefore the Priest Need Not Refuse the
Earthly Reward of His Efforts if It Is Given to Him**
in a lawful manner. With Paul he can say to his flock:
" If we have sown for you spiritual things, is it a great
matter if we reap from you carnal things?" (1 Cor.
9:11.) But the shepherd must not set his heart on
these good things from the herd to such an extent as
to injure his apostolic spirit. He should not be disap-
proved of if he rejoices in his daily bread and does not
disdain to win respect and tributes from his parish,
and if in the midst of all his devotion to his office, he
cherishes a well-ordered desire for better benefices,
special authority, and those dignities, titles, decorations

and insignia by which even the Church herself recognizes and seeks to satisfy the craving of the human heart for honours. For after all, in the eyes of the Church these are but an anticipation of the distribution of rank—by which " star differs from star in glory " (1 Cor. 15:41) which will take place in heaven. The heavenly Father has reserved to Himself the conferring of these honours, and He determines them according to the degree to which we have drunk from the cup which He has given to His Son to drink (Mt. 20:22 f.).

Reading : 1 Cor. 9:3-14.

PART FIVE

THE CATHOLIC PRIESTHOOD
IN RELATION TO
THE MOST HOLY TRINITY

THE CATHOLIC PRIESTHOOD IN
RELATION TO THE MOST HOLY TRNIIY

1. GLORIFIES THE FATHER

76th Consideration

> " In this is my Father glorified, that
> you may bear very much fruit, and be-
> come my disciples " (Jn. 15: 8).

Manifold blessings flow from the Catholic priesthood,
if the graces of ordination become effective in the
offices for which they are meant—blessings for
humanity and for the Church; blessings for the priest
personally. We have considered all this in the foregoing
Considerations (Nos. 56 to 75). But that is not all.
The benign influence of the faithfully used graces of
the Sacrament of Holy Orders goes even beyond all
created things and reaches up to the throne of the
Most High; and from there is answered with new
blessings.

In John 15:8 our Lord says: " In this is my Father
glorified, that you may bear very much fruit, and
become my disciples."

Let us consider then: *That the heavenly Father is
glorified in the gift and the service of the sacred priesthood.*

**I. The Glory of the Father Is Indeed the Final End
of All the Priestly Action of Christ.** That is why He
said, looking back on His earthly life and its task: " I
have glorified thee on earth; I have accomplished the

work that thou hast given me to do " (Jn. 17:4). By saying, shortly afterwards, of His Apostles : " Even as thou hast sent me into the world, so I also have sent them into the world," He revealed the fact that all the works of His apostolic servants too must, in the final resort, have for their aim the glory of the heavenly Father.

II. Now, How Does the Priestly Disciple of Christ Glorify the Father? The Son sees the glorification of the Father by the bearers of the apostolic office in *two things which they achieve.* The first consists of the *much fruit* which their priestly service produces. This is the fruit of all the sanctification of the Church and of her members, including the priest himself, such as we have considered already. It is simply the sanctification of the world by the *ministerium apostolicum.* The other achievement consists *in the progress of the discipleship of Christ in the priests themselves.* To be sure, the Apostles had already been a long while in the relationship of disciples to Christ. Nevertheless, our Lord spoke to the Eleven at the Last Supper of their yet " *becoming* " disciples. For the relationship of disciple is something capable of development, and the more they become the disciples of Jesus, the greater is that transformation which takes place in them, by which they glorify the heavenly Father.

How precisely the glorification takes place through these two achievements Jesus shows in the parable of the vinestalk and the vine. In fact, this parable, too, was spoken in the first place with a view to purifying the relationship of the Apostles to their missionary task, and not as an explanation of the life of grace in

general, as it is generally, if uncritically, assumed nowadays to be. If the vine, on the vinestalk Christ, brings
forth much fruit for the sanctification of the world, this is
for the glory of the Father, because the Father is the
vinedresser who has planted and reared the vinestalk,
who cares and purifies the vine on the vinestalk, and
waits for the grapes to grow sweet and ripe and ready
to be carried home. The grape is the glory of the vinedresser, for it is the result of his industry and skill.
Similarly, the fruit of apostolic labours is the glory of
the Father, in its blessedness and beneficence, and
does not arise from the will and action of the servant
of Christ but from the wisdom, power, goodness, holiness, and mercy of the heavenly vinedresser (Rom.
9:16). That is why the Master says: " In this is my
Father glorified, that you may bear very much fruit."
But the Father is also glorified by the progressive
action of their becoming disciples. For in the eyes of
the heavenly Father the preciousness of the fruit of
the vinestalk depends on the vine taking as much sap
as possible from the vinestalk on which it grows; the
pastoral work of the servant of Christ is valuable in the
measure that it is animated by the spirit which animates the Heart of the Son of God. This spirit is
none other than that love of the Son of the Father
which caused Him, during His earthly life, to seek not
His own will but the will of Him who sent Him. The
more our priestly service is animated by this venera-
tion of the Heart of Jesus for His heavenly Father,
the more do we glorify the Father: " For God . . .
has shone in our hearts, to give enlightenment concerning the knowledge of the glory of God, shining
on the face of Christ Jesus " (2 Cor. 4:6).

III. " Whosoever Shall Glorify Me, Him Will I Glorify " (1 Kings 2:30). God does not allow Himself to be exceeded in generosity. Therefore, He raises up into His glory those who glorify Him. He does this in the next life to an extent for which no earthly thoughts can find words; but even on earth He honours those who think of His glory *by making Himself their servant,* so to speak. " My Father will love him," Jesus says of the disciple who fulfils His orders (Jn. 14:23). And the more the Father loves the apostolic messenger of His Son, the more He will become accessible to him and the more ready He will be to grant his petitions. That is why the influence of the loved disciple of Christ will become stronger and stronger with the heavenly Father, so much so that eventually he will not even have to appeal to Jesus in order to obtain what he wants from the Father: " In that day you shall ask in my name; and I do not say to you that I will ask the Father for you; for the Father himself loves you because you have loved me, and have believed that I came forth from God. . . ." " Amen, amen, I say to you, if you ask the Father anything in my name, *he* will give it to you. . . ." " Ask, and you shall receive, that your joy may be full " (Jn. 16:26 f., 23, 24). Paul experienced this love of the Father in his apostolic life, and he confesses this in the deep and comforting words: " And those whom he has predestined, them he has also called; and those whom he has called, them he has also justified, and those whom he has justified, them he has also glorified" (Rom. 8:30).

Reading : Rom. 8:28-30.

II. SERVES IN THE JOY OF THE SON

77th Consideration

> "These things I have spoken to you
> that my joy may be in you, and that
> your joy may be made full" (Jn. 15: 11).

The glory of the heavenly Father is the basic intention of the Heart of Jesus. When His disciples place themselves in the service of this aim, they give their Master consolation and joy, in fact they earn His gratitude. He shows this by a gift in return. He gives His zealous apostolic servant *the joy which is His*.

Let us therefore consider that: *The Catholic priesthood serves in the joy of the Son of God.*

I. The Joy of the Son of God. This joy is the joy of *Oneness* with the Father and in His yet being *another than* the Father. He is another as a person, who is different from the Father. He is one with the Father in manifold ways. He is this in the possession of the same divine nature; and as God made man in that oneness in thinking, desiring and loving, as He himself described it in the testimony concerning His relation to the Father which He pronounced before the Jews after His healing of the man at the Pool of Bethsaida who had been an invalid for thirty-eight years. His joy, furthermore, is everything which He has done, during His ministry in the world, for the honour of His heavenly Father and the salvation of lost humanity, and which He still continues to do as the glorified Christ, and will do until the end of the world.

That is the joy of Jesus. The Church thinks of this joy when she bids us pray: " *Per gaudia tua, libera nos, Jesu!* " For the Lord Himself tell us that His joys are communicable, naturally not in the plenitude in which the Son of the heavenly Father, in His capacity of Incarnate God, is capable of enjoying them, but in the capacity to which a limited vessel, as our human nature is even when exalted by grace, can receive them.

II. That He Might Convey These Joys to His Apostolic Servants is the other reason beside the glory of the Father which made Jesus send the disciples into the world. Therefore, He gave them His instructions as to how they should bear witness of Him in the world: " These things I have spoken to you [the things I have just explained and all my instructions during the years of your apostolic training] that my joy may be in you, and that your joy may be made full." The apostolic ways are ways of trouble, struggle, privation and vilification, they are the ways which the Incarnate God trod in His earthly life and which led Him to Gethsemane and Golgotha, and yet were ways of joy. " He who sent me is with me; he has not left me alone, because I do always the things that are pleasing to him " (Jn. 8:29). Hence, His joy in those hours was the oneness with the Father. This joy is the sap of the vinestalk of Christ; He can the more plenteously communicate it to the vine the more the vine is animated with the urge to form the fruit of the apostolic work which the Lord has given it to do. Finally, the joy of Jesus makes our joy " full." For the joys of Jesus cannot disappoint; they do not arise from illusory and transitory things as earthly joys do. They spring from unerring insight into the true nature of things and their value.

III. "If Anyone Thirst, Let Him Come to Me and Drink!" (Jn. 7:37.) The servant of Christ becomes like the vine which withers up and is of no more use but to be thrown away and burned if he ceases to live from the joy which comes from Jesus, the vinestalk. When this happens he falls a victim to the withering effect of apostolic labours. But if he drinks daily from the springs of living waters which flow from the Heart of Jesus into those who seek refreshment in It (72nd Consideration), he is able to cope with the trials his work presents. He can then say with Paul: "Blessed be the God and Father of our Lord Jesus Christ, the Father of mercies and the God of all comfort, who comforts us in all our afflictions, that we also may be able to comfort those who are in any distress by the comfort wherewith we ourselves are comforted by God. For as the sufferings of Christ abound in us, so also through Christ does our comfort abound" (2 Cor. 1:3 ff.). The servants of Christ who act in accordance with these instructions experience the fulfilment of the words of the Psalmist: "They have their fill of the prime gifts of your house; from your delightful stream you give them to drink. For with you is the fountain of life, and in your light we shall see light" (Ps. 35:9-10).

Reading: Jn. 7:37-39.

III. CARRIES THE FLAME OF THE HOLY SPIRIT INTO
THE WORLD

78th Consideration

> " And there appeared to them parted
> tongues as of fire, which settled upon
> each of them " (Acts. 2: 3).

In His farewell discourses Jesus said to the Apostles:
"I will ask the Father and he will give you another
Advocate to dwell with you forever, the Spirit of
truth " (J. 14: 16 f.). Earlier He had announced: " I
have come to cast fire upon the earth, and what will I
but that it be kindled?" (Lk. 12:49.)

Since the Lord fulfilled these promises ten days after
His Ascension, *the Catholic priesthood bears hidden
within it the flame of the Holy Spirit, for the sanctification of the world.*

I. **The Holy Spirit as Pentecostal Gift.** According
to the divine decree the Holy Spirit is co-ordinated
with creation *in a number of ways.* Even before the
"Let there be " of God resounded, the Holy Spirit
swept over the void of unformed possibilities and laid
in it the form, order, and reason of the things that were
to be created. Everywhere that there is life, in matter
and in spirit, in nature and in supernature, He is forma-
tively active. Through the merits of Christ He becomes
co-ordinated, as a gift of the Redemption, to everyone
who accepts with faith the message of salvation, and
He enables him to become a child of God, " born again
by water and the Holy Spirit," and to be taught by

Him " to receive a spirit of adoption as sons by virtue of which we cry ' Abba! Father!' " (Rom. 8:15).

But the Holy Spirit comes at *Pentecost* to begin *His task of assistance,* for which the Incarnate God had asked for Him from the Father and by which He is to help the messengers of Christ to bear witness for Christ " in Jerusalem and in all Judea and Samaria and even to the very ends of the earth " (Acts 1:8). They had already received from the Master the order to bear this witness, but they were to delay beginning to carry out this order until the Holy Spirit would have come upon them: " And while eating with them he charged them not to depart from Jerusalem, but to wait for the promise of the Father, ' of which you have heard,' said he, ' by my mouth; for John indeed baptized with water, but you shall be baptized with the Holy Spirit not many days hence' " (Acts 1:4 f.). And a few days afterwards Christ, having ascended into heaven, fulfilled His promise: " And there appeared to them parted tongues as of fire, which settled upon each of them."

II. The Pentecostal Fire of the Holy Spirit Must Be Preserved to the Church, and Through Her to the World.

For it is the real fruit of the Redemption, through which all the other graces of the Redemption are conveyed to us. If it were quenched mankind would sink back into the old " darkness of the shadow of death "—separation from God. Therefore, Jesus asked for the Paraclete, so that He should remain " forever " with the messengers of the Redemption, and make their joyful tidings come true to the end of time. Hence, the tongues as of fire had to pass on from those on whom

they had descended on the day of Pentecost to the
others who took over their mission when the Twelve
left this earthly battleground, and carried it farther into
the world and among the human race. The Pentecostal
fire still remains in the world, and it passes on from
bearer to bearer in the saving mystery of holy orders.
And once someone has received it, it remains in him
unquenchable, not for his own sake but for the sake
of the Church and the world into which the Father
sent His Son, that He might save it. What an inven-
tion of divine love is the Sacrament of Holy Orders!
Jesus Himself stands before us in the person of the
officiating bishop and calls down from heaven the
Pentecostal fire for which Christendom prays:
" Accipite Spiritum Sanctum in vobis Paraclitum: ille
est, quem Pater mittet vobis . . . Alleluia " (Words of
the Rite of Ordination, after Jn. 14:16). From this day
onwards the ordained person goes through the world
a vessel in which is hidden the unquenchable flame of
the first Pentecost.

**III. In the Renewal and Continuance of the Sacred
Priesthood the Holy Spirit Gives to the Church the
Enduring Joy of Pentecost.** In Pentecost week the
Church expresses in the following words the joy of the
primitive Church at the descent of the Holy Spirit on
the Apostles: " Fire from heaven came down, not
destroying but enlightening, not consuming, but illuminating. And it found pure vessels in the hearts of the
disciples: then it gave them gifts of grace, Alleluia!
Alleluia! To those whom it found in harmonious love:

—It flooded them with the enlightening stream of the divine pleasure—and gave them the gifts of grace, Alleluia! Alleluia!"

What began on the first Pentecost continues without ceasing in the Kingdom of God: the coming of the Holy Spirit to those on whom the followers of the first who received Him lay their hands, and the going forth into the world of those thus blessed to put the power from above into action, for the salvation of the world.

Reading: Acts 2:32-33.

EPILOGUE: Stir Up the Fire!

79th Consideration

> " For this reason I admonish thee to
> stir up the grace of God which is in thee
> by the laying on of my hands " (2 Tim.
> 1: 6).

It has been the aim of this book to bring to the minds of the priests who read it the true nature of their calling. It is essentially a gift: *the gift of the grace of ordination. To see this gift and to use it as it is meant to be used so that it achieves its end—this is the essence of a rightly lived priestly life.* When a priest proves inadequate to his calling, this always means that he has lost the vision and apprehension of the grace of ordination, and that he has eyes only for his own wishes, abilities and advantage ; that he is no longer serving the blessed gift of the Holy Spirit, but rather his own self-love under its many guises. Meanwhile, the gift of the Holy Spirit is growing cold under the ashes of worldly cares and in the suffocating air of smugness and complacency, until at last it only glimmers on, hidden and ineffectual even if unquenchable, in the depths of his subconscious spiritual life, a heavenly spark from which light and warmth could stream forth if a fresh breath of wind should fan it once more to a flame.

That is why the Church sends out to all the ordained servants of her Bridegroom the Apostle's warning cry: *Stir up the grace of God which is in thee !*

I. This Is the Call Which She Sends Out to Those Concerned for the Priesthood of Today. For the world is crying out for the " good priest "; and that is certainly a happy omen. For implicit in this demand (whether spoken or unspoken) is the admission that the self-sufficient human spirit has lost credit and that mankind is ready to accept God's wisdom and strength, if only He sends it by the right kind of minister. But what kind of minister can win the confidence of the man of today? Opinions are sharply divided. All sorts of people voice their wishes, and these wishes almost unanimously concern the human side of the priest; the *divine* in him is hardly taken into account at all. One person finds him acceptable if he shows a broad-minded spirit towards questions of the day; if he furthers, from the " spiritual standpoint," the things which are valued at the moment. The priest who is interested in social welfare meets with his particular approval. The next person wants his clergyman to be purely " the man of God," but he must far excel the clerical average *in verbis, et signis, et factis,* and leave it completely in the shade in achievement, if indeed he does not actually disapprove of it.

Opposed to these present-day views of the priest stands the devout reverence of sound Catholicism, which sees in the priest, not so much the quality of the person as the value of *the grace of ordination* which it has pleased the Holy Spirit to entrust to him. The right-thinking Catholic respects the grace of ordination; he is glad if the human vessel is of Christian nobility or even greatness; but he does not reverence it the less if the vessel is of simple average quality or even leaves much to be desired in the matter of worthiness.

We should recall how the saint of Assisi used often to say: " If I were to meet at the same moment a saint just come down from heaven and a poor simple priest, I would first show honour to the priest and would immediately kiss his hands. I would say, ' Oh, have patience a moment, St. Lawrence, for the hands of this priest touch the Word of Life and they have something which is above all human value ' " (*Vita* II, n. 201). That something which is *" above all human value "* in the priest is the grace of ordination, and it is this in every priest.

II. But the Grace of Ordination Does Not Have the Same Illuminating Power in All Priests. In one it may be a faint spark, in another a friendly fire, in a third a conflagration. If the fire of the grace of ordination has died down to a faint spark of the grace of the worldly priest, it cannot fulfil its task and becomes the accuser of its bearer. It accuses him by his flock, in which the spirit of Christ is falling away because it cannot be kept alight by the fire which should be visible in its shepherd. It accuses him by his high-priestly Master because the " angel of the church " has become a fading star by which the flock can no longer find its way (Apoc. 2:19, 20; 2:1). In the great, apostolic, souls of the Church's history: in Paul, Boniface, Francis Xavier, the grace of ordination became a raging conflagration at which whole peoples caught the fire of faith in the message of salvation. God can send souls of fire like these into the darkness of our day, and perhaps He would be more likely to do so if only we asked for them more urgently and prayed for them more fervently. But when He does

send them, we must not love the darkness more than
the light. The grace of ordination is a friendly fire in
the priest who so dispenses the mysteries of the New
Covenant that he can say in conscience, with the
Apostle of the Gentiles: "I give thanks to my God
always concerning you for the grace of God which was
given you in Christ Jesus, because in everything you
have been enriched in him, in all utterance and in all
knowledge; even as the witness to the Christ has been
made so firm in you that you lack no grace, while
awaiting the appearance of our Lord Jesus Christ" (1
Cor. 1 : 4-7). Happy the pastor of souls who can bid
farewell to his parish in these terms!

III.   Therefore : Resuscites Gratiam, Quae Est in Te !
Renew the illuminating power of the grace of ordination in you if it is covered with the ashes of worldliness or flickering out in the suffocating air of self-
complacence. The Seer of the Apocalypse had to write
to the Angel of Ephesus (was it Timothy, grown
weary, to whom Paul had written the "*resuscites*"
letter?): "Thus says he who holds the seven stars in
his right hand, who walks in the midst of the seven
golden lamp-stands. . . . I have against thee, that thou
hast left *thy first love*. Remember therefore whence
thou hast fallen, and repent and do the former works;
or else I will come to thee, and will move thy lampstand out of its place, unless thou repentest" (Apoc.
2 : 1, 4 f.). The High Priest Himself watches His
servants and will not tolerate it if they allow the fire
of the Holy Spirit to grow cold within them. The Considerations in this book aim at serving this solicitude
of Christ. They will have attained their aim if the

priests who read them renew the holy ardour in which
we should pray, imbued with the spirit of the Church:

> "Jesus, our High Priest, do Thou live in me; let
> my spirit grow so warm at the living flame of
> Thy love that it may blaze into a perfect fire.
> May it glow on the altar of my heart, may it
> burn into the marrow of my bones, may it flame
> up in the hidden depths of my soul. On the day
> of my temporal end, grant that I may be perfected
> in Thee, who with the Father and the Holy
> Ghost, livest and reignest God, forever and ever,
> Amen."

Reading: Consecration of Priests to the Most Sacred
Heart of Jesus, by Pope St. Pius X.